Playing the Field

Playing the Field

Why Sports Teams Move and Cities Fight to Keep Them

CHARLES C. EUCHNER

THE JOHNS HOPKINS UNIVERSITY PRESS
Baltimore and London

Johns Hopkins Paperbacks edition, 1994
03 02 01 00 99 98 97 96 95 94   5 4 3 2 1

The Johns Hopkins University Press
2715 North Charles Street
Baltimore, Maryland 21218-4319
The Johns Hopkins Press Ltd., London

Photographs reproduced by permission: Frontispiece, Tom Harney
(1989); p. 2, Tom Harney (1991); p. 22, Neil A. Meyerhoff (© 1992);
p. 52, Tom Harney (1987); p. 78, Amateur Athletic Foundation of
Los Angeles (Robert Hagedohm AAF/LPI 1984); p. 102, Neil A.
Meyerhoff (© 1992); p. 132, Tom Harney (1989); p. 160, Tom
Harney (1990).

Library of Congress Cataloging-in-Publication Data
Euchner, Charles C.
    Playing the field : why sports teams move and cities fight to keep
them / Charles C. Euchner.
        p.   cm.
    Includes bibliographical references and index.
    ISBN 0-8018-4572-6 (alk. paper)   0-8018-4973-X (pbk.: alk.
paper)
    1. Sports—Political aspects—United States—Case studies.
2. Sports—Economic aspects—United States—Case studies.
3. Sports franchises—United States—Location—Case studies.
4. Metropolitan areas—United States—Case Studies.
I. Title.GV706.35.E93   1993
796'.0973—dc20   92-43276

A catalog record for this book is available from the British Library

For my parents

Perry C. Euchner, Jr. and
Gale Young Euchner

Contents

Preface

When I look out the window of my apartment study, I can see Boston's Fenway Park. On game days, I get regular updates of the score, the ball-strike count, and batting averages from the scoreboard visible from my window. The roar of the crowd, audible from a couple blocks away, provides alerts of the excitement on the field. Organ music offers a prelude to the game, as well as intermittent serenades.

A neighborhood park is something special, for both passionate sports fans and more casual observers. The rhythms of the season make for a pleasant sense of stability and routine. The excitement of a pennant race reverberates on the street and among the neighbors. It is hard for any lifelong baseball fan not to engage in gloppy sentimentality about the game and the stadium: *Just think,* Babe Ruth used to play there, and Ted Williams, and Carl Yastrzemski, and . . .

But professional sports, like much of our popular culture, can be understood only partly through its folklore and continuing excitement. Baseball and football are not only cultural institutions but also hardcore businesses. These sports are not very big, really, compared to the television industry or the steel industry or even the pork and beans industry, but they are still big enough to warrant careful analysis. As businesses, sports leagues can be as conniving, deceitful, and manipulative as they are allowed to be. Politicians always lurk nearby, seeking to exploit both the cultural and the economic dimensions of sports for their own purposes. Many people still think John V. Lindsay won reelection as New York's mayor in 1969 on the strength of the civic goodwill that followed the "Amazin' Mets" world championship.

Fans do not like to acknowledge the more cold-blooded aspects of sports. Baseball especially is prone to the lyric incantations that are intended to deny the greed, corruption, and blackmail pervasive in sports. Sports sentimentalism is reminiscent of a Victorian prude's reaction to the theory of evolution: "Descended from apes! My dear, let us hope that it is not true, but if it is, let us pray that it will not become generally known." The people who run professional and college sports are aware of the public's desire to believe the mythology surrounding the games. The romanticism of sports has spawned smaller industries in films, bubble gum cards, caps, sportswear, videos, books, and magazines.

This book attempts to analyze some of the aspects of professional sports that most fans would rather not consider. Specifically, I want to explore the feverish competition among North American cities to attract professional sports teams. In the last decade, virtually all the big cities in the United States, and a few small cities as well, have battled with each other for the right to host big league franchises. While facing staggering social and fiscal crises, cities spend hundreds of millions of dollars to build new stadiums and offer other enticements to private franchise owners. Municipal officials often push for stadiums and other favors to teams despite intense opposition in the neighborhoods and general opposition across the city.

Some of the most storied franchises in sports, like the Oakland Raiders and Baltimore Colts of the National Football League, have shifted to other cities regardless of years of loyalty from the hometown fans. Perhaps more important than the actual moves have been the threatened moves. By simply exploring options for playing in other cities—by playing the field, so to speak—teams have gotten all manner of largess. New stadiums are only the beginning. The willingness to threaten departure has secured for teams a variety of land deals, lower taxes, more revenues from parking and concessions, control of stadium operations, guraranteed ticket sales, renovation of stadiums with luxury seating, control over neighborhoods and transportation systems. The list goes on.

A sports image sometimes used to describe unfair political confrontations—the "uneven playing field"—helps get at the dynamic of city-franchise relations. To extend the metaphor, cities appear to play defense most of the time. City officials react to the offensive strategies of team owners, but it is hard for them to anticipate these maneuvers or develop an effective defense ahead of time. Franchises can pick and choose when to execute their plays; that timing advantage enables the teams to control the terms of debate. Teams skillfully divide and distract political opponents. Teams can often get players from the municipality's side to join their cause. With influential government allies, teams also can do a complete "end run" around the political process; special authorities and indirect taxes can help proposals for stadiums and other benefits avoid normal political scrutiny. City officials do not seem able to confront teams authoritatively.

Boosters make grand claims for a sports team's effects on the city, based as much on their own wishful thinking as on hard data. If you build it, boosters say of a proposed stadium, the city will experience an economic renaissance. All kinds of wild numbers get thrown about as evidence of the economic growth that sports supposedly creates. Sports nuts, particularly those who write for newspapers or read scores for television stations, agree vociferously. That unreality makes the pro-sports arguments difficult to confront.

The claims are all a bit unreal, like the games themselves. Curiously, one of the reasons sports development manages to succeed in the contentious urban political system is not that it is so important but that it is in many ways nebulous and relatively unimportant. Opponents of new stadiums or other franchise benefits have testified that their activism was cut short by the realization that more important problems were begging for attention. Problems with drugs, schools, homelessness, and AIDS loom so large that it often seems foolish politically to get in a lather about a silly sports stadium.

To the dedicated fan, the sports industry's willingness to abandon a community not only exhibits bad faith but is irrational over the long term. When Al Davis moved the Oakland Raiders to Los Angeles, he rebuffed the sport's most loyal fans and also created distractions that hurt the team's fortunes on the field. Football's Colts and Cardinals, while enriching themselves, have been failures on the field since their moves. If the White Sox had moved from Chicago to Florida, they would have left behind both the nation's third largest market and one of baseball's greatest traditions. But as destructive as "gypsy franchises" can be in the long term, there is much gain to be had in the short term. That is why the sports industry is so unsettled.

Acknowledgments

Thanks are in order for those who helped me along the way.

Matthew A. Crenson, my graduate school advisor at the Johns Hopkins University, was terrific. Throughout my years in Baltimore, Professor Crenson and I had an extended conversation about urban politics and society. It was a wonderful way to become part of the academic enterprise. I hope the conversation will continue in the years to come. Professor Crenson is smart, open-minded, excited by intellectual inquiry, and patient. Goodness, he is patient. His extended comments on earlier versions of this essay improved the manuscript in every way.

Francis E. Rourke, my second dissertation reader at Hopkins, was also very helpful. With wit and wisdom, he picked out the trouble spots and suggested ways to fix them. Throughout my time at Hopkins, he challenged and amused me. I only hope his endurance of the Orioles will be rewarded soon with a world championship.

Dennis Judd of the University of Missouri at St. Louis read the complete draft and offered good suggestions to improve it. He also offered the kind of encouragement that only an accomplished scholar can give.

Linda Kowalcky of the University of St. Louis at Missouri, Timothy L. Smith of the Johns Hopkins University, James Nickell of St. Mary's College of Maryland, and Oliver Williams of the University of Pennsylvania read and critiqued some chapters. Discussions of papers at the American Political Science Association (1991) and Southern Political Science Association (1988), Barnard College (1989), the University of Alberta (1990), and the College of the Holy Cross (1990) provided new insights.

David Whitford, a fellow traveler in the study of sports as a business and a friend, read parts of the manuscript and offered findings from his research for *Playing Hardball*, a forthcoming book on baseball expansion.

My colleagues and students at Holy Cross College have my sincere appreciation for the serious but enjoyable atmosphere that they have offered me over the past two years. I feel lucky to be part of the place.

The stories told in this book are enhanced by the photography of Tom Harney. Tom's photo essay of Chicago's old Comiskey Park extends back two decades. The photographs will be part of a forthcoming collection tentatively entitled *Fans*. His work expresses some of the bittersweet feelings that only a fan and an urbanite can know.

I owe thanks to my editors at the Johns Hopkins University Press. Henry Tom showed interest in the project back in its formative stages and has been with me all the way. The copyeditor, Anne Whitmore, has been superb. She scrutinized this manuscript actively, not only fixing awkward phrasing but also challenging me to develop some important ideas better. Even though she did not intrude on the text, her presence is important on virtually every page. She also has a great sense of humor, which made the whole process easier.

Playing the Field

Sports Politics: Teams, Local Identity, and Urban Development

> We're going to do whatever it takes to keep the
> Redskins here. Sports has become an industry, and to
> the extent that we can guarantee jobs for District
> residents, we will do whatever it takes, including
> building the stadium ourselves.
> —Sharon Pratt Dixon, Mayor of Washington, D.C.,
>   May 1991

> Just build it.
> —Al Davis, managing general partner of the Raiders, to
>   Mayor Henry Cisneros on the subject of a new stadium
>   in San Antonio

As the Chicago White Sox threatened in 1988 to move to Florida unless the Illinois legislature approved funding for a new stadium, labor activist Thomas H. Geoghegan tried to convince state and municipal officials to resist the team's demands. The White Sox had broken two previous commitments—first, to stay if the city built luxury seating at Comiskey Park; second, to accept the terms outlined in 1986 state legislation for a new stadium—and Geoghegan privately urged a friend in city hall to avoid taking the team's latest bait. Forget the team's demands at the state capital, he said; before entering into negotiations, insist that the team meet its obligations.

Opponents of a possible White Sox move from Chicago's South Side, Geoghegan said, should "hit the White Sox from all sides" to convince them that a move would pose serious risks. "The point is to treat the Sox like any other runaway shop. Tell the Sox owners, in effect, 'Look, we want to cooperate, but if you try to leave, we'll either stop you, or make it very, very costly.' "[1] Geoghegan, who also wrote to the state's deputy attorney general, said the city could charge the team with violating several informal contracts. "The city lavishes services and infrastructure on these teams, and I was arguing this was unjust enrichment," he later recalled.[2]

Government officials did not follow Geoghegan's advice. Even more distressing to the quixotic young lawyer, the officials undermined the efforts of community groups from what Geoghegan wryly called the "black, sulfurous, White Sox anti-world" of the South Side.[3] The Chicago government, then drifting under Interim Mayor Eugene Sawyer, accepted the terms specified by the White Sox. The new Comiskey Park opened in 1991.

Chicago's decision to accede to the White Sox' demands is typical of the relations between cities and professional sports franchises. Municipal officials negotiate with teams, but they negotiate from a position of weakness. Negotiations take place on a proverbial uneven playing field. Cities in decline, desperate for some visible sign of economic and social rejuvenation, are especially prone to manipulation. Occasionally, someone like Geoghegan will suggest confronting the team or the league and demanding that professional sports live up to its formal and informal commitments to the city, but cities usually shy away from tough tactics.[4] Most public officials place such importance in professional franchises that they lack the combative spirit to take on the sports industry.

An Age of Mobility

In the 1980s, professional sports franchises engaged in an unprecedented series of skirmishes over the terms of their location in host cities. One expert claimed, "In football and baseball, there is now a sense of instability unlike any other since the late 1950s, when the Dodgers, Giants, Athletics, and Browns all moved."[5] Previous periods in sports history had seen franchise shifts; in fact, in the formative years of professional sports, the shifts were so common that few teams even had permanent playing fields. But in the modern era, teams are considered permanent parts of the civic order. Beyond breaking emotional attachments, team transfers (and threats to move) now involve billions of dollars and significant parcels of urban real estate.

Team movement was hardly the only source of upheaval and controversy in professional and amateur sports during the 1980s. Players went on strike, teams moved broadcasts from network to cable television, drug use and gambling threatened the integrity of competition, franchise partners squabbled and sued one another, owners and commissioners dueled. Players, with their astronomical salaries and coterie of agents and lawyers, seemed to become more and more remote from fans. These were all part of a larger transformation of professional sports from a game played for modest profits into a modern, rationalized industry involving billions of dollars.

However upsetting all these developments may be, the transfer of a sports franchise produces the most devastating effects. Psychologists have compared the loss of a sports franchise to the trauma experienced at the death of a loved one.[6] Popular opinion holds that teams have a responsibility to the city, that sports is as much a matter of community and culture as it is industry and commerce. By their own reckonings, teams are integral parts of their communities because, as one study put it, they provide "a sense of continuity and unity in a discontinuous and increasingly atomized society."[7] When teams move or threaten to move, they upset a fragile relationship—a relationship based increasingly on profit seeking but undergirded by the lore of community values.

At some point in the past decade, virtually all professional franchises publicly threatened to move to a different city in order to extract the benefits they desired from local governments. Including shifts from in town to suburbia, fifteen teams moved to different sites between 1970 and 1990, and others got new stadiums after threatening to move. Even such tradition-bound clubs as the New York Yankees, who stayed in the Bronx, thought of pulling up stakes; and the Baltimore Colts actually did move to Indianapolis. Among the biggest losers in stadium politics have been the nation's biggest cities: New York, Los Angeles, Chicago, Detroit, Oakland, and Baltimore. The winners have included both big cities, like Los Angeles and New Orleans, and suburban jurisdictions, like Foxboro, Massachusetts, and Pontiac, Michigan.

The nation's emerging urban areas in the South and West, from Tampa to Seattle, were most active in forcing major league cities to fight to retain sports franchises. Those emerging cities made serious offers to franchises, thereby exerting pressure on the cities hosting teams: either yield to the teams' demands for new stadiums and other benefits or risk losing the team to a city willing to meet the demands. The competition among cities has extended to the lower levels of organized sports. Minor league and spring training baseball cities, once backwaters, have been forced by competition to construct modern facilities in order to attract or retain teams. Many of the cities use the facilities as part of their development efforts.[8]

Since the Dodgers moved west in 1957, American cities have spent billions of dollars constructing sports stadiums; 70 percent of today's stadiums were publicly financed. Only one new facility, Joe Robbie Stadium in Dade County, Florida, was privately financed, and it still required significant public expenditures for land and infrastructure.[9] Cities have been innovative in their financing of new facilities. The use of tax increment financing, which involves taxing businesses that directly benefit from new construction, is one popular idea. Another is the use of lotteries to finance sports; a Maryland lottery will pay $16 million of the annual $17 million in interest payments incurred in construction of the new Camden Yards ballpark.[10]

Building stadiums and courting sports franchises have become major parts of city agendas as the emphasis of urban leaders has shifted from redistribution to development. In the 1960s and 1970s, mayoral agendas were dominated by social programs designed to address inequality. Spurred by the civil rights movement and inner-city riots, mayors like John Lindsay of New York, Coleman Young of Detroit, and Kenneth Gibson of Newark attempted to reshape the power structures of their cities and empower the poor. Even mayors who rejected that agenda, Frank Rizzo of Philadelphia and Sam Yorty of Los Angeles for instance, acted within the parameters of the redistributive agenda. As economic stagnation and fiscal crisis jarred cities in the 1970s and 1980s, the agenda shifted to development issues. Mayors Edward Koch of New York, William Hudnut of Indianapolis, Federico Pena of Denver, and other mayors argued that the local government's primary job was to generate economic growth. Rather than change the system, they sought to jump-start it. Even progressive mayors like Raymond Flynn of Boston emphasized that growth was a necessary precondition to programs to deal with homelessness, education, and other concerns.

Once cities decided to stress economic development, and sports franchises became a means to that end, a cutthroat competition among cities for teams was inevitable. An undersupply of baseball and football teams meant that the teams would enjoy the upper hand in negotiations. During the past decade, more than two dozen cities have sought major league baseball franchises (for an enumeration of the cities, see Table 1), but only two to six new teams are likely to be added by the end of the century. Likewise, fifteen localities sought football teams when only two to four clubs realistically can be added to the National Football League this century. Such counts of cities do not include the literally dozens of suburban and rural areas that are potential sites for big league baseball and football. Such exurban sites add an important dimension to the supply-

and-demand equation, since they serve as a reserve that strengthens the already formidable bargaining positions of team owners. The only cities now hosting major professional teams that have not faced some threat are Cincinnati, Kansas City, and San Diego—all cities with relatively new facilities, built in the 1970s. If teams were publicly owned, there would be little pressure to constantly upgrade facilities, but both baseball and football ban community ownership. The National Football League requires that one person have operating control of the team. It allows Green Bay's public ownership of the Packers because of a grandfather clause written during the league's formative stages. Major League Baseball rejected Joan Kroc's offer to give the city of San Diego ownership of the Padres in 1990.

The public discussion in negotiations over franchise demands is restricted. Downtown business interests and sports fans usually form alliances with elected officials eager to show a "can-do" approach to local government. Because the sports industry controls the pace and the content of much of the debate, it is difficult for government or community actors to address the many issues comprehensively. Boosters of stadiums are usually involved at all stages, while opponents are involved at only selected stages.

The most comprehensive public debates occur during occasional referendum campaigns. Recently, referendums for new stadiums were defeated in New Jersey, San Francisco (three times), Santa Clara County, San Jose, Oklahoma City, and Miami (three times). In 1987 a vote on a new stadium in Baltimore was blocked on a state constitutional technicality. A rare instance of a stadium proposal's being approved in a referendum was the 1990 vote in Ohio for a new facility in Cleveland, on which the vote was 51.7 percent in favor to 48.3 percent against. Interestingly, residents of Cleveland itself rejected the $344-million plan by a 54.6 to 45.4 margin. A previous referendum had failed, but the pro-stadium forces enjoyed statewide support from politicians and there were threats from both the Indians franchise and the Commissioner of Baseball that the team would leave unless a new park was built. The opposition was badly organized and was hobbled by an inept campaign.[11]

The most dramatic franchise move in recent years—as seismic as the Brooklyn Dodgers' move to Los Angeles after the 1957 season—was the transfer of the Oakland Raiders football team to Los Angeles. Following four years of negotiations and legal battles, the court gave permission for the move in 1982. Al Davis, managing general partner of the Raiders, sought the nation's second-largest market, Los Angeles, because of its glamour, economic dynamism, promises of stadium renovation and

Table 1. Supply and Demand of Professional Baseball and Football Franchises,
          1980–June 1992

Cities	Teams in residence	Activity
Albuquerque	None	Seeks B[1]
Alexandria, Va.	None	In 1992 governor proposes building F[2] stadium
Anaheim	B F	Lured F Rams in 1978; F threatened to leave over stadium development dispute in 1988
Arlington, Tex.	B	Plans new B stadium
Atlanta	B F	Opened new F stadium in 1992; plans new B stadium in conjunction with 1996 Olympic games
Austin, Tex.	None	May ally with San Antonio to seek F
Baltimore	B	Opened a B stadium in 1992; seeks F; plans F stadium
Birmingham, Ala.	None	Seeks B and F; considers building stadium
Boston	B	Considers building F stadium; occasional talk of building new B stadium
Buffalo	F	Seeks B; built new stadiums for B and F
Casa Grande, Ariz.	None	Sought F; considered stadium
Charlotte	None	Seeks B or F; plans stadium
Chicago	B(2) F	Opened B stadium in 1991; plans F stadium
Cincinnati	B F	No recent developments
Cleveland	B F	Building B stadium; plans new F stadium
Columbus, Ohio	None	Seeks B or F; considers stadium; attempted to lure F Cardinals in 1987–88
Denver	B F	Awarded expansion B; plans new stadium
Detroit	B	Plans new B stadium; location under dispute
East Rutherford, N.J.	F (2)	Lured F Giants and Jets from N.Y.; referendum defeated B stadium proposal
Fort Lauderdale	None	Seeks B and F; plans new stadium
Foxboro, Mass.	F	F team threatens to move
Green Bay, Wisc.	F	Occasional stadium renovations; team plays some games in Milwaukee
Honolulu	None	Seeks F
Houston	B F	Plans stadium renovations to keep F; occasional threats by B to move, calls for new B stadium
Indianapolis	F	Lured F Colts from Baltimore with new stadium in 1984; seeks B; occasional proposals for new B stadium
Irving, Tex.	F	Occasional proposals for new F stadium; F lured from Dallas
Jacksonville	None	Seeks F; regular talk of building new stadium
Kansas City	B F	No recent developments
Knoxville	None	Considers alliance with Memphis and Nashville to seek expansion F
Los Angeles	B F	Competes to keep F; plans for $200 million renovation in doubt; talk of new stadium
Louisville	None	Seeks B and F, considers stadium

Cities	Teams in residence	Activity
Memphis	None	Seeks B and F; considers stadium
Miami	B F	Awarded expansion B; new F stadium opened in 1987
Milwaukee	B F	Considers new stadium; shares F with Green Bay
Minneapolis	B F	B and F play in new domed facility
Montreal	B	B occasionally considers moving
Nashville	None	Seeks B and F; considers new stadium or renovation
New Orleans	F	Seeks B; renovates Superdome; F considers move
New York	B(2)	Considers new F stadium
Norfolk	None	Considers stadium
Oakland	B	Lost F to Los Angeles, 1982; seeks F
Oklahoma City	None	Seeks F; considers stadium
Orlando	None	Seeks B and F; considers stadium
Philadelphia	B F	Almost lost F; renovates stadium
Phoenix	F	Seeks B; lured F from St. Louis, 1988; building new stadium
Pittsburgh	B F	Almost lost B; mayor proposed new stadium, retracted after opposition
Portland, Oreg.	None	Seeks B or F; considers stadium
Raleigh-Durham	None	Seeks F; considers stadium
Sacramento	None	Seeks B and F; developer proposes new stadium; attempted to entice F Raiders
St. Louis	B	Lost F to Phoenix in 1988; new F stadium due to open in 1995; seeks F
St. Petersburg	None	Seeks B; opened dome in 1987 without tenant
Salem, Oreg.	None	Sought F; gave up in 1991
San Antonio	None	Seeks F, possibly with Austin; plans stadium
San Diego	B F	No recent developments
San Francisco	B F	B attempted move to St. Petersburg, 1992; two B stadium proposals defeated in referendum
San Jose	None	Proposed B stadium defeated in referendum
Santa Clara Co., Calif.	None	Proposed B stadium defeated in referendum
Seattle	B F	Almost lost B; new dome opened in 1977
Tampa	F	Seeks B, now in alliance with St. Petersburg; considered stadium
Toronto	B	Opened new dome in 1989 to keep B
Tucson	None	Sought F; considers stadium
Vancouver, B.C.	None	Opened new stadium in 1983; seeks B
Washington, D.C.	F	Seeks B; mayor committed to building new stadium
Worcester	None	Seeks F; considers stadium

Sources: Newspaper reports, personal interviews

[1]B denotes Major League Baseball team   [2]F denotes National Football League team

greater ticket receipts, and potential for superprofits from cable television.

Like the Dodgers before them, the Raiders had become a symbol of the hardscrabble, working-class city that struggled for respectability in the shadow of a more glamorous neighbor.[12] Oakland had supported the Raiders with an unparalleled thirteen straight years of stadium sellouts. Despite this, in 1980, after talks on a new lease for the Oakland–Alameda County Coliseum failed, the Raiders' management moved the team south. Announcement of the transfer followed years of bitterness, miscommunication, isolation, and posturing during negotiations with the coliseum commissions of both Oakland and Los Angeles.

Remarkably, soon after the Raiders won a series of bitter legal battles and moved to Los Angeles, Davis actively considered another move. By the summer of 1989, Los Angeles was being challenged by three other California cities for the right to host the Raiders. Oakland, Sacramento, and Irwindale, as well as Los Angeles, put together packages worth between $200 million and $600 million for the Raiders to play in their cities. Cities outside California, such as New York and Jacksonville, were poised to make offers should those contenders fail to satisfy Davis. In 1990, Davis announced that he would move the Raiders back to Oakland in time for the 1992 season, contingent upon passage of a lucrative agreement by Oakland authorities.

In the end, the Raiders did not move back to Oakland, but even the possibility of such a move indicates the peculiar nature of the sports business. It is too simple to say that sports is a soulless business enterprise obsessed with the bottom line. Sports politics seems to involve two intertwined dynamics. First, civic elites are so attracted to professional sports that they seem willing to do whatever it takes to become part of the competition for a franchise. Major league sports brings a special status to a city. Whatever may be wrong with the city, having a big league club insures regular national attention. The quintessential example of this desire to "play in the major leagues" is the gift of $10 million from the city of Irwindale, California, to the Los Angeles Raiders, just to get telephone calls returned.

Second, once competition for teams develops, the logic of sequential political deliberation takes over. The sports industry, exploiting its monopoly position, is able to *steer* the process, and the franchises clearly enjoy an advantage. But because the process of negotiation is so drawn-out and sports issues are not addressed in a comprehensive fashion, events and actors large and small can change the whole course of the situation. The possible return of the Raiders to Oakland could not have been predicted because of the twists and turns taken by the long course of negotiation. Another unpredictable outcome was the case of the Chicago White Sox, whose intense desire to get out of an inner-city neighborhood eventually led to construction of a new stadium in that same neighborhood.

A Most Peculiar Industry

The character of the sports industry determines the parameters for the politics of sports in American cities. The sports industry is unique. The character of the product, the organizational structure of the producer, and the historical bonds between industry and community are all peculiar. A city does not treat a major league baseball franchise the same way it treats a "major league" paper mill or cannery. The usual assumptions about public-private relations do not hold to the sports industry.

One of the most important aspects of the professional baseball and football leagues is their monopoly, or cartel, status. Major League Baseball and the National Football League both exercise near-total domination of their professional and even amateur sports. For the most part, these leagues operate without the usual constraints of antitrust law. They exercise extraordinary control over the markets for labor (players) and consumers (fans). This control affects these sports in matters ranging from broadcasting contracts to player salaries to playing facilities.

Professional leagues consciously exploit their monopoly status. For years, the leagues enjoyed absolute control over labor. Player movement was restricted absolutely in baseball by the "reserve clause," by which teams reserved the right to renew player contracts indefinitely according to the previous terms of employment. Unlike the case in virtually every other labor market, players could not move where the conditions of employment were most agreeable. Football similarly bound players to teams through the "Rozelle rule." That rule—fiat, really, by Commissioner Pete Rozelle—guaranteed so much compensation to teams losing players to free agency that most franchises did not find it advantageous to raid other teams. Football's subsequent free-agent system, which allowed teams to protect thirty-seven players from the open market, is another example of football's internal cooperation.

In recent years, the control of organized sports over the labor market has weakened; but at the same time, the leagues have developed even more extraordinary control over the rest of the sports industry. As player salaries have skyrocketed, teams have become more aggressive in seeking out greater revenues. Organized sports has sought additional revenues from two sources in particular: broadcasting and state and local governments. Network broadcasting revenues for baseball teams, for example, increased from $3.3 million in 1981 to $14 million a decade later, and local cable television contracts provided a handsome supplement to those revenues. Localities have provided greater financial opportunities in the form of new stadiums and renovation of old stadiums. Especially important are the revenues from "skyboxes," luxury seating that brings in as much as $16 million annually, and a variety of other benefits ranging from tax concessions to real estate partnerships. Professional sports has become a more formidable player in the sports politics game because of these aggressive growth strategies.

Sports franchises are difficult for local politicians to confront because the symbolism and ritual of sports are so powerful. Sports is vivid; it provides intense bursts of action that most other activities lack. The sports event has the potential to hold the rapt attention of spectators because of the intensity of competition. Neal Offen writes: "Sports is a world speeded up and a world of absolutes. There is good and bad, black and white, right and wrong. It's not gray and tentative like the real world. It's hyperlife under glass."[13] Perhaps just as important, sports is vivid because it occurs at a distance. Sports separates or "brackets" the performers and the spectators. The "star system" that dominates the sports industry and other entertainment industries creates unreal and even mythic figures. Sports is also a vehicle through which cities develop what Alan Ingham and his associates have called "contrived community." The bracketed performances of athletes, the star system, and the contrived community combine to separate sports from real life and from meaningful political engagement.

The emotional hold a team has on its home city stems partly from its ability to embody and enhance the city's identity. Whether on the playing field or as the object of competition with a city that hopes to lure them away, the "home" team is a symbol for the whole community. "By virtue of having a professional team, they are distinguished from dozens of other cities as 'major league' towns."[14] This identity can overwhelm all the other ways that a city's residents think about themselves; it therefore can obscure other possible emblems of civic identity, large and small. A city's identification with a sports team creates vivid symbolism of a common interest, but it also washes away other less dramatic concerns that might be more important for the community, like schools, parks, housing, and libraries.

Competitive sports exemplifies the city's engagement with the external world. To an extent, cities understand themselves by way of contrast to other cities. As Alfred Schutz and Thomas Luckmann suggest, self-identity develops "only in various stages of concrete apprehension and typification of the Other."[15] The images that people develop of "the Other" may be inaccurate, and they may produce inaccurate self-images, but those images are vivid nonetheless. Sports is unusual as a business in being a vehicle for this self-image. Other businesses, having more mundane and complicated interactions with the external world, cannot perform this function. It is hard to imagine Baltimoreans rooting for the Esskay meat company, a local firm, over a rival cold-cuts firm like Oscar Mayer of Madison, Wisconsin. The two firms do not carry the city's name and do not confront each other as symbols of their communities the way sports teams do. Such firms compete indirectly, and the results are inconclusive at any given moment. Each firm can prosper without "defeating" the other. This comparison of the sports and meat industries may seem fanciful, but it illustrates some of the uniqueness of the sports industry—and that uniqueness may, in turn, explain something about why other industries do not attract such great attention in city politics.[16]

The Urban Process

Sports politics is difficult business not only because of the powerful inherent appeal of sports but also because of the complexity of urban society. As urban theorists beginning with Georg Simmel and Louis Wirth have argued, the city presents an overwhelming array of phenomena. No one can take it all in at once without being thrown into confusion. A bewildering system of local government, shaped by a complicated system of federalism, exacerbates the situation. Symbolic politics—such as a mayor's well-publicized attempt to attract or retain a team—offers the city a sharp focal point in the hopeless confusion of urban affairs.

Amidst the confusion, the public seeks some kind of signal that the polity is capable of shaping its destiny. Murray Edelman writes, "Because it is apparently intolerable for men to admit the key role of accident, or ignorance, and of unplanned processes in their affairs, the leader serves a vital purpose by personalizing and reifying the processes."[17] Management of a few ultimately symbolic issues can provide a palliative for a failure to address complex and contradictory problems like housing, transportation, health care, unemployment, drugs, and education and training. Even efforts of dubious merit, such as construction of a new stadium where an adequate one exists, can be sources of public support when they are addressed decisively. When Maryland's governor, William Donald Schaefer, abandoned his moral and fiscal pretenses and attempted to lure the St. Louis Cardinals football team to Baltimore, he received praise from even the most cynical observers, because he was doing his best to be a "winner" on an issue at the top of the public agenda. One otherwise critical Baltimore journalist wrote of Schaefer's efforts, "Having ethics [is] not as good as having a football team" and "It's a dirty job, but the governor's got to do it."[18]

Any industry's interaction with the municipal government would provide a worthwhile focus of study. The factor that most sets the sports industry apart is probably the leagues' monopoly power, which allows the franchise to control the tempo and scope of political confrontations along the sequence of events. Ironically, sports franchises may exert greater leverage over city government than other interests do because of their overall economic *in*significance. Since a franchise's demands do not directly affect many interests, opponents of stadium projects have difficulty developing coalitions to oppose them.[19]

The specific characteristics of industries are often ignored by both students and practitioners of urban politics. The urban affairs literature explores a wide variety of groups in the city but usually fails to examine the distinctive characteristics of various industries. An implicit assumption of the scholarly literature is that all businesses pursue similar strategies in their quest for profits. Paul E. Peterson, for example, argues that development policies take precedence over others in city politics. Development policies are those designed to attract business firms, investment capital, and prosperous taxpayers.[20] Peterson does not distinguish among the different demands and rewards that different sorts of industries present to a city. The particular aspects of the industries—and how they interact with the city—are lost in the generalizations about developmental politics.

Peterson is not the only scholar to gloss over the particularities of different actors' involvement in urban politics. Conservatives, like Charles M. Tiebout, Marxist theorists, like James O'Connor, and even more subtle and nuanced observers, like Jane Jacobs, also have a tendency to generalize about urban industries and institutions.[21] The failure to address the different needs and strategies of businesses produces a determinist understanding of urban processes. The generalizations understate the complexity of cities and their enterprises.

Some urban scholars have focused on particular cities and attempted to determine the wisest strategies for developing the local economic base. These studies pay attention to the common demands that manufacturing and service economies make on the local political system. John Mollenkopf's study of development politics in Boston and San Francisco is a good example of this approach.[22] The closest that urban studies literature comes to exploring the peculiarities of development is to discuss dominant industries.[23] Bryan D. Jones and Lynn W. Bachelor's analysis of the automobile industry in Detroit is a notable example.[24] For the most part, however, studies contain the tacit assumption that a city can devise an economic development policy that will appeal to a wide range of industries.

Sports is not a dominant industry in any city, yet it receives the kind of attention that one might expect to be lavished on major producers and employers. At the very least, the attention paid to sports far exceeds its importance to the city economy. Why does sports attract this kind of attention? What does it say about the urban process?

The American governmental system is uniquely fragmented. Unlike countries such as France and Great Britain, which manage local affairs in a more or less coherent way, the United States seems designed to be confusing and contradictory. American cities compete with each other in a sometimes cannibalistic way. Contradictory U.S. policies and a dynamic economic and social system further fragment policymaking on issues from poverty to housing. In addition, a tradition of privatism creates suspicion of attempts to give the public sector greater authority.

How one perceives city government depends on which level of it one is analyzing. Douglas Yates argues that local government is fragmented and overloaded—and therefore "ungovernable"—because of the extraordinary access that the recipients of city services have to the producers of those services.[25] City government has the task of implementing, directly, the policies of the federal and state governments. The "street-level bureaucracy," says Yates, gives citizens innumerable points of access to the city government, and citizens constantly use those openings to overwhelm the government with demands and complaints.

Matthew A. Crenson, on the other hand, focuses on the higher levels of the system.[26] City politics, he says, is driven by the interaction of elite established interest groups and high-level city officials, not by citizens incessantly making demands on the producers of city policies. As theories of collective action suggest, elites have a better chance of making an impact than do the direct recipients of city services, because it is easier for them to organize. Not only is it easier to pull together a small group of like-minded people at the elite levels of the city, but the rewards are much more significant and discernible. Recipients of services at the street level may indeed bombard the system with demands and complaints, but those interactions are uncoordinated and fragmentary. Coherence is far more likely at the top than at the bottom of the system.

Yates and Crenson present two ends of the same system. Yates describes the demand side—the citizens pressing demands on the "street-level bureaucracy," which consists of the foot soldiers rather than the generals of city government. Crenson describes the supply side of urban government—the policy-making bureaucracy and its organized interests, the "issue networks"[27] of people activated by the material interests of city government and equipped with knowledge of the policy area's arcane vocabulary and difficult institutional channels. The two levels of urban government do interact, but usually according to their own separate logics and in the interest of their own constituencies.

Sports politics takes place at the intersection of these two streams of urban affairs. Cities seeking some kind of affirmation—especially the more dependent, desperate cities—feel compelled to compete for the privilege of hosting professional sports franchises. A team's value as a symbol offers a way for city officials to lift themselves above the chaos and ungovernability of everyday affairs. At the same time, sports offers numerous rewards for politically connected interests.

The Legacy of the Dodgers

Political disputes over sports stadiums and team location emerged in the 1950s, when the economic growth of the South and West created pressure on the leagues to expand into those sports-barren regions. The team transfers of that period were prompted by the desire of emerging cities to gain "major league" status. Suburbanization and the growth of broadcasting pivotally influenced the moves. Without doubt, the most emotional and controversial transfers were the moves of the Brooklyn Dodgers and New York Giants to Los Angeles and San Francisco after the 1957 season.

Until the post–World War II years, the Mississippi River was the western border of major league sports. The first extension of the sports map was the move of the NFL's Cleveland Rams to Los Angeles in 1947. Then, in the early 1950s, three baseball teams—the St. Louis Browns, the Boston Braves, and the Philadelphia Athletics—moved to new cities. None of those franchise shifts produce a sustained or emotional reaction, because the life of the teams had already expired, for all practical purposes. The clubs were receiving poor local support, and, besides, each of the cities still hosted another major league team. The new host cities— Baltimore, Milwaukee, and Kansas City—showed the kind of enthusiastic support that the old cities had not provided for years. Baseball replaced three oversaturated markets with six well-served markets.

The moves highlighted not only the changing shape of professional sports but also the transformation of the metropolis. The postwar years brought suburbanization and the decay of the nation's older urban areas, as many businesses sought to escape the real and perceived inadequacies and dangers of the inner city. At the same time, demographic shifts shaped new markets for professional sports and the major sports leagues gained greater control over their sports. The NFL overtook collegiate competition nationwide as the superior brand of football. Meanwhile, major league baseball gained dominance over the minor leagues, which had once been independent and some of which offered a calibre of play equal to that of the majors. As demand for access to the sports expanded, fewer actors controlled the supply of teams.

The 1957 shift of the New York Giants and Brooklyn Dodgers to California provoked a bitter and long-lasting reaction that could have threatened the future of the major leagues. Even though the Dodgers had long threatened to move, the transfer came as a great shock. When the Dodgers moved west, one fan remembers, "if you were in Behan's Bar and Grill, you'd have thought it was a wake. This was like seceding from the union."[28] The venerable columnist Arthur Daley wrote, "The only word that fits the Dodgers is greed."[29] Claims of betrayal can still be heard in New York today.

Dodgers owner Walter O'Malley had lobbied the government of New York City for years for help in obtaining enough land to construct a new stadium to replace rickety old Ebbets Field. O'Malley planned to build the new stadium with his own money; he wanted the city to use its powers of eminent domain to clear enough land for the project. O'Malley insisted that the team be kept in Brooklyn, the borough that had supported the team for decades. Anyplace else, even elsewhere in New York City, would violate the Brooklyn community as much as a transcontinental move would. Locating the stadium in Brooklyn would have followed a European style of urban development, with various modes of regional transportation feeding into a tightly knit development project.[30] The city's master builder, Robert Moses, had other ideas: he wanted the Dodgers to move to the neighboring New York City borough of Queens, where the team would play at a multipurpose suburban-style facility dependent almost wholly on automobile transport.

Moses was not O'Malley's only source of resistance. Moving forward on a project as big as a new stadium required agreement by state officials, regional authorities, city leaders, and borough officials. The support of party leaders and federal agencies also was necessary to the success of the project. The city's decision-making process, a growing public suspicion of public works projects, and conflicting political pressures contributed to the city's sluggish response to O'Malley's demands. O'Malley told a congressional committee:

> Mayor Wagner [Robert, Jr.] has been most cooperative, Mr. Chairman. He, however, is the mayor of the whole city and he can't get into a political hassle just over Brooklyn. . . . If the man in Queens won't vote for this to be done in Brooklyn and the man in Bronx won't vote for it, then Mr. Moses gets disgusted with the whole thing and says let's put them over in Flushing Meadow [Queens], that is what we've got.[31]

City officials were so confident that the Dodgers would stay in Brooklyn that they were not aggressive in their negotiations. In the terminology of Albert O. Hirschman, the city's disbelief of the Dodgers' threat to "exit" reduced the impact of the team's "voice" in lobbying the city to help it clear land for a new stadium.[32] The city's political leaders, particularly Moses, were almost willful in their refusal to transcend the fragmented system of government in New York for this cause, as they had done on dozens of housing, highway, bridge, beach, and park projects in the previous three decades.

Los Angeles faced many of the same constraints in attempting to lure the Dodgers but benefited from having a three hundred–acre parcel of land, which was the product of a previous political deadlock. The city itself exercised little authority in the political decisions that substantively affected it. Los Angeles County, which included some four thousand square miles and seventy-seven incorporated cities, was the encompassing jurisdiction. The site of Dodger Stadium, the Chavez Ravine, originally was intended for public housing; but the county's voters, armed with the progressive legacy of the referendum and convinced that such a public use was evidence of "creeping socialism," rejected plans for the city housing authority to proceed with the project. The county's political system, then, made the Dodgers' move possible by prematurely clearing land for the large project. The county gave the land to O'Malley, and O'Malley built his own stadium.

California's complex system of government later threatened construction of the stadium and the Dodgers' continued residence.[33] O'Malley had to deal with the state, county, and city governments, the courts, voter referendums, and neighborhood activists before final approval of construction in the Chavez Ravine was possible. The land deal required a two-thirds majority approval by the city council. Opposition came from neighboring San Diego's baseball interests, who feared the effect of major league baseball in Los Angeles on their own aspirations to be part of a new major league, based on the Class AAA Pacific Coast League.

The moves of the Dodgers and the Giants involved virtually all of the major issues important in stadium politics today. Issues of public versus private development, eminent domain, competing economic development strategies, neighborhood resistance, fragmented local political processes all remain crucial elements of stadium politics. Most important, the long, drawn-out series of threats and negotiations—in which the owner of a franchise ratchets up demands by entertaining the competing bids of two or more cities—still drives stadium politics.

Los Angeles has remained at the center of stadium and franchise relocation activity today. The city has been both winner and loser in the franchise game of musical chairs. After drawing the Rams from Cleveland in 1947 and the Dodgers in 1956, the city experienced years of growth and security. Major League Baseball granted Los Angeles an expansion team in 1961; that team, the Angels, moved to Anaheim in 1966. In the 1980s, the Rams also moved to Anaheim, then Los Angeles lured the Raiders away from Oakland. Shortly thereafter, the Raiders started to discuss a possible move from Los Angeles.

L.A.'s checkered sports history encapsules the changing nature of the relationship between sports and cities. The area includes both inner-city (the south-central neighborhood) and suburban sprawl (Anaheim, Irwindale). It has experienced both nonpartisan government efficiency (Los Angeles Memorial Coliseum Commission) and endless political bickering (ditto). It has incorporated sports traditions (the Dodgers) and relentlessly ripped apart others (the Raiders). L.A. in some respects sets the standards for the rest of professional sports, but it also lags behind in important ways. It has been a world leader, hosting two Olympic Games, yet is incapable of even regional leadership, losing numerous collegiate as well as professional teams.

Other cities have played important roles in recent sports history, reflecting the changing nature of both American cities and organized sports. Baltimore typifies the struggles of a small market and the logical response—regionalization, a recent trend. St. Louis invented the modern baseball farm system; it also managed to be both winner and loser of the same Cardinals football franchise. Chicago has been the most stable big city, but its experience shows the complex conflicts of interest that are created by the presence of many franchises from different sports in the same city. Chicago's relationships with its teams represent the informal bonds between city and family-owned teams (the Wrigleys' Cubs, the Halases' Bears) as well as the more bottom-line relationship between city and corporate owners (Jerry Reinsdorf and Edward Einhorn's White Sox).

St. Petersburg, Chicago's rival for the White Sox franchise, typifies the rise of the Sun Belt and the potential for extension of the major leagues into less-urban communities. Irwindale, California's bid for the Raiders epitomized the shift of sports outside the city; had that town won the franchise, it would have been the first big league city to have more starting players than cops.

Sports and the Dependent City

Even though sports plays a relatively minor role in urban fortunes, confronting the sports industry could provide some clues for how cities might deal with other dilemmas. The politics surrounding franchise movement prominently underscores the dependence of cities in the modern era. Cities are not authoritative governmental structures but rather secondary institutions in an international, bureaucratic, corporate system of economics and politics. Outside forces set the parameters of possible action by cities. The powerlessness of municipal officials vis-à-vis sports franchises and leagues—from Baltimore to Los Angeles, Chicago to St. Petersburg—testifies to the limits of localism.

Before engaging in negotiations with franchises, cities might find it advantageous to establish ground rules for the negotiations. For example, by insisting that all the relevent issues will be put on the table at the beginning, cities might avoid many surprises and arbitrary decisions. The standards of negotiation might be given some unofficial sanction by an organization like the League of Cities or the Chamber of Commerce and might be submitted to the major league organizations. Like the SALT II treaty—never ratified but followed by both sides—such standards might succeed through the power of public pressure. If nothing else, public standards might make it easier to establish the truth of a claim or the fairness of a demand made by either side.

Cities could also lead the way toward a national sports policy. Legislation to regulate franchise relocation was introduced in Congress in 1984–85 but failed. That legislation could be revived and tied to madates for league expansion. Omnibus legislation to address additional facets of the sports industry—also cable television, amateur sports, labor relations, gambling, drugs, and violence—might find a significant constituency at a time of public disillusionment with the industry. Congress has some important trump cards, such as broadcasting and antitrust law, that could provide enough leverage to open some long-dormant questions. Traditionally, Congress has allowed professional leagues great freedom, but it has also intervened when the interests of national or local constitutents were at stake. Congress pressured the leagues to expand several times in the last three decades, and to make their games widely available on television.

Whatever cities do to take on the sports industry, they will be vulnerable unless they improve their economic and political conditions apart from sports. Cities are most vulnerable to the relocation threats of businesses—manufacturing and sevice firms as well as sports francishes—when they do not have the fundamental building blocks of urban prosperity and a good quality of life. Good schools, health care, roads, utilities, and recreation facilities ideally can make a city strong enough that it does not need to beseech sports teams or other firms to locate there.

Cities may find it wise to concentrate on the thousands of small and large ways of building community. Parks, libraries, schools, PTAs, theater, churches, political parties, unions, street festivals, neighborhood associations, music, voluntarism—this is the stuff of a more vibrant community. A professional sports franchise can only serve as a pale substitute for community when these other ingredients are missing. In many American cities the more complex web of community activities often gets short shrift.

Sports as an Industry

Football is a joke. The Giants have been a total
mediocrity for fifteen years; the Raiders have been a
major factor; yet the Giants earn more than the
Raiders. No one can say we haven't put an exciting
team on the field. We've got the best record in football.
It isn't fair that we should be earning less than a lot of
clubs that don't feel any need to perform. They suffer
no penalty for their incompetence.
—Al Davis, managing general partner, Los Angeles Raiders

Sports politics today turns on one simple fact: more cities want big league
franchises than can ever hope to get them. The shortage of teams is built
into the structure of organized baseball and football and has been reinforced by individual and collective decisions of the franchises. Nothing
less than a fundamental change in the conception of professional sports
can alter the built-in shortage of teams in these two major professional
sports.

The major leagues of baseball and football operate in thirty-seven host
cities, but the demand for teams is not fully met in those cities, and more
than a dozen other communities also seek entry into the major professional
sports leagues.[1] In recent years, the number of unsatisfied jurisdictions
has increased because of a changing conception of what constitutes a
potential franchise site. Until the 1970s, sizable cities with large markets
were considered the only viable sites for teams. The twin influences of
the highway and television, however, have brought suburbs and even
rural areas into contention for franchises. Dozens of cities, suburbs, and
even small towns now seek teams.

Even though teams infrequently move, threats of transfers drive cities into expensive bidding wars. Dozens of reports circulate each year about possible franchise shifts. Amid the constant rumors of moves, every host city realizes it could lose its franchise. The number of cities seeking teams is so large that franchises always have plausible alternatives for their current sites.

Major League Baseball and the National Football League do much to create excess demand but appear unwilling to meet the demand by expanding their operations. The leagues have promised Congress, the players unions, and specific cities that they would add teams, but action is delayed by difficulties with labor negotiations, television contracts, minor league development, and lawsuits. Critics charge that both sports will limit expansion to strengthen the leverage they get from being monopolies. Donald Fehr, the executive director of the Major League Baseball Players Association, argues:

> The owners have never been interested in expansion. . . . There's no question there ought to be one, maybe two, teams in Florida. I mean, there's a great baseball tradition here. It's about the third most populous state in the country and they can't figure out how to put a baseball team anywhere in the state? Why is that? The reason is that if you put a team in Tampa, [owners like the Chicago White Sox Jerry] Reinsdorf can't extort money from the city of Chicago by threatening to move to Tampa. That's worth more to him than any number of expansion teams are ever going to be worth. And for that, they're not going to expand.[2]

In June 1990 Major League Baseball announced it would add two teams in 1993. The announcement came as congressional leaders threatened to examine baseball's special antitrust status. Football also has pledged to expand by two teams before the end of the century, although its plans have been interrupted by labor difficulties. The demand for franchises in both sports is still high. In 1991, eighteen ownership groups from ten cities competed for baseball expansion teams that cost $95 million apiece.

Throughout the 1980s, as franchises have either moved or threatened to move, Congress has considered legislation to regulate professional sports. The bills usually come from members of Congress whose states or districts are threatened by moves. One bill would have forced the leagues to expand by granting franchises to cities previously abandoned by the leagues in franchise moves. Other bills would have established procedures to protect host cities. One approach would establish federal guidelines for the city-franchise relationship, making specific demands of teams seeking to move. Another approach would have given leagues authority to regulate transfers with broad antitrust exemptions; major league baseball already enjoys formal protection as a monopoly, and other sports have sought for decades to match it. None of the bills addressed the full range of relevent issues, such as broadcasting contracts, revenue sharing, collective bargaining, and the suburbanization of sports. None of the meansures passed.

The leagues' monopoly status, control of the supply of teams, and tax benefits depend on the subtle interaction of the leagues and their member franchises. The only interference in this arrangement is the players' growing strength vis-à-vis the owners. Owner-player disputes, however, do not concern the structure of the industry but rather how monopoly profits will be divided. Union strength, in fact, works to the overall advantage of the owners insofar as it channels criticism and challenges toward the distribution of wealth rather than the league's fundamental structure.

The league is a successful cartel because the whole reinforces the actions of the parts and the parts reinforce the actions of the whole. The league organizations offer a base of operations with "major league" legitimacy and television revenues. Individual franchises build on that base by attempting to gain advantages over other clubs in the form of better stadium leases, local broadcasting deals, and arrangements with local public and private institutions. Leagues encourage teams to negotiate better deals with local governments as a way of driving up what is considered the "minimum" standards for all teams. The more frequently teams are up for sale, especially since they are limited in absolute numbers, the greater the pool of potential buyers.

Beyond its monopolistic nature, other peculiarities of the sports industry affect the negotiations between cities and teams. Franchise turnover produces a steady influx of new ownership groups, which usually want to negotiate new arrangements with their stadium landlords, in turn producing more intercity bidding for franchises. Team sales are encouraged by the unique prerogative of franchises to depreciate players salaries for five years; this gives owners at least some incentive to sell the team after five years. As new owners negotiate more lucrative deals with local authorities, other teams in the league seek similar advantages just to keep pace. The cycle of some teams gaining business advantages over other teams, and those other teams playing catch-up, begins anew.

The turnover of sports franchises has a direct bearing on the city-franchise relationship in another way. Owners feel that to maximize the sale price of their team for prospective local buyers, they must shop the team around to other cities. Pirates President Carl Barger argues: "You have to use the threat of relocation as leverage to attract local ownership. Without it, a team cannot be sold for a fair price."[3]

The Economic Base of Professional Sports

The economics of sports has changed dramatically in two related ways in the last several decades. First, sports has "commodified"—that is, it has become increasingly bound up with the larger process of economic production and distribution, part of the powerful recreation and entertainment sector of the economy. Second, sports has "delocalized": like manufacturing and other sectors, sports has become less dependent on attachment to a specific place.

For much of human history, sports has represented a release from the demands of economic production, something separate from the cash nexus; but in recent years, recreational activities have become a growing part of the economy.[4] Because of commodification, virtually every aspect of sports and recreation is now part of the economic process.[5] This change has profoundly affected the character of sports. Most adults, for example, can remember a time when sports were informal pastimes, with ad hoc rules, minimal supervision, and rudimentary equipment. Even youth sports today are dominated by organizations and firms that produce the means by which children play. Little leagues for sports at all levels, camps, training facilities, tennis and golf and swimming lessons, uniforms and other sportswear, health and nutrition aids, drugs, and a proliferation of equipment have turned youth into consumers of sport. It is now almost unthinkable to play a sport without becoming part of the economics-sports nexus.

The same holds for sports spectatorship. To be sure, sports spectatorship has long been a pecuniary affair.[6] It has long been normal for fans to pay for tickets, refreshments, and souvenirs. The nature of spectatorship has changed remarkably, however. Fans are not just avid followers of teams, but also full-fledged buyers and sellers of commodities—what might be called "fansumers." As the sports industry provides more products and services to the fan, the fan is drawn into more and more consumer relationships. The simple act of attending a game has been complicated by the need for an automobile and the costly incidental purchases at the game. Many fans also buy expensive team-promoting sportswear and equipment, publications, access to cable television sports programming, admission to special events like "fantasy camps" and cruises, and a variety of souvenirs.[7] One indication of the high stakes of this game is the ongoing battle among producers of bubble-gum cards.[8] Franchises are so concerned about fansumers that they have submitted their operations to the rigors of modern marketing. "Teams are starting to understand that they're not just competing against other teams," says Andy Dolich, vice-president for marketing for the Oakland Athletics. "Teams that understand they are part of the whole entertainment firmament seem to generate the most success."[9]

As sports has been increasingly defined by consumerism, it has also decentralized. In their marketing strategies, franchises have taken to heart the adage about hunting—duck hunters should go where the ducks are. Sports franchises orient their marketing efforts to exurban areas because that is where they can find the most attractive fansumers.

Sports marketing has shifted from blue-collar urban workers to upscale groups with more disposable income—in other words, the booming areas of the suburbs in the North and the new cities of the South and West. This shift is in part a response to the greater ability of suburban fans to afford tickets and concessions, the orientation toward automobile transportation, and the greater advertising revenues possible with upscale markets. In recent years, the makeup of baseball and football fans who attend games has shifted toward to the white middle class. Owners are aware that studies show higher levels of fan support among populations with more whites than blacks.[10] Only 6.8 percent of all baseball fans who attended games in 1986 were black (12 percent of the total population was black). The skewing of sport toward wealthier groups may affect major league rosters: more white players survive in baseball with inferior statistics.[11] Discrimination against minorities regularly shows up in studies of fans' attitudes and spending preferences.[12]

The targeting of affluent markets has transformed teams from local to regional enterprises. Many teams now downplay their home towns in order to appeal to the entire region. The Baltimore Orioles, whose fan base extends to Pennsylvania, Washington, D.C., Virginia, West Virginia, and the Carolinas, urge fans to visit "Birdland" rather than Baltimore. When the team decided in 1988 to redesign its uniforms, management's first requirement was that the word *Baltimore* not appear on them. (The city's name was restored when the logo was again redesigned in 1992.[13]) Team surveys show that 25 percent of the team's fans come from Washington, D.C., and its suburbs. The team president, Lawrence Lucchino, acknowledges the delocalizing strategy: "We embarked on a regionalization campaign. It didn't take a Harvard business and marketing genius to realize there was a great opportunity available in areas like Washington; York, Pennsylvania; and Annapolis. Regionalization became our watchword."[14] The site selected for the team's new stadium was on the southern edge of the city, a half-hour drive closer to Washington, D.C. than was Memorial Stadium.

In their pitches to the leagues, cities seeking to attract teams increasingly stress the larger regions from which they can draw and the affluent consumers accessible in exurban areas. In the 1991 competition for two NFL expansion teams, San Antonio emphasized that its broadcasting area extends as far as Austin. Memphis, Nashville, and Knoxville formed a Tennessee consortium in the same competition. When groups from Miami and Denver were awarded baseball expansion teams in 1991, they decided to call their teams by the names of their states rather than their cities, for marketing reasons.

The Chicago White Sox, traditionally the emblem of the city's working-class stiffs, has shifted its main marketing focus to middle-class suburbanites. The team has targeted its advertising appeals to suburbanites. In a move that angered many long-time fans, the White Sox in 1985 shifted most local broadcast operations from commercial to cable television. The team planned to move to suburban Addison until an anti-stadium movement blocked the move. The inner-city park that a state authority recently built for the White Sox is designed to attract suburban fans. White Sox officials have been so blunt in their efforts to attract suburbanites that they have antagonized the Chicagoans who have supported the team for decades.[15]

Professional sports leagues since the 1970s have pursued explicit and implicit policies of suburbanization. Prior to 1960, none of the twenty-eight franchises in major league baseball or the National Football League were located outside of a central city. By 1990, however, eleven teams played outside the inner city, and as many as a half-dozen others were considering such a move. The NFL even encourages moves within a seventy-five-mile radius of the team's current site. Commissioner Rozelle explained the logic of the suburban policy:

> The Giants' move to the Meadowlands, across the river to New Jersey, was a move of six or seven miles from Times Square. . . . I don't think there's any question that the Giants are getting the same support that they got from New Yorkers. They're on the same television channel in New York, and I don't think it makes much difference if you're moving to a better facility in the suburbs. . . . I think that a suburban move by any of our clubs, such as we've had in the past . . . is justified. I realize the city may be concerned, but I'm saying the Jets' fans will be serviced as they have been in the past on the same television station— if they were to move.[16]

City governments place a high priority on keeping teams within the city limits, but even when they succeed in doing so they must make concessions to suburbanization. New city stadiums are designed for the convenience of suburbanites. The new structures typically lie at the city's edge, more closely tied to outlying areas by a tangle of highways than to the city itself. Unlike old parks, which were wedged into a tight, neighborhood space with proximity to houses and small businesses, the new facilities are usually surrounded by acres of parking lots. The lots sometimes serve the central business district, which is the part of the city most commonly used by white-collar suburbanites. Pittsburgh's stadium parking lots are used by downtown workers during business hours. Public transportation to the stadium is limited. In every way, the new stadiums are places for outsiders to come, spend their money, and leave; they are not integrated with other urban institutions and even do much to destroy tight-knit neighborhood patterns.

The Importance of Being Broadcast

Revenues from national and local television contracts—once a minor supplement to the revenue gained from ticket sales and related activities at the stadium—now constitute the major source of financial support for professional sports. As a league's television contract goes, so goes the league.

A television audience's demographic characteristics are often more important than the size of the audience. Broadcasters stand to earn more in advertising revenues if they provide upscale audiences. Television and stadium audiences overlap, but they are not the same; leagues must balance their appeal to the stadium fan and to the television fan without unduly antagonizing either. Increasingly, however, the television fan has become the preferred customer. Leagues schedule games to occur in "prime time." They also stress the star system in marketing the club.[17] Players like Joe Montana, Dwight Gooden, and José Canseco are glamourized to sell the product to important television audiences. To reach large, upscale audiences attractive to advertisers, teams develop public relations campaigns that address middle- and upper-class fans and ignore less affluent groups.

The nationalization of sports has profoundly undermined a team's relationship with the local community and also with local industries. One scholar suggests that the shift from local to national television broadcasting may have been partly responsible for the monopolization of the beer industry by a few large breweries. Breweries and other local industries used campaigns tied to the local sports team to develop markets within the community. The sports franchises and other local businesses were, in other words, symbiotic. With the emergence of network broadcasting, however, national advertisers came to dominate marketing to sports consumers. At the same time, national breweries came to dominate the beer industry and killed off many local breweries.[18]

Network television has supplied most of the recent wealth in professional sports; regional broadcasting has added to revenues of baseball teams. Some 60.5 million viewers watched football in 1987, while baseball attracted 57.7 million viewers. But the network ratings fell in the 1980s as a result of a proliferation of sports and other entertainment programming on local and cable television. Sports as a whole lost 4 percent of its national network ratings from 1986 to 1987, with a 4.3 percent decline in football and an 8.3 percent decline in baseball.[19] The percentage points represent tens of millions of viewers. With national network ratings in decline, experts expect baseball and football to shift more games, including playoff and championship contests, to cable television.

Cable television has extended the possibilities of broadcasting. About 60 percent of all homes in the U.S. were wired for cable in the late 1980s. Affluent homes dominate cable hookups. Cable offers opportunities for sports growth for two reasons. First, cable can accommodate dozens of channels and thereby broadcast several times as much programming as over-the-air television. Second, since viewers pay for access, cable television produces more total revenue. Consumers pay different rates according to the number of channels they wish to receive. Most sports programming on cable is offered as part of premium packages, which cost subscribers more than the basic package. One cable option that may transform the sports industry is pay-per-view television, in which cable companies transmit programs such as concerts and sporting events to specific homes in return for separate charges. Industry experts speculate that major events soon will be broadcast on a pay-per-view basis. If only half of the homes that normally watch the Super Bowl paid $5 for pay-per-view transmission, the revenues would be greater than $100 million, not including advertising revenues.[20] The three networks now pay just over four times that amount—$423 million—for broadcasting sixty-four regular season games, nine playoff games, and the Super Bowl.

Shifting braodcasts to cable television does risk losing fan support. Broadcasts on "free" network television make events available to all fans. It is, in a way, free advertising of the product—the team and the sport. The existence of diehard fans is what keeps stadiums full, commercial rates high, and sales of souvenirs and concessions up. The NFL owes much of its success, for instance, to ABC's "Monday Night Football" telecasts.[21] Not everyone has access to cable; urbanites, in fact, have gone longest without the service. Professional football and baseball already have alienated fans by shifting many games to cable.

Industry analysts predict that pay-per-view cable will be incorporated into the broadcasting strategies of professional sports. The sports organizations must guard against causing such a tilt toward elite audiences that they undermine their broad bases of fan support. One journalist proposed using pay-per-view TV as a way to reinforce network broadcasting and local followings.[22] Under this proposal, the 15 million U.S. households with pay-per-view capacity could elect to see games offered to other television markets by the networks. For example, if a Bengals-Raiders game were offered by the Washington NBC affiliate, fans in Washington more interested in a game offered at the same time by another NBC affiliate could buy access to that other broadcast. Only games offered by network affiliates could be purchased by the viewer, so the networks' market share would not be undermined. In addition, pay-per-view as a network supplement could enable fans to see local games that are "blacked out" of the hometown broadcast area.

The NFL has treated the pay-per-view concept gingerly. League officials are wary of giving Congress or other critics a pretext for examining a wide range of sports issues, from labor relations to franchise relocation. However the leagues decide to deal with broadcasting, it will shape the industry for decades to come. Donald Fehr, the baseball players' bargaining representative, states bluntly: "The biggest issue in the industry is the nature of the restructuring of broadcasting. Currently, teams share the revenue from the networks, and we don't even know if networks will be involved with TV after 1993."[23]

Sports broadcasting can damage lower levels of competition because of the emphasis it puts on regional and national rather than local teams. Fans are less attracted to local college and minor league teams when the airwaves are saturated with major league teams and a trip to the stadium is just an automobile ride away. When televised broadcasts of major league baseball began, many minor leagues and their teams foundered. The number of minor league clubs declined from 450 in 1959 to 148 twenty years later. With the introduction of major league baseball to Florida in 1993, the demise of the eight-team Florida State League may not be far behind.[24] However, with a reorientation in marketing, many minor leagues have thrived in recent years, even though others were suffering.[25]

One study concludes that the possibility of greater television revenues was an important factor in at least half of baseball's franchise transfers.[26] New broadcasting markets were leading considerations for the Dodgers and Giants' moves to California, the Braves' move from Milwaukee to Atlanta, and the Washington Senators' moves to Minnesota and then Texas. The Chicago White Sox nearly moved to Florida in 1988; perhaps the attraction most strongly "pulling" the Sox was the prospect of a statewide television contract. The Seattle Mariners' relatively meager local television revenues prompted owner Jeff Smulyan to put the team on the market; if it had not found a local buyer it would have moved to another city with better television potential.

Broadcasting combines with other initiatives to expand its profit-making opportunities. Baseball has used Third World countries as grounds for recruiting players for years.[27] The foreign reach of North American sports expanded from inputs to outputs when the National Football League in 1989 announced formation of an international league, which would play games in West Germany, Great Britain, and Italy. The NFL has broadcast the annual Super Bowl across the globe since the 1970s. It also stages exhibitions at London's Wembley Stadium and broadcasts delayed tapes of games and highlights every week.[28] With the European Economic Community's reduction of trading barriers among its twelve countries in 1992, experts expect the television industry to change fundamentally. Global sports advertising, which totaled $8 billion in all media in 1987, could increase to $50 billion in the year 2000. Sports producers in the United States would likely hold the advantage early in the development of worldwide broadcasting. A sports trade journal notes that

> what is developing globally is the setup of a classic product—in this case [sports in] the United States—dominating a market but becoming a mature brand with little prospect for expansion. What happens then is the inevitable whittling away of its control of the market. Export could turn to import, and suddenly the sports world will have to consider such things as a sports balance of trade.[29]

Such a scenario suggests that someday baseball's World Series may actually live up to its name.

The Leagues and Stadium Politics

A league is a collection of separate teams, a necessary system for organizing regular contests that lead to a championship. In many ways a league is a natural monopoly. Leagues require cooperation among their members in order to schedule games, establish common rules and standards, and maintain a fairly even distribution of talent and therefore interesting contests. Many leagues faltered in their nascent stages because a few teams became so dominant that the contests provided little interest. Saying that leagues require cooperation, however, is not to say that they need to collude on all important issues. Individual franchises could be allowed to operate on their own in everything except scheduling, game rules, and some labor issues.

The national organizations of baseball and football negotiate network contracts for each season, then divide the proceeds evenly among their teams. This profit-sharing is important for two reasons. First, it serves as insurance against economic volatility. The fortunes of franchises can change rapidly, and the income from television limits potential losses. Second, the system equalizes resources so that a few teams do not dominate—and suffocate—the league.

Within this somewhat socialistic system, however, the profit incentive remains. Even though the league's viability depends on cooperation, each team has a separate interest in performing better than opponents. The one-upmanship has short- and long-term aspects, and success on the field is important for both. In the short term, teams want to increase their yearly revenue; winning usually produces a financial boon, with better ticket prices and sales. In the long term, success increases the franchise's value. Most team owners are going to make their biggest profits on the sale of the team. Glamourous teams like the San Francisco Forty-Niners and the Dallas Cowboys are worth significantly more than teams from areas of comparable size like the Indianapolis Colts and the New England Patriots. The desire to win puts an upward pressure on player salaries. The NFL has formal and informal mechanisms to control salaries, but the 1991 league payroll of $693 million represented a 29-percent increase from the previous year.[30]

In the attempt to balance increases in expenses like player salaries, luxury seating, usually called skyboxes, has become one of the greatest sources of extra revenue in both baseball and football. Corporations and wealthy patrons can rent these glass-enclosed luxury suites—which typically provide plush seating for eight to twelve spectators, with a bar and restaurant—for $40,000 to $75,000 apiece. The highest current prices for skyboxes are the $100,000 to $225,000 at Toronto's new SkyDome. Most important, skybox revenues are exempt from the league's revenue-sharing requirements for ticket sales, so the revenues go directly into the team's or local government's coffers. Skyboxes provide millions in additional revenues yearly.[31] Such funds could be important in bidding for top players and in financing player development programs or simply in keeping a favorable ledger. In the 1980s, teams aggressively sought access to skybox revenues—demanding that local governments or businesses build the units in the stadiums. The teams often insisted on whole new facilities, to better accommodate skybox construction.

Skyboxes were introduced at the Houston Astrodome in 1965, but the skybox boom did not occur until the 1980s. Luxury seating has become a crucial strategy for overcoming the equality of team revenues that revenue-sharing produces, especially in the NFL. The 215 skyboxes at Joe Robbie Stadium outside Maimi bring in almost $9 million a year, and 10,000 unenclosed luxury seats earn another $10 million. A proposal for a new stadium for the Washington Redskins estimates annual revenue from luxury seating at $58 million, including $21 million from 300 skyboxes. Luxury suites usually are leased for five or ten years. The Dallas Cowboys have begun to sell skyboxes outright rather than simply lease them. For the cost of purchase, fans can "literally live with the Cowboys. They don't even have to cut the lawn, and they can usually resell at a profit."[32]

Skybox revenues may be more sensitive to larger economic trends than ticket and concession revenues. The exorbitant cost of luxury seating may be one of the first expenses eliminated during corporate cutbacks of discretionary spending. The experience of Texas teams during the 1980s slump in oil prices provides some evidence. In 1986 the Cowboys opened 120 new suites on the top level of the stadium; 70 of those seats were vacant two years later. Major sports boosters reduce their activity during economic slumps. "People who would buy season tickets to the Oilers, Astros, Rockets, and Cougars . . . would cut it down to maybe one sport," said one analyst. Teams that required long-term commitments to skyboxes were hit hardest.[33] Skyboxes are also vulnerable to changes in the federal tax laws, which have in the past provided deductions for businesses renting luxury seating to entertain clients. Corporations now account for about half of the gate receipts of many franchises.

The rising cost of franchises makes yearly profitability more important. Modern owners expect to see fast returns on their investments, whereas owners a generation ago were content to receive small but stable returns. The debt that many owners assume to buy teams increases pressures for success on the field and in the ledger books. This more intense financial concern causes teams to demand improvements in stadium and broadcast contracts. Teams can add millions a year to their coffers by renting luxury suites at stadiums; but these often require construction of a brand new stadium, since facilities built as recently as the 1970s do not have the structural capacity for such seating. Stadiums located close to suburban markets can produce stronger revenue streams. Parking, concessions, taxes, and real-estate development are also important considerations in the aggressive search for profits.

One way to cut costs and increase revenues simultaneously is to negotiate better lease agreements with state and local governments. By threatening to move the team to a city that offers better terms, clubs can gain concessions on rent, ticket revenues, sales of novelties and food, parking, and land. Some teams have exerted enough leverage to gain rent-free leases, and others have gained valuable land for parking and development. Most teams signing new leases exact from the local government and businesses guarantees of specified attendance levels. Teams cannot constantly move around, lest they undermine the league's base of devoted fans, but they can always hint or threaten to move.

Even though it would be unthinkable for all the threatening teams to move, cities do take seriously the immediate danger of their franchises' relocation. In the absence of equitable standards and coordination for expansions, municipalities tend to confront only what is most immediate to them—that is, the threat of a team move. Leases involve so many intricate financial matters that there is almost always room for new concessions. If a team strikes a good balance between public threats and private negotiation, it can gain a favorable deal with the local government—and an even better deal with another jurisdiction.

Sports as a Monopoly

Despite acknowledging that professional sports leagues are monopolistic, the federal courts have refused to confront the leagues. The courts at different times have reasoned that the cultural value of sport is too great for the judiciary to tamper with it, that Congress should be the body to regulate the sports industry, and that monopoly control is necessary for the leagues' survival.[34] In the absence of blatant abuses, the leagues will probably retain monopoly control.[35]

Monopolistic tendencies manifest themselves in different ways. Strictly speaking, *monopoly* refers to total control of product markets, *monopsony* to mastery of labor markets, and *oligopoly* to near-total mastery of markets through collusion with other producers. At various times, baseball and football have exhibited the characteristics of all three economic conditions. Baseball's reserve clause created a monopsony, binding employees to employers for as long as those employers wished to control them. If major league baseball were not also a monopoly, it might not have been a monopsony; the lack of rival leagues gave players little choice in their employment. In another sense, baseball can be considered an oligopoly, in that it acts in concert with other professional sports, such as football, on matters like broadcasting and stadiums and thereby colludes to restrict access. Baseball is also oligopolistic when the individual teams are considered separate enterprises and collude on important matters.

Theories on the harmfulness of monopolies vary. Some critics of monopolies argue that a monopoly can defeat any competitor with the blunt use of force and that a monopoly can thwart competition just by presenting such an intimidating posture that potential rivals will not even attempt a challenge. To protect the consumer, they say, the government should vigorously enforce antitrust laws against combinations and takeovers of industries. Only when the consumer has a meaningful choice, and producers must strive to expand options for the consumer, can the consumer and society be served. Among the important questions this interpretation poses are just how much choice the consumer needs and how much competition is necessary for consumer sovereignty.[36]

Others dispute the argument for government action by questioning the ability of monopolies to maintain control for long. Even if an entire industry falls under the sway of one provider, like the league, it is questionable whether the industry can strive without being responsive to the consumer. The baseball industry may be a monopoly, but it must respond not only to its own customers but also to the rest of the entertainment industry and to the construction, transportation, and media industries. Baseball has responded to the consumers of the larger entertainment market with suburban stadiums, network and cable television contracts, and even rule changes (such as the controversial designated hitter rule and the instant replay rule in baseball and football). Even artificially high prices can benefit consumers, according to this school of thought, since minimum ticket prices may be necessary to maintain a strong overall team product.[37]

The experience of baseball and football should cast some doubts on both of these analyses of monopolies. In each side's rush to argue that monopolies dominate the market without attention to consumer demands, or that monopolies cannot control markets for long, a more complex understanding is lost. An industry may be both unitary and fragmented, and this mixture might best serve the industry's overall interests.

That baseball and football are monopolies tends to put their actions beyond the control of outside forces. The teams cooperate on a wide range of issues, not only to assure order and a viable product, but also to address common challenges. Television contracts and standards for stadiums are examples of collective policies that enhance the profit-making potential of all clubs. Even the competition among franchises for the best players and playing facilities, which exists within this system of cooperation, can yield collective benefits. Al Davis's decision to move the Raiders from Oakland to Los Angeles, for example, endangered the organizational structure and prerogatives of the NFL, but it opened the door for later moves by the Colts and Cardinals and it increased the bargaining power of all franchises vis-à-vis cities. The NFL also used the occasion to argue for antitrust exemptions from Congress. In such cases, the cartel's apparent instability ultimately can give it greater strength and cohesion.

The stadium issue is a classic illustration of internal unrest producing greater cohesion. The teams demand better lease terms in order to gain an advantage over rivals. A new stadium might provide the kind of revenues that the team can use to become dominant or competitive in league play. At a certain moment, this break from the ranks is a threat. If the Los Angeles Rams negotiate a stadium lease that gives them tens of millions of dollars more each year than the rest of the teams in the league, they gain an important advantage. They could become the dominant team in the league. But as other cities use the Rams' advantage as a new minimum standard for the whole industry, the cartel as a whole is strengthened.

The only immediate danger to the cartel is the possibility of outside governmental action. This danger, however, is minimized by the symbolic and emotional bond between political jurisdictions and professional sports teams and by a policy discourse that tends to isolate one or two aspects of the overall problem—like an owner's personality—rather than seriously confronting the leagues. At no time in modern debates over the development of sports policy has the fundamental character of the industry been questioned.

The Legal Privileges of Sports

Debate about the monopoly status of professional sports has turned on narrow legal and economic interpretations. Specifically, judges and scholars debate how the Sherman Antitrust Act should apply to sports. Several questions are at issue. First, should it be the leagues or their teams that are considered the main economic units of the sport? Second, what kinds of restraint of trade are relevant? Third, should the government oppose all monopolistic practices, or should it allow those that can be shown to serve consumer interests? Just what is the consumer interest? Finally, do some unique industries deserve exemption from antitrust scrutiny?

The antitrust laws are designed to block attempts by businesses to become monopolies and restrain the activities of competitors or potential competitors. The exemptions given to professional sports established the notion that the only viable form of team sports competition is the self-contained league. This has allowed dominant leagues to smother their competition and manipulate cities.

Baseball's privileged antitrust status stems from a narrow interpretation of the notions of commerce and interstate commerce. In *Federal Baseball Club* v. *National League* in 1922, the Supreme Court held that since baseball was played within the borders of a single state, it was an intrastate activity not subject to federal statutes. The Court also maintained that baseball was more a game or amusement than a business and therefore not subject to antitrust scrutiny. The Court concluded that interstate transportation for league play was purely incidental to the game. The decision, written by Oliver Wendell Holmes, relied on the *Paul* (1868) precedent, which held that the insurance industry did not engage in commerce but an activity incidental to commerce. The Court has broadened its definitions of interstate commerce since 1922, but baseball's antitrust exemption stands. In *South-Eastern Underwriters* (1944), another insurance case, the Court overturned seventy-five years of precedent and found that the insurance industry was indeed engaged in interstate commerce and was therefore subject to Sections 1 and 2 of the Sherman Antitrust Act.[38] In the *Gardella* (1949), *Martin* (1949), and *Toolson* (1952) cases, the Court decided that baseball was interstate commerce after all, but the Court also said baseball's special place as the "national pastime," and the force of the judicial doctrine of *stare decisis*, mitigated against overturning *Federal Baseball Club*. If baseball's special antitrust status were to be ended, Congress would have to do it.

Other sports do not enjoy baseball's blanket antitrust immunity but have a variety of protections. The National Football League gained major antitrust exemptions in the 1960s that enabled it to conclude a national television contract and merge with the upstart American Football League.

Under the labor-law exemption, a business can use collective bargaining agreements to supersede antitrust law. As long as the labor agreement is not in itself a management conspiracy to monopolize commerce or adversely affect entities not party to the agreement, the league can "immunize" itself from some antitrust challenges. A number of labor rights can be forfeited under quid pro quo arrangements. The federal courts in *Mackey* v. *National Football League* declared that the so-called Rozelle Rule, which required compensation to teams whose players signed with another franchise, was a restraint of trade only because it was not a labor provision bargained "at arm's length" with player representatives. In addition, courts do not consider some provisions of a collective bargaining agreement to be permanent, since the players who were party to the agreement are replaced by new generations of players. Nonbargaining players—that is, members of scholastic or other leagues—may not be bound by the agreement.[39]

The NFL has attempted to gain even broader authority over its affairs by claiming to be a single entity. A league cannot function without some kind of cooperation among franchises. If the teams are considered separate firms, they may be judged to be illegally conspiring when they act in concert—for example, when they vote to forbid the transfer of a franchise from one city to another. If, however, the league is considered a single firm, in competition with other entertainment industries, such as other sports, film, television, music, circuses, amusement parks, publishing, and so on, then the league's internal cooperation can be considered proper, not much different from a chain store's management of franchises or a law firm's management of divisions.

The courts' answer to the single entity question, perhaps the most important currently in professional sports, is that in some respects the league can be considered a single entity and in others it should be considered a collection of competitors. The logic of this position is expressed by legal scholar John C. Weistart:

> It does not seem inevitable that a sports league would be treated as a single entity for all decisions that it makes in connection with its operation. One could imagine, for example, that the antitrust liability of the league might vary depending on whether the clubs involved were buying uniforms, assigning players, or allocating franchises. It should be clear that the clubs within a league involve themselves in a variety of different markets and take actions which affect third parties who have varying degrees of closeness to the league's management.[40]

According to this logic, the league should be allowed to cooperate to provide a product—teams of relatively equal strength competing for a league championship—but that league may not otherwise restrain trade. Monopolization of television revenues or collusion to deny franchises to cities and to squeeze exorbitant benefits out of cities presently in the league should be considered restraint of trade. The league may constitute a single entity in many of its endeavors, but that status should not immunize the league in the whole range of its actions.[41]

Other considerations are also important for the resolution of antitrust issues. One issue is the legal standard of judgment. Two approaches—

the "per se" standard, which means a simple determination of monopoly control, and the "rule of reason," a balancing of several legitimate but conflicting interests—dominate legal proceedings.[42] With a per se standard, determining whether sports leagues act as monopolies is an all-or-nothing matter and sports might require radical restructuring to avoid antitrust violations. The rule of reason would allow leagues to be judged according to a wide range of criteria, as Weistart suggests.

Baseball has retained its privileged status because of its strong symbolic hold as the "national pastime" and the leagues' skill in responding to occasional challenges from Congress. When Congress threatens to eliminate the antitrust protection, baseball expands into new territories. Members of Congress can be mollified by the addition of new teams, just as they often are gratified by the construction of new military bases, veterans' hospitals, or water reclamation projects in their districts.

Team Profits and Franchise Relocation

The most prominent argument for monopoly control of professional sports, after the contention that leagues require cooperation, is that the sports industry is a financial burden. Year after year, leagues release statements that claim millions of dollars in losses for their franchises.

It is difficult to assess the cries of fiscal woe, because all but one professional team, the Green Bay Packers of the NFL, are privately held corporations unwilling to release important financial information. Information about the general revenues and expenses of teams is not difficult to find. Public information abounds about player salaries, lease terms, and television and ticket revenues, but it is hard to put into context. The way franchises use their sports assets to feed outside enterprises, such as broadcasting, publishing, and beer companies, is difficult to analyze. Reckoning profitability is complicated by the mysteries of the tax system and arcane accounting and management practices.

A 1988 survey by the *Los Angeles Times* found that only seven of the NFL's twenty-eight teams earned profits in the 1987 season,[43] but the calculations are flawed in a number of ways. First, the vast majority of the teams' losses were attributable to $30 million the clubs had to pay to the Los Angeles Raiders as damages stemming from the 1982 antitrust suit and the lost television revenues from the 1987 players' strike. Second, revenues were underestimated, because of incomplete information about the franchises' revenues from concessions and luxury seating. Third, the study does not consider the millions of dollars of tax benefits that many franchises receive for depreciation of assets (player contracts and equipment), paper losses, and portfolios. Finally, the wide array of ancillary benefits that franchise owners can receive, such as land and development deals and tie-ins with other businesses, were not considered.

The annual reports of the football team from the smallest market indicate a potential for small but steady profits even in an era of growing player salaries. The Green Bay Packers' 1989 annual report[44] indicates a profit of $433,989, its lowest in recent years. A 60-percent increase in salaries over the previous three years had reduced the team's overall profits. But the Packers' profitability may be underestimated in team statements. Published accounts indicate that the club earns more than $1 million annually from interest on a reserve capital account of $15.1 million.[45] With television contracts scheduled to climb from $17 million in 1987 to $39 million in 1993, the club could add significantly to its profit margin, especially with prudence in managing its payroll. Other teams may be in a more profitable position. The Packers list close to $7 million in annual overhead expenses; many clubs have practically no overhead expenses, since they have bargained favorable leases with their home jurisdictions. Furthermore, the Packers report less than $1 million in income from private boxes, while other NFL clubs make up to $15 million.[46]

Because of the secrecy of the sports franchises, inconclusive evidence must suffice in discussing profitability. As a general rule, professional sports is a profitable business. Every team does not do well every year, but with decent marketing, reasonable cost controls, and an occasional winning team, every franchise can succeed financially. Some teams are more financially successful when they are losing than when winning, since it is easier then to control player salaries. Poorly performing teams also make a more compelling case for public support, including construction of a new stadium, since they can claim a "crisis" situation.

A survey by *Financial World* magazine, probably the most extensive examination of the finances of professional sports franchises, found that 79 of the 102 baseball, football, basketball, and hockey teams made money in 1991. Total revenues were $4.34 billion and operating income was $560 million.[47] Those estimates, however, are probably pessimistic, because they do not include calculations of depreciation, interest, and expansion-related fees. Various accounting methods that could yield millions to the teams also are not taken into account.[48]

The total revenues of baseball teams in 1991 ranged between $38.8 million (Brewers) and $90 million (Yankees). All teams received $15.5 million from national broadcasting contracts, as well as $3.7 million per team in licensing fees. Gate receipts ranged from about $12 million to $28 million. Stadium advertising, parking, and concession sales brought in another $3 million to $10 million. Luxury seating brought teams varying amounts from nothing to $5 million. The greatest differences in team revenues were from local broadcasting deals. The New York Yankees received about $40 million from cable and over-air television stations, while the Seattle Mariners received only about $5 million.

The total expenses of baseball teams in 1991 extended from a low of $31.5 million (Astros) to a high of $72 million (Dodgers), mostly because of different payrolls. The minor league systems cost from $3.5 million to $5 million. Rent of stadiums ranged from nothing at all to $3 million; the average was around $2 million. (Some cities have actually paid teams to play at their stadium.) The average cost of player development was $5 million. Player salaries account for the widest disparities in team expenses. The Oakland Athletics ($39.2 million) and Los Angeles Dodgers ($36 million) had baseball's largest payrolls in 1991; the Houston Astros ($12.1 million) and Seattle Mariners ($17.4 million) had the smallest. Payment to Major League Baseball's central fund amounted to $2.3 million. Office expenses and player disability insurance cost another $3 million to $5 million.

The profitability of NFL teams is more straightforward, because revenues are shared more equally. Total revenues in 1991 ranged from $45 million (Packers) to $66 million (Dolphins). Broadcasting revenues from regular-season and post-season games are shared equally, with each team receiving $30 million in 1991. Each team can arrange its own pre-season broadcasting deals, which can produce $2 million or so. Ticket revenues are split between home and away teams on a 60-40 basis, but because of different seating capacities and ticket prices, revenues vary. In 1991 gate receipts varied from $8 million to $12 million. NFL teams each got $1.7 million in licensing fees. Team revenues from advertising, parking, and concessions averaged around $1 million. The biggest revenue disparities came from luxury seating, with some teams receiving nothing and others making anywhere from $5 million to $16 million.

The total expenses of football teams in 1991 ran from $41.8 million (Buccaneers) to $52.2 million (Forty-Niners). Stadium rents averaged about $1.6 million, extending from no rent to $2.3 million for the Dolphins. Salaries account for most of the differences. Player costs ranged from a low of $19 million (Steelers) to $32.6 million (Forty-Niners), with an average of just under $25 million. Teams also vary in the annual debt service they owe for purchase of the team and related assets.

In addition to these constant revenues and expenses, the leagues have one-time revenues and costs. In 1993, for example, baseball teams will have $190 million to divvy up from the entry fees of the two expansion teams. On the other side of the ledger, teams owe players $280 million in damages for their collusion to hold down salaries in the mid-1980s. NFL teams had to make a one-time payment totaling $50 million in damages to the Los Angeles Memorial Coliseum Commission and the Raiders franchise for attempting to block the franchise's move from Oakland to Los Angeles. Football teams will also have to pay four players $1.62 million each as a result of a free-agency case decided in 1992.

Baseball executives often express alarm at the growing disparity between the revenues of franchises from large and small media markets. The size of the market—ranging from 3.3 million in San Diego to 24.6 million in New York—determines the local broadcasting fees teams can obtain. In 1991, Commissioner Francis T. Vincent, Jr., warned that "baseball is poised for a catastrophe, and it might not be far off."[49] The fear is that the competitive balance among clubs will be upset as teams from profitable markets like New York and Los Angeles spend millions to secure the best players. The claim may have some validity, but it ignores research findings that show little correlation between salaries and performance.[50] It is possible to put together a competitive, profitable baseball team with less money. In fact, spending millions often handicaps wealthy teams by draining resources and limiting their roster flexibility.[51] Baseball has experienced its greatest balance of team talent since the beginning of open bidding for players.

To the extent that the gap in local broadcasting revenues is a problem for baseball, it is one that the industry can correct without demanding new stadiums and subsidies from local governments. One union official's comment would be just as appropriate coming from a local government official: "If there's really a problem with small-market clubs, why don't the clubs solve it instead of asking us to?"[52] The National Basketball Association has become immensely profitable with a team salary cap. Pooling some or all of the local television revenues and distributing them among all teams is another idea, albeit an unpopular one among large-market owners. The owners proposed a revenue-sharing arrangement that would allocate a certain percentage of the team's revenues to salaries in 1989; the players' union rejected it at the time but might bargain over such an arrangement in the future. In 1982, the NFL players' union proposed using a fixed percentage of gross receipts for player salaries, to be paid from a league pool according to a wage scale involving seniority and performance standards.[53] One innovative idea was broached by *Forbes* magazine: loosen the restrictions on player sales. In 1976 baseball commissioner Bowie Kuhn set a $400,000 limit on player sales, and the limit has not been revised to conform with new economic realities. If the limit were raised to $4 million, small-market teams would have the flexibility and moveable assets they need to stay competitive.[54] It is a variation on the St. Louis Cardinals' strategy of the 1940s and 1950s to become one of baseball's most profitable franchises, that is, developing talent in the minor leagues and then making money with sales of contracts.

Owners might take the free-market prescription a step further by ending broadcasting market exclusivity for teams. The reason New York's Yankees and Mets make such vast revenues from local broadcasting rights is that they have a total claim on the biggest market in the nation. If teams could put together broadcasting packages to market for nationwide over-air syndication or cable programming, good teams from smaller markets, like the Pittsburgh Pirates or the Baltimore Orioles, could compete more fairly for broadcasting revenues against teams from major markets.[55] Teams might devise rivalry packages—blocks of games involving old or new rivals, like the Giants against the Dodgers or the Orioles against the Blue Jays—which could be sold regionally or nationally. Groupings might highlight marquee players or critical series.

To confront salary inflation, owners might adopt another radical market approach: end all restrictions on player mobility. The sports industry has always attempted to restrict players' ability to offer their services on the open market, fearing that bidding wars would cause salaries to escalate. Both baseball and football have systems of limited free agency, in which only players meeting certain criteria may sell themselves to the highest bidders. But by limiting the number of superior free agents to a couple dozen each year, the owners are restricting the supply of a precious commodity; and as any Economics 100 student knows, low supply and high demand cause high prices. In baseball, the salaries bargained in the restricted pool of free agents are extended to the rest of the labor market through arbitration. The owners might actually control salaries better by allowing market forces to work than by attempting to restrict access to the labor market.

The most profitable teams either pay low salaries or have an unusually large cash flow. Cash flow comes from lucrative broadcasting deals and luxury seating at the stadium. A particularly competitive team and a new facility can temporarily boost public interest and profits. Teams suffer when they are forced to pay high salaries but are unable to generate the attendance or broadcasting revenues to pay those salaries. With neither the limited salary structure of the losers nor the exceptional drawing power of the winners, they can be squeezed by salaries. The Pittsburgh Pirates are a prime example of a team that proved lucrative during a period of low salaries and then was forced to raise salaries after many players performed well. The Pirate payroll increased from $4 million in 1987 to

$7.7 million in 1988, $11.9 million in 1989, and $24.9 million in 1991.[56] In 1992, however, the Pirates managed to purge their payroll of some high salaries and still finish at the top of their division.

The Tax Privileges of Sports

Sports franchises offer a wide range of the tax and bookkeeping benefits to their owners.[57] *Fortune* magazine notes:

> When a team is successful, its returns are in a class with those found in the sort of real estate deal that generates cash flow, tax benefits, and long-term appreciation. . . . Professional sports teams qualify for so many tax benefits as to render their "book" profit or loss figures meaningless.[58]

Partners in money-losing franchises can use losses to offset tax liabilities in other enterprises. The national tax reform of 1986 eliminated benefits for individuals who are "passive" (noncontrolling) investors, but the break still applies to corporations. James F. Ambrose notes that a "truly profitable operation can appear on paper to be most unprofitable."[59] George Steinbrenner, the owner of the New York Yankees, is reported to have used the extensive profits from the franchise to revive his American Ship Building Company.[60] Edward DeBartolo secretly transferred ownership of football's San Francisco Forty-Niners to his father's real estate company to exploit the potential for paper tax losses.[61]

The size of a team's tax benefits depends on how its expenditures are classified: as current expenses, capital assets, or nondepreciable assets. Firms can deduct the cost of current expenses, and they can deduct the cost of capital assets over five years. The logic behind deductions for "depreciation" of capital costs is that assets such as machinery lose value over time and need to be replaced, often at considerable cost, so the government should help the firm recover losses from the deterioration or depreciation of assets. If a $1-million machine lasts only five years, for example, the firm can be said to "lose" $200,000 per year. Sports franchises depreciate the "value" of players. Baseball franchises could capitalize the costs of training players in the minor leagues, but then they would not be able to depreciate players at the major league level, so they treat the lower costs of minor league development as a current expense.

Professional sports is the only business in which salaries may be claimed as depreciable assets. For example, suppose a franchise is bought for $10.8 million and, with total player wages of $10.2 million, the owner makes a profit of $100,000 in the first year of operation. Using the Accelerated Cost Recovery System for figuring depreciation of assets, the owner can claim that he actually lost $1.545 million in the first year. In the second year, the owner can claim losses of $2.166 million.[62] Owners can claim depreciation of assets for five years after buying a franchise. The New York Mets deducted $9 million annually for player depreciation in the early 1980s. In 1976 Congress passed the Tax Reform Act, which places a 50-percent limit on the portion of the franchise price that can be attributed to player salaries (prior to the tax reform some 90 percent of the purchase price of a team could be allocated for depreciation over a seven-year period). Still, the remaining deductions are worth millions. Bowie Kuhn estimated in 1976 that baseball clubs deducted an average of 7 percent of total expenses.[63]

The tax benefits from depreciation last only five years, but there are ways to extend them. It is not unusual for ownership groups to buy each other out to extend tax benefits. In 1986, the Doubleday Company sold the New York Mets to two of its principal stockholders, Nelson Doubleday, Jr., and Fred Wilpon. Although the management did not change, the franchise technically had a new owner. Not coincidentally, the change in ownership came six years after the Doubleday Company first bought the club.

It is not just player contracts but also other intangible assets that are depreciated by sports franchises. Just about any aspect of the franchise can be depreciated—the franchise itself, contracts such as leases, concession and broadcasting agreements, files containing scouting reports, and customer lists. Gerald W. Scully, the author of the most authoritative study of baseball economics, argues that the depreciation claims of sports franchises lack legitimacy:

> The economic basis for the amortization of player contracts, broadcast and concession agreements, stadium leases, the franchise, and so on is by no means obvious. None of these contracts really are wasting assets. As the contracts expire, they are renewed. Clubs have valuable rights to sell. As players are traded or retire, they are replaced with new players, much as in any business. Further, clubs already deduct the training expenses associated with player development as these costs are accrued. There is no economic justification for the amortization of player contracts or other intangible assets in sports.[64]

Until 1986, another important question for franchises was whether transactions are taxed as capital gains or ordinary income; capital gains rates were more favorable. In 1971 the IRS ruled that the money franchises get from the entrance fee for expansion teams and the surrender of territorial

Table 2. Amortization of Chicago Cubs Baseball Team, 1982

Item	Allocation (thousands)	Percentage	Life (years)
Stadium	$7,611.6	32.3	20.0
Baseball equipment	1,910.6	8.1	8.0
Office equipment	207.2	0.9	10.0
Leasehold improvements	12.6	—	18.0
Concessions agreement	595.4	2.5	12.0
Landlease leasehold	1,389.3	5.9	31.0
Computer software	5.5	—	5.0
Scouting reports	258.0	1.1	3.5
Customer files	223.3	0.9	5.0
Player contracts	8,947.4	37.9	7.0
Franchise	1,250.3	5.3	40.0
Other assets	1,186.0	5.0	—
Total	23,597.2		

Source: Gerald W. Scully, *The Business of Major League Baseball* (Chicago: University of Chicago Press, 1989), p. 131, from data provided by Roger G. Noll.

rights should be considered capital gains.[65] The Tax Reform Act of 1986 eliminated the differential taxation of ordinary income and capital gains. Since 1989, President George Bush has made cuts in the rates of capital gains taxes a top priority. That legislation so far has failed in the Congress.

The key question is what part of a team's overall value should be attributed to the cost of the player contracts and what part should be attributed to other factors, such as membership in the exclusive league, use of the team name, lease of the stadium, and so on. The more the owners can claim the team value rests with the player contracts, the more they can deduct as capital gains.

"Subchapter S Corporation," a provision of the federal tax code, enables a club owner to combine the tax advantages and liabilities of many different enterprises to produce the best possible mix for tax purposes. The owner can manipulate accounting formulas by selectively including different parts of the operation in various enterprises when figuring tax liability. The reported losses for the franchise can reduce the amount of overall income that is subject to taxation. The IRS has restricted the manipulation of multifaceted business operations, but the practice is still common. The New York Yankees partnership reorganized in 1991 to allow limited partners to claim losses on their personal income tax statements.[66]

Hidden earnings also come to franchises through write-offs for inflated administrative costs, circuitous interest payments, and sometimes abnormally high rents that some teams charge themselves for the use of the stadium.[67] In addition, team owners can increase paper losses by paying themselves excessive salaries[68] and making low-interest "loans" to affiliated businesses. The New York Mets, for example, were reported to list their everyday management costs at $15 million,[69] a figure most experts consider inflated. Paul Beeston, the vice-president of business operations for the Toronto Blue Jays, candidly acknowledges: "Anyone who quotes profits of a baseball club is missing the point. Under generally accepted accounting principles, I can turn a $4 million profit into a $2 million loss, and I can get every national accounting firm to agree with me."[70]

The most important trend in sports ownership is making teams parts of conglomerates (combinations of unrelated businesses). Just as investors develop balanced portfolios to cushion their investment against risks, businesses combine the operations of disparate industries. Conglomerates not only avoid putting all one's eggs in one basket but also reinforce the activities in one field with the activities in another. A hotel chain may enter the restaurant business, or a construction firm may invest in real estate. One business can help another without having the expenses show up on the ledger. The same use of conglomerates has become important to sports.

Ownership of a professional team can provide handsome ancillary benefits. Ted Turner, the owner of the Atlanta Braves baseball and Atlanta Hawks basketball teams uses them as inexpensive programming material for his cable television station. The Tribune Company, the owner of the Chicago Cubs, owns several broadcasting outlets, including a cable television station, as well as the Midwest's most influential newspaper. The Chicago White Sox created a cable network to broadcast games; the Sox ledger shows no broadcasting revenues even though the Sox network benefits from free programming. The Texas Rangers are partly owned by Gaylord Broadcasting, which broadcasts Rangers games.

Purveyors of alcoholic beverages figure prominently among team owners. A distillery once owned the Montreal Expos. The owners of the St. Louis Cardinals and Toronto Blue Jays are brewers and use their teams to promote their beers. The Cardinals' late owner, Augustus Busch, was known to use his position to pressure other teams to sell his beer in their stadiums. Busch told his board of directors that he bought the Cardinals for promotional purposes. Sales of Budweiser were 6 million barrels in 1953, the year Busch acquired the team; they were 35 million by 1978 and 70 million by 1988.[71] One of the new expansion teams, the Colorado Rockies, is partly owned by the Coors Brewing Company, which has the concession for beer at the stadium. Fast-food restaurateurs own the Detroit Tigers and San Diego Padres. The Nintendo Corporation bought the Seattle Mariners in 1992 as a way of solidifying its position in the economy of the American Northwest. Baseball franchise owners are involved in a number of other sports, such as basketball, hockey, thoroughbred racing, prizefighting, tennis, and soccer.

Team ownership can provide leverage with which to acquire other assets. Carroll Rosenbloom, owner of the Los Angeles Rams football team, gained control of ninety-five acres of choice real estate as partial compensation for moving his franchise to Anaheim. Al Davis, owner of the Raiders, would have won the rights to develop real estate near a proposed new stadium in Irwindale if he had moved his team. Art Modell, Cleveland Browns owner, leveraged a takeover of the Cleveland Stadium Corporation and then sold a parcel of land to the corporation for $4 million, almost five times what he had paid for it three years before.[72] Teams also serve as collateral for other investments. The Sullivan family in New England, Modell in Cleveland, and Joe Robbie in Miami all used sports assets to leverage development in other businesses.

As investments major sports franchises are unparalleled in their profitability. Because the supply of teams is limited and a team provides great prestige for the owner, the value of franchises has increased as much as ten times during the 1970s and 1980s alone. The New England Patriots and Seattle Seahawks sold for about $80 million each in 1988; fourteen years earlier, controlling shares in the Seahawks were bought for $8.16 million. The sale price of the New York Mets jumped from $20 million to $85 million between 1980 and 1986. The Seattle Mariners, probably the worst team in baseball since its founding, increased in value from $11 million to $106 million between 1978 and 1992.[73] The Houston Astros were sold for $125 million in 1992. The entry fees for each of the two major league baseball teams to be added in 1993 was $95 million. One sports consultant estimated that baseball's most lucrative franchises, the Los Angeles Dodgers and the New York Mets and New York Yankees, could sell for $200 million; the Kansas City Royals and St. Louis Cardinals could sell for at least $100 million. The imbalance in supply and demand keeps franchise values high.

Ownership of a team confers important psychic benefits. Says an analyst for the Peat, Marwick, and Main accounting firm, "We are amazed at the frequency with which the transaction cost is determined long before due diligence has been undertaken, which tells us that a great deal of the value determination is on the part of the egos or the prestige or the interest of the owners themselves." The prestige that team ownership confers can help an entrepreneur gain the exposure he needs to improve his client list or partnerships. Venture capitalist Eli Jacobs, said an associate, bought the Baltimore Orioles because his "mission is to get the important people of the world to know who he is."[74]

The Leagues and Cities

Until there is reform of the structure of major league sports in the United States, cities will always be confronting the dilemma of subsidizing or losing itinerant teams. The teams hold all the advantages in negotiations with cities, chief among them being a highly desirable product in artificially short supply.

Longstanding practices often appear to be the natural or at least the logical way of operating. Leaders and vested interests often argue that their organizations' procedures constitute the only viable, legitimate way to operate. But all institutions, including sports leagues, are the results of long histories; the league is not a necessary structure for all times but part of an evolutionary process.

Sports organizations in the rest of the world differ from those in the United States. Soccer in other nations operates under a club system that assures an ample supply of teams and team loyalty to the city and neighborhood. Most cities have several clubs, and even small cities have clubs. Clubs are arranged hierarchically; teams rise into higher divisions or fall into lower divisions if they do particularly well or poorly, so the system is competitive throughout. Clubs are publicly owned and operated; fans buy shares of stock, and vote on team policy. The largest Brazilian soccer team, the Corinthians of Sao Paulo, has 150,000 dues-paying members. Fans play an important role in management. They influence policy on player salaries, the hiring of players and coaches, and investments. Clubs perform many functions; team receipts not only pay salaries, but also finance a variety of youth sports programs, dances, fashion shows, and picnics. Profits are ploughed back into the club. The organization even provides a place for businessmen and politicians to make connections and develop community followings. Soccer teams in Brazil help to integrate a variety of activities within the community.[75]

Unlike the European and Latin soccer leagues, the major leagues of baseball and football in the United States enjoy monopoly status as the superior brand of competition. This gives the leagues extraordinary power in their relations with cities, because it makes them unique and impossible to duplicate. That one fact is at the heart of the sports dilemmas facing cities in the 1990s.

3

Local Political Economy
and Sports

> The interest of the dealers . . . in any particular
> branch of trade or manufactures, is always in some
> respects different from, or even opposite to, that of the
> public.
> —Adam Smith

"Like all social structures," Paul E. Peterson writes in an influential study of urban politics, "cities have interests." The city's interests, Peterson argues, lie in developing a strong economic base. The city needs businesses to provide livelihoods for its citizens and to support a wide range of public services. Even though the city's different groups have distinct interests, they share the common goal of improving the city's competitive position in the larger economy. "All members of the city thus come to share an interest in policies that affect the well-being of that territory."[1]

To improve its market position, the city must develop its export capacity by assembling a productive package of land, labor, and capital. Peterson has a strict and simple test for a city's policies for economic development: efficiency. "By efficiency I am referring to a state in which no person can be made better off without some other person being made worse off," he says.[2] To make an efficient polity, local governments need to develop aggressive "developmental" policies (those which seek to attract or develop industry) and perform a variety of "allocational" tasks (housekeeping chores like police, fire protection, and garbage and sewer services). The city cannot prosper, however, if it pursues ambitious "redistributive" policies that tend to undermine the city's economic foundation.

"Because the beneficiaries of the policy are different from the taxpayers, any increase in the tax rate for redistributive services is likely to have particularly harmful economic consequences."[3] Peterson goes so far as to state that developmental policies are uncontroversial because they benefit all groups in the city:

> When developmental policies are considered, attempts to ascertain the power of one or another individual or group are probably pointless, if not misleading. In this policy arena the city as a whole has an interest that needs to be protected and enhanced. Policies of benefit to the city contribute to the prosperity of all residents. Downtown business benefits, but so do laborers desiring higher wages, homeowners hoping house values will rise, the unemployed seeking new jobs, and politicians aiming for reelection. Those who seem to have "power" over developmental policies are those who do the most to secure these benefits for all members of the city.[4]

At first glance, Peterson seems right when he says development policies are uncontroversial. Even though there are always dissenters—in the case of sports, usually the people in the neighborhoods affected by a new stadium—it often appears that community consensus and even outright enthusiasm prevail for development projects, like stadium construction. Local newspapers, the "statesmen" of local affairs,[5] usually portray widespread agreement on stadium and other development projects.

Ultimately, however, Peterson's account is inadequate, because it ignores the disparate effects of development. The structure of local government and a regular process of economic restructuring lead cities to pursue large-scale projects like stadiums. Bruce Kidd's lament about Toronto's politics holds equally for many American cities: "There is no political machinery to develop programs on the basis of collectively determined and anticipated need."[6]

Most arguments for building stadiums and hosting professional baseball and football teams depend on a promise of economic development. The key stage in public campaigns for stadiums is the release of official studies that estimate how many millions of dollars a sports team "contributes" to the city's economy.[7] With severe declines in federal aid to cities during the 1980s and with fiscal stress a chronic condition for many municipalities,[8] local leaders are determined to promote economic development as a means of generating local tax revenues, providing income-producing jobs for an increasingly poor population, and projecting images of themselves as engineers of an "urban renaissance." Anything city leaders can do to demonstrate a reversal or even a slowdown of urban decline is important because it reduces anxieties and complaints among the city's many disgruntled groups.[9]

Some state and municipal leaders have made professional sports the centerpiece of plans to revive the local economy. Governor Rudy Perpich of Minnesota, for example, envisioned the Hubert Humphrey Metrodome as the lynchpin of a plan to revive downtown Minneapolis. Reshaping the urban space and spurring consumer buying were the strategy's two prongs. Sometimes officials just point to a boost in morale and image to justify sports-oriented development. The head of Perpich's task force on economic revitalization put the case in public relations terms: "It is almost worse for a city's image to lose a major league team than to have never had one at all."[10] Gregg Lukenbill, the organizer of an effort to bring an NFL team to Sacramento, gushed, "The Raiders coming to Sacramento would be an event of the magnitude of the Gold Rush."[11] The idea is that status as a "major league" city will help a municipality attract businesses and citizens.

Cities have invested hundreds of millions to support teams.[12] The biggest investment was Toronto's expenditure of $500 million to build a stadium complex, completed in 1989, for its baseball team, the Blue Jays, and the Canadian Football League Alouettes. Oakland in 1990 offered guarantees worth almost $600 million in its bid to lure the National Football League's Raiders back from Los Angeles. Irwindale, a town in Los Angeles County, gave the Raiders a nonrefundable fee of $10 million in 1987 to consider it as their home; in addition, the town offered the team 160 acres of free land plus more than $110 million in loans to construct a new stadium. Seattle's Mariners got use of the new Kingdome rent free, plus a 40-percent share of revenues produced by the stadium's elite "suites," and the right to break the lease if the team does not draw 1.4 million spectators each year. In an unsuccessful attempt to lure the Mariners, Indianapolis had offered a package that included a guarantee of 2 million in attendance.

Baltimore and Indianapolis both offered Colts owner Robert Irsay a loan at an interest rate below the market level to induce him to locate his team in their cities. The Florida state and St. Petersburg city governments together arranged for construction of a new domed stadium in order simple to attract a baseball team, without having a commitment from any team. When the Chicago White Sox showed interest, the Illinois and Chicago governments and a private consortium guaranteed minimum ticket sales and a television package that would cover the entire state. These are just a few examples of the largesse state and local governments are willing to provide to attract or retain a team.

The Local Polity

Cities are state-chartered public corporations with a blend of political and economic imperatives subject to the particular attributes of the territory. A city's economic and political realms interact with each other in countless complex ways. They are in sync on a number of issues but are also in constant tension with each other. This tension stems from their different sources of authority and, more importantly, different mechanisms of accountability. Economic organizations are geared toward market competition and profit making, while government actors are geared toward democratic processes and bureaucratic authority.

In general, the economic sphere tends to dominate and direct the political sphere.[13] There are two explanations for this. A neo-Marxian argument is that the economic sphere takes precedence because of the specific "regime" of capitalism. Capitalism is inherently so dynamic and expansionistic that economic powers gain control over society's major resources and processes. Unlike the more stolid public sector, private firms have an extraordinary capacity for transformation and mobility. The search for new markets and the confrontation with market competitors impel "perpetual revolutions in the productive forces," to use David Harvey's words.[14] Private interests have such flexibility, innovativeness, and coherent control over resources that they can respond quickly to new circumstances.

Another explanation for economic dominance, developed in rational choice theory, is that cities are immobile while private firms can move from place to place. Government depends on the private sector not only to create wealth but also to provide campaign and other support for politicians. To again use Albert O. Hirschman's terms, private actors have an "exit" option that public actors lack; their "voice," therefore, becomes all the more potent.[15] If firms were more closely tied to a community—for example, by strong plant-relocation or eminent domain restrictions—they would not have the leverage to extract great concessions from government.

In the American political system, public control of the economy is further undermined by legal limits and an ideology of privatism. Since revolutionary times, Americans have been suspicious of public authority. The development of a capitalist ideology has reinforced this suspicion of government. That ideology asserts that selfish private interests, played out in a market system, order social resources and energies to the benefit of the larger community. Peterson's argument is just one example of such thinking.[16]

The reaction of elected officials and others to the demands of itinerant businesses stems from the structure of local government. Douglas Yates and Matthew A. Crenson argue that urban government is distinctive because of the nature of administration and pressure politics at the local level. At higher levels of government, agencies paint policy in broad strokes and leave it to others to define the details in the implementation process, but municipal government is all about service delivery. That emphasis on implementation creates great opportunity for collective action among some elite groups but makes effective organization nearly impossible for others.

Building on a theory of "street-level bureaucracy" developed by Michael Lipsky,[17] Yates argues that the city is "ungovernable," because its administrative apparatus is too susceptible to pressure politics. City agencies are responsible for direct delivery of services—for operating schools, running fire departments, managing police and criminal justice systems, operating mass transportation systems, picking up garbage, and maintaining streets and sewers. Service delivery occurs face to face; for that reason, the city government is bombarded by citizen demands. Intensifying the pressure on local government is the fact that government goods and services are divisible. Urban administrators "can make countless small adjustments and reallocations both in their deployment of street-level bureaucrats and in their definition of what service policies and procedures should be followed in a particular neighborhood."[18] Because street-level bureaucrats can make such small discriminations, citizens constantly pressure service providers and their superiors in agencies. Citizen action, however, is fragmentary on most issues—including the matter of neighborhood preservation from stadium construction.

The upshot, according to Yates, is that big-city politics is fragmented, unstable, erratic, uncertain—out of control. A mayor hoping to gain control of the huge local bureaucracy perceives agitated citizens, narrow-minded bureaucrats, minimal resources, and problems whose complexity extends to the four corners of the globe. The best a mayor can hope to do is to cope, to temper the conflict of the city. Just to improve some basic aspects of service-delivery is an enormous job. Even with more influence over the street-level bureaucrats, it would be difficult for a mayor to penetrate the complex relationship that develops between those bureaucrats and their clients. Yates writes:

> Given the complexity and ambiguity of these service problems, the lack of clear-cut rules dealing with them, and the absence of a controlling hierarchy that would tightly constrain his discretion, the urban foot soldier handle[s] many service demands through mutual bargaining and

adjustment. . . . Thus, in the history of American cities, services have often not been delivered so much as they have been bought, sold, and negotiated.[19]

Because of the many constraints, Yates writes, solving urban problems has become the stuff of campaign rhetoric, not reality.

Crenson agrees that local government has distinctive traits, but he emphasizes the difficulty ordinary citizens have in *effectively* organizing themselves to pressure the government. While the national government is organized to serve formal interest groups and associations directly (note the "constituent" departments of agriculture, commerce, labor, housing, and veterans' affairs), local government is organized along functional lines (with departments of education, police, fire, sanitation, sewage, and so on). The organized clients of federal agencies are eager to deal with those agencies, because they have common interests and the clients get direct material benefits or important prerogatives from the agencies. The less-organized clients of urban administration, on the other hand, often would rather avoid municipal authorities. Urban groups are more diffuse and ill defined, and they find the citywide impacts of urban administration difficult to gauge.[20]

The distinctive structure of city government affects political disputes in two ways, according to Crenson. First, because municipal agencies are not captives of their clients (the street-level recipients of services), managers of those agencies can act as brokers among clients. Even if they can never develop the policy coherence they might like, agency managers and bureaucrats can bring a degree of order to the city. Second, as a result of the lack of power at the street level, influence tends to go to the suppliers rather than the clients of municipal goods and services. Teachers unions, for example, tend to have more influence in school politics than students and parents. The same dynamic works with sports politics. Battles over proposals to contruct sports stadiums are decided not on the influence of people at the grass roots, but on the maneuverings of a few major suppliers (banks, construction companies, unions, real estate interests, and so on). Crenson writes:

> While the incentives to organize are usually invisible, elusive, or diffuse for the consumers of municipal outputs, they can be powerful and distinct for the suppliers of municipal inputs. Those who provide labor, credit, materials, or contractual services to municipal government rarely need worry that their rewards will escape into the hands of the public at large.[21]

City politics, Crenson says, "is like an assembly line run in reverse."[22] The provision of public services and facilities seems to be driven more by the desire to supply than by the demand of consumers. Executive leadership in the city is geared toward enticement and management of the suppliers; mayors often try to control the bureaucracy and its attendant demand side, but the problems are beyond their grasp. Elite business firms also exert direct pressure on municipal agencies in their capacity as recipients of services. Major businesses receive speedier service than ordinary citizens on their demands concerning police, roads, and other infrastructure and planning issues.

The use of special authorities and ad hoc commissions further restricts access by citizens to decision-making processes. Baltimore, Boston, and other cities have established special funds in order to pursue public policies without having to respond to public pressures. Many stadium projects are managed by authorities, bodies to which the state gives the power to acquire land, let contracts, and even raise revenues but which are not accountable to elected officials or the public directly. As one activist noted, "ad-hocery runs wild."[23]

Elites have the small numbers, great clout, and vision to coordinate and press their demands on the city government. They have frequent disagreements and feuds, but they can act with purpose and dispatch. The principal bidder for the construction management job at Baltimore's Camden Yards baseball stadium, for example, was the Whiting Turner Contracting Company, whose president was a close political ally of Governor William Donald Schaefer and part-owner of the Baltimore and Ohio Railroad warehouse adjacent to the stadium site.[24] The diffused general citizenry, however, do not have the time, resources, or common purpose to make an impressive impact on city policy. They are dispersed and therefore relatively powerless.

Yates and Crenson appear to be at odds with each other about the nature of local government—Yates stressing the disorder at the bottom, Crenson stressing the order at the top—but they are really just talking about different aspects of the government. Yates stresses the ungovernability of the city from the standpoint of the bureaucrats and mayor, who are constantly reacting to demands. Because local politics is so fragmented, Crenson adds, concerted action can come only from suppliers— the people who do big business with the city—who are few enough in number to coordinate their actions.

This analysis suggests a number of explanations of stadium politics. Projects like stadiums will be enthusiastically received by the elites of the urban scene. Banks, real estate developers, elements of the tourism industry like restaurants and hotels, insurance companies, construction firms, bond brokers, all would favor large-scale projects and might have a direct interest in stadium construction. They also are major players in political campaigns and hence have enormous influence with officials seeking reelection. To the extent that there is a "countervailing force" to these groups, it is similar groups with interests in different places, like the suburbs.

Movements against stadium construction (and for different spending priorities) are difficult to organize. Citizens can make the argument that sports and stadiums are poor development tools and that $200 million can be better spent on education, police, or housing programs; but such arguments often carry little weight, because the results of such spending are undramatic and recipients of the services are unorganized and sometimes even hostile. There is no guarantee that spending the money on education, for example, would markedly improve schools; the money, after all, would not transform the system but would go to the same bureaucracy and neighborhoods, without alleviating the problems of poverty and alienation they are experiencing. Why, then, bother to shift the $200 million from the stadium project to the education system? In order for collective action in favor of such a shift to develop, people must somehow connect their own situation with the larger forces operating in the city.[25]

The City's Economic Ground

What makes urban economies vibrant—why enterprises thrive in, and flock to, particular places—is a question of academic and policy dispute, but certain principles find widespread acceptance. It is accepted that, to gain any control over its destiny, a city must be attractive to mutually reinforcing, high-value–producing economic activities. The controversy concerns how best to reach this condition.

The starting point of classical urban economics is geography. Urban development stems from favorable geography, resources, or position in the systems of transportation and communication. Cities rise to prominence because of the convergence of varied manufacturing and commercial activities that a particular geographic setting facilitates. For example, New York and Baltimore in the 1800s were premier commercial centers because as major ports they had access to world markets and resources. St. Louis and New Orleans thrived because of the trade on the Mississippi River. People and businesses naturally settled in those cities because of economic convenience.

Government intervention augments natural advantage. Houston became the leading port of Texas, surpassing Galveston, when the U.S. Congress financed construction of a canal from that landlocked city to the Gulf of Mexico. Likewise, California and the rest of the West began to flourish when the Congress funded dams and irrigation projects. Governmental provision of highways, canals, port improvements, airports, and research and development facilities have served to create nodes in national and international economic systems. Without government money, Los Angeles would be a barren desert rather than an economic and cultural power.

The chief task for cities is to develop exports. No city can be self-sufficient: the international division of labor makes such an ideal not only unattainable but also probably unworthy of pursuit. In a self-contained economy, as Paul Peterson notes, "residents, in effect, are simply taking in one another's laundry."[26] But if the city is part of a wider economic system, it can attain a strategic position that gives it strength and flexibility within that system. By developing import-replacement capacity, the city not only minimizes the dislocations of a volatile economy but ensures that it has the capacity to influence the larger economic system.

An understanding of the conditions of the production process—what happens before import and export—is often missing from analyses of local economics. Cities are systems of numerous industries with myriad parts. Producers determine their locations according to the relative advantages spaces offer and the organizational costs associated with shifting operations. New, innovative industries often take root on the outskirts of cities because such areas offer access to materials and expertise and also provide territory that can be shaped to the industries' specific needs. Even with an overall trend toward decentralization, economies still need agglomeration within certain industries or sets of industries. Michael Storper and Richard Walker describe the process of economic transformation from old to new markets and production methods as "recentering."[27]

The main requirements for a healthy local economy, Storper and Walker argue, are innovation, close-knittedness, adaptability, and new markets. Development requires an environment in which people are clustered enough and diverse enough for coordinated activity and where the urban form accommodates production and distribution requirements. Diversity also can spur entrepreneurial activity. Production centers develop in territories that present unique "windows of locational opportunity" for emerging economic processes. Storper and Walker write:

> As the agglomerated territorial complex grows, spinning off new activities and firms, it . . . creates its own locational specifications: a network

of intermediate buyers and sellers, users and suppliers of each of these products. Linkages, and the spatial relations necessary to their fulfillment, this can develop simultaneously; location is not something that follows once input-output coefficients are established.[28]

The economic center of gravity constantly shifts. Industries and governments find different spatial configurations useful at different times. At one point, a firm will find a concentration of labor and resources good cause to center its operations in an urban location; at other times, an exurban site might be preferable because of larger and cheaper plots of land, favorable development policies, or less combative labor relations. Economic growth occurs where there are sufficient "locational capabilities," say Storper and Walker, which means "the capacity of a plant, firm, or industry to secure what it needs—labor, suppliers, buyers—at a given location."[29]

The boom-bust cycle is a key factor in shaping the processes of investment in some places and disinvestment in others. In boom times, as a general rule, policy makers are often content to step aside and let private actors run the show. Firms produce according to a fairly well established economic "ground." In bust times, the government tends to be more active. The government uses a variety of policy tools—monetary policy, investment incentives, direct spending—to create a growth-oriented environment. This involves literally remaking the urban geography, as well as remaking the technological and educational resources available for a new round of economic growth.

David Harvey argues that the urban economy includes three circuits.[30] The primary circuit is simply production. The secondary circuit is the fund of fixed capital (machines, factories, tools, roads, sewers) and consumption capital (homes, automobiles, appliances, sidewalks) that provides the environment in which the economy operates. The tertiary circuit is a range of long-term investments in education, research and development, health care, and so on, that could make the first two circuits operate more efficiently.

The three circuits operate interactively. Each is necessary for the other two to operate. For example, a manufacturer's production of commodities (primary loop) depends on the availability of roads to get products to market (secondary) and the housing and education of its workers (tertiary). Another function of the second and third circuits is to absorb excess capacities; still another is to develop strategies to pursue new economic activity. If a local market is glutted, government-directed "switching" to the secondary circuit can pave the way for new production activities. For example, building or extending roads and airports can expand the potential market for products. Research can create new possibilities of growth. In this way, crises are overcome with new activity. Of course, switching circuits itself requires time and energy and involves dislocations.

The switching process enables cities to transform themselves, make themselves over for a new stage of development. Old cities, with their ossified physical form and entrenched political and economic structures, often present obstacles to new processes and technology. Stadium building may be considered part of this switching process. The business community promotes sports and stadiums because they represent not just ways to absorb excess capacity or promote direct spending in building, financial, and service industries, but also because they can serve as magnets of new activity. Baltimore's decision to build a new stadium, for example, not only spurred immediate spending and development downtown but also opened the old stadium site for new development. Also, developers began lobbying to turn the Memorial Stadium area into a new research park, perhaps linked to nearby hospitals or the Johns Hopkins University.

Private developers and urban planners alike tend to favor major economic projects—both for their direct spending boost and their long-term reshaping of the urban environment. Other things being equal, great profits from large-scale development projects are preferred to the modest profits from small-scale projects. Because of the need of the local political economy to intensify land values, projects with potentially large rewards are more attractive to economic and political elites. Stadiums, convention centers, and office buildings—projects involving large parcels of land and construction that could intensify land use and land values—get priority.

Even if stadiums do not strengthen the overall local economy, they do represent a boost in direct spending and perhaps even enough economic leverage to transform whole neighborhoods. Stadiums, convention centers, and other large projects have been important parts of Harvey's secondary circuit of capital. These projects are usually part of a larger downtown restructuring intended to attract or retain capital in a competitive regional or national economy. Such investments may be to the detriment of the local economy in the long run, but they have the immediate effect of answering some of the growth needs of some sectors.

Peterson maintains that the entire city benefits from major development projects, since the economic activity itself adds to the economic pie. But gigantism in urban development may suffocate other economic activities that could enable the development of mutually reinforcing economic activities.[31] Furthermore, as Crenson would point out, some people win more than others. The winners include elites who benefit from a general improvement in the economic climate (banks, real estate interests, newspapers, retail outlets), groups with a direct stake in the projects (banks, construction firms, unions), and people able to take advantage of spillover activities (neighboring businesses, homeowners who benefit from increased real estate values).[32]

High-risk and (for the firms involved) high-yield investments like stadiums require the help of the government. Major projects that transform urban space are "lumpy," one-shot investments, and usually require more up-front money than investors are willing to provide. State and local governments play a crucial part by bankrolling large projects. In 1978, for example, state and local governments sold $48-billion worth of bonds for the construction of schools, highways, hospitals, housing, sewer and water mains, and other public works.[33] The use of industrial bonds for commercial projects rose from $6.2 billion in 1975 to $44 billion in 1982.[34]

In judging the wisdom of stadiums and other large-scale projects, the important question is not just whether the projects can give a quick boost to a local economy but whether they can contribute to an import-replacing, linkage-rich city. The city develops by initiating and mastering, then spinning off, production processes. Only by attaining versatility can a city survive the tumult of the larger economy.

The suburban-style stadium prevalent in the 1970s and 1980s, which was cut off from the rest of local urban setting, would not appear conducive to local development, since fans leave the premises from a parking lot immediately after a sporting event.[35] Sports is an entertainment industry that does not create the need for a wide range of interconnected activities, spinoff firms in the same general line of work, common labor markets, and connections to outside industries.

The models offered by Toronto, Anaheim, and Orlando may be more useful. Those cities have created entertainment complexes as a major part of development efforts; sport in those cities is part of a larger, integrated production of new value that involves many people or that can create or expand markets. Still, such operations are usually so large in scale that they depend on outside suppliers and labor markets, so revenues at the complexes leak outside the immediate area. These complexes tend to be cut off from more linked economic activities in the city.

Parking lots alone can destroy the capacity for linkage-rich space. Thomas Fiorini of the Cincinnati Department of Economic Development notes, "If you're in the shadow of a stadium it's hard to get to your business because of the traffic the day of an event";[36] yet the rest of the time, the area reserved for parking is dead space, not conducive to sustained economic or social interaction. The most economically productive stadiums would cause visitors to come to the city to see games, and then keep them in the neighborhood after the game. Even better, the stadium might somehow help give rise to a variety of new economic activities. The stadium would be part of a centering process in which a wide range of firms would find advantages in the stadium neighborhood.[37]

If a city used $200 million to rehabilitate existing housing stock, rather than to build a new stadium, the economy would benefit not only from the economic investment but also from the greater tax revenues and rootedness of residents. For the most part, the benefits of that kind of development would be diffuse, not concentrated. But as much as housing renovations projects might help the overall economy, they might not attract as much political support from major real estate interests as projects like stadiums, since the latter intensify land use and land values in a more dramatic way. Large-scale development entails reshaping the geographic and social makeup of the city. Whole neighborhoods are transformed and resources that might otherwise be used for maintenance and rehabilitation are shifted from other neighborhoods.[38]

Sports as a Development Strategy

The simplistic assumption that stadiums will revive urban economies is well expressed by a *Time* magazine headline: "Rx for Cities: Build a Dome."[39] That assumption has to be tested according to the previous analysis of clustered, linkage-rich development.

Major development projects contribute to economic growth in three ways. First, they stimulate direct spending. Stadium boosters argue that the direct revenues emanating from stadium construction and operation exceed the costs of stadium construction and maintenance. Second, there are indirect benefits and there is a multiplier effect. Advocates of stadiums maintain that these produce revenues that exceed construction costs. Finally, the cluster of activity and innovation associated with a new development project gives a city the reputation of a vibrant and reliable place to do business. The city's "major league status" is said to attract economic enterprises, producing an overall growth rate that pays for the construction costs.

Sports and Direct Spending

As a producer of direct spending, the sports industry plays only a small part in the local economy. The late Senator Sam Ervin, putting sports into perspective nationally, declared that "The professional sports industry is about the size of the pork and beans industry."[40]

Studies of stadium economics for two cities concluded that sporting and other events held in those proposed stadiums could produce only enough revenue to pay for the operating costs, not the capital, infrastructure, and land costs necessary to build the stadiums. A study conducted for the Buffalo, New York, city government, for example, concluded:

> Most major sports facilities are not self-sufficient from an economic standpoint, at least in the initial years of operation. While rentals from users of the facility could be substantial, it is unlikely that these revenues would be sufficient to support the cost of operation and debt service . . . no matter whether the large rental generators, such as baseball or football, are present or not. In almost every case, some type of public financial support is required.[41]

Indeed, if the cost of constructing and operating a sports facility required less money than was generated by the facility, private interests rather than state and local governments could be expected to dominate stadium construction. That is clearly not the case. Of the stadiums built since 1965, only one was privately financed; that one, Joe Robbie Stadium in Dade County, Florida, benefited from millions in public expenditures for land and infrastructure. The Chicago Bears football team plans to build its own facility but will require similar land and infrastructure subsidies.

Examples abound of cities burdened by annual operating deficits in their stadiums. Annual losses at the New Orleans Superdome and the Pontiac, Michigan, Silverdome are $3 million and $1 million, respectively. The Florida Suncoast Dome in St. Petersburg ran an operating deficit of $1.3 million in its first year, in addition to $7.7 million in debt payments. The stadium, which hosted twenty-seven events, has not been able to attract a sports franchise as a permanent tenant. The deficits would likely remain or even worsen with a baseball franchise, since the stadium can charge rent for concerts and revivals but would not be able to get much if any rent from a team.[42]

A study by economist Dean Baim of fourteen cities with sports franchises found no direct gains to most cities as a result of the franchises. The one facility that showed an "unambiguously positive value" was Dodger Stadium in Los Angeles, which was privately built and pays annual property taxes of almost $400,000. Two other facilities that show less definite gains, California's Anaheim Stadium and Denver's Mile High Stadium, also "reflect minimal investment by municipal authorities."[43] An earlier analysis, by Benjamin A. Okner, also concluded that direct benefits from facilities are rare. Though now outdated, the study contains revealing data: In 1970-71, about 17 percent of the cities enjoyed a net gain on their facilities. Some 20 percent had losses in excess of $1 million, 17 percent had losses of $500,000 to $1 million, and the rest had lesser losses.[44] That was before the explosion in stadium costs and interest rates.

Another study, by Robert A. Baade and Richard F. Dye, underscores just how difficult it is for a stadium to make ends meet. As a rule of thumb, Baade and Dye state that for every $1 million of debt for stadium construction, two dates per year of large-crowd activities are necessary.[45] A $100-million stadium would require 200 large-crowd events—baseball and football games, tractor pulls, religious revivals, and concerts—to pay its own way. One difficulty with this requirement is that stadiums built in the late 1980s usually cost considerably more than $100 million. Toronto's domed stadium cost at least $400 million, and Baltimore's new open stadium cost over $200 million including expenditures for land acquisition and infrastructure. A further difficulty is that no stadiums are able to book so many dates. Scheduling conflicts, the need for maintenance, weather problems in most stadiums, and the limited number of entertainment events available for stadiums make it a rarity for a stadium to hold even 150 events in a year.

Another cause of these large debts is miscalculation of stadium costs. Construction estimates are notoriously inaccurate, because of the many aspects of such projects (land acquisition, infrastructure augmentation, consulting fees, parking lots). Later choices among design options, and political pressures also drive up costs. Cost estimates can vary by as much as two or three times. The original cost estimate for constructing Baltimore's Camden Yards stadium was $60 million; it eventually cost over $100 million, not including land acquisition and preparation. The variation can be greater for parts of projects. For example, the cost estimates for new parking lots for Busch Stadium in St. Louis ranged between $9.8 million and $52.3 million in 1985.[46] The renovation of Yankee Stadium cost $120 million, almost five times the original $24-million estimate.[47]

Stadium projects also can harm a city's already vulnerable capital spending program. At the same time Toronto debated whether to build a new domed stadium, which ended up costing close to $400 million, the city's budget for parks acquisition and maintenance was being squeezed. One city official estimated that the city needed 700 new acres of parkland to keep pace with demand, but the city had a budget of just $500,000 for parks acquisition. Other infrastructure needs that went begging included public transportation, housing rehabilitation, and expansion of the sewer system.[48]

Most major American cities have experienced increasing fiscal stress in the years since New York City almost defaulted in 1975. Cities have suffered, not only because of the decline in revenues stemming from the exodus of industry outside the traditional inner city, but also from tax-reduction movements such as Proposition 13 in California and Proposition 2 1/2 in Massachusetts. The effect has been cutbacks in basic services, like police and fire protection, and a steady decline in spending for the city's built environment, or infrastructure. Capital spending by state and local government has declined from a high of $35.9 billion in 1968 to $22.6 billion in 1982—in constant 1972 dollars, a decline of 37 percent. In per capita terms, spending on infrastructure has declined from $179 to $95.90 during the same period. The Reagan administration's cutbacks in aid to states and localities exacerbated the capital-investment crisis: federal monies accounted for 35 percent of all state and local public construction funds in 1982, compared to 40 percent in the 1970s.[49]

Stadium construction can cost more than half the annual capital budget for major cities. Because those costs are stretched over a number of years, the total annual burden is a fraction of that figure, depending on the length of amortization and the interest rates on bonds. The percentage of total capital budget devoted to stadiums varies inversely with the size of the city. For example, Chicago spent $1.07 billion in 1980 on capital projects, or $150 per capita; a $100-million stadium would impose a burden of $14 per capita on the city. Indianapolis, in the same year, spent $154.86 million, or $131 per person, on capital projects; a $100-million stadium there would cost $84.60 per capita.[50] Money spent on stadiums is money not available for other infrastructure projects, and most U.S. cities are in a state of crisis regarding the condition of roads, water and sewer mains, bridges and tunnels, and subways.[51]

To the extent that a team and its stadium attract outside consumer spending rather than develop a base for more permanent and rooted economic activity, economic gains will be limited. Rather than spurring industries that will develop strong export potential, recreational service industries tend to rearrange what has already been produced. Mark Schneider and Fabio Fernandez argue that for service industries to promote growth, they have to be part of a well-balanced mix of manufacturing and service activities, government policies, and modern infrastructure. If a service industry does not feed into these other activities, its positive impact will be minimal.[52]

The Multiplier Effect

The second and more prominent claim for sports facilities is that they have a multiplier effect on local economic activity. This argument is also used on behalf of municipal projects like convention centers, urban malls, and office buildings.[53] A professional sports franchise, according to this argument, brings in millions of dollars that stimulate other economic activity in the city. For example, a family coming to Baltimore to see an Orioles game spends money not only on tickets but also for parking, food and souvenirs at the game, restaurants and hotels after the game, and gasoline and other travel necessities on the way home. In addition, stadium employees spend money on goods and services in the city, giving the whole local economy a boost.

Economists differ on the size of the multiplier effect of different economic activities. The multiplier in stadium debates is usually set at 1.5 or 2, and sometimes as high as 3.2. A study of sports in Philadelphia used a 1.7 multiplier, and a study on Chicago sports economics used a 3.2 multiplier. An accurate estimate of the multiplier depends on an assessment of the amount of further local spending that an initial expenditure produces; the more that spending "leaks" to the outside economy, the lower the multiplier. Large cities tend to capture more of the spending generated by stadiums or convention centers since more local businesses exist near the facility. Wilbur R. Thompson warns against overestimating multipliers:

> A local multiplier is much lower than the national multiplier, probably ranging from a value of perhaps one-half as large in a million-plus population urban area down to perhaps one-quarter as large in an urban area of 50,000 population. Unlike the national case, where the multiplier must be at least 1 and is probably rarely less than 2, the local multiplier could easily be less than 1. To illustrate, a (deficit-financed) depression public works project (e.g., a new civic auditorium) might cost $1 million but over one-half this amount might be lost to the local economy immediately through the purchase of imported building materials, and the one-half that remained in (construction worker) wages and (building contractor) profits might be respent in such a way that less than one-half [is] added to wages and profits in the local service industries in each ensuing round of respending. The local multiplier would then be less than $1/2 + 1/4 + 1/8 + \ldots$, or less than 1, a very expensive way to buy local recovery.[54]

To determine the multiplier effect, it is necessary to add up the activities that can be associated with stadium events. A club hires thousands of people to serve as vendors, ushers, and ticket takers. It purchases advertising and printing, pays the taxes on ticket sales. Sales of food and souvenirs run in the millions of dollars per year. There is also advertising on the television and radio stations that broadcast games. Visiting teams spend hundreds of thousands of dollars a year on their visits to a city. The multiplier on these activities could add up to millions of dollars—if the money is kept in the city. But there is little evidence that that is the case.

Many new baseball parks are located within city limits, with direct access to the highways that surround the city. These stadiums might be considered urban parks, but they are not part of a complex urban fabric linking many urban institutions. These stadiums are designed for quick entry and exit of suburban fans with automobiles. Even though they are technically inner-city parks, their urban integration is limited to supplying parking facilities close to the downtown business district. Parks such as Pittsburgh's Three Rivers Stadium and New York's Shea Stadium fit this description. Another example is the new stadium in Chicago. As journalist Peter Richmond notes, "Never have city and stadium been so detached from each other: The garages will attach to the park by elevated walkways, and thus fans who arrive by car will have the privilege of never actually setting foot on the South Side of Chicago."[55]

For the local economy, the ideal enterprise would at the same time attract outside actors that would play a permanent role in the local economy and also develop some local autonomy. If an enterprise is just an interchangeable part in the larger economy, locals are likely to have less control over their own destiny. Robert Baade and Richard Dye write: "The imposition of a suburban ballpark model on an urban neighborhood will minimize the chance for ancillary development. . . . A channeling of fans through carefully planned commercial corridors could help maximize secondary economic activity."[56] Despite this finding, most new stadiums are suburban in their basic design, cut off from the city's economic flows.

Because of the fragmentation and dispersal of the production process, and because many workers commute from outside the city, the one-shot boost delievered by these projects may go to outsiders as much as urbanites.[57] John Kasarda has noted the tendency for such development projects to be isolated from the flows of the urban economy.[58] Expenditures for construction machinery and parts, contracts for accounting and architecture, and salaries for blue-collar construction workers frequently transfer the city's money to the suburbs or beyond. The concern about outsiders benefiting has led to proposals that specific percentages of construction contracts and jobs be set aside for city residents.

Many economists are skeptical about the claims for a sports multiplier effect. A study of the impact of the Dallas Cowboys and the Texas Rangers on the local economies found their effect to be small.[59] The study compared Irving and Arlington, the teams' respective host cities, with seven other cities and towns. The analysis found that general economic trends and tax policy accounted for whatever increased economic activity had taken place. Furthermore, whatever economic benefits resulted "spilled over the boundaries . . . affecting the economies of many different cities in the region."[60]

Robert Baade's studies are the most extensive explorations of the sports multiplier question. Baade argues that stadiums and sports at best make a small contribution to the local economy and at worst actually detract from the local economy. According to Baade, "the construction or renovation might well have a positive effect on the economy in the stadium's immediate neighborhood. But at what cost to the rest of the city or to the region as a whole? Perhaps a new restaurant will open up in the vicinity of a new sports stadium; it is, however, just as likely that an established restaurant fifteen blocks away will close its doors as a result. Is this what stadium proponents call 'economic growth'?"[61]

The biggest problem with the multiplier argument is its assumption that the spending that occurs at the stadium would not occur elsewhere in the local economy without a sports team—in other words, the dollars spent at a game would not otherwise be part of the urban economy. To use the economic terminology, the analyses assume an increase in aggregate consumer demand. On the contrary, it is more reasonable to assume that money spent on game tickets, parking, and so on, might instead be spent somewhere else in the city if there were no local team. If a family could not see the Orioles in Baltimore, for example, they might instead opt to visit Harborplace, Little Italy, museums, concerts, street fairs, or movie theaters. As a matter of fact, concern about a possible decline in museum attendance and other activities near Lake Michigan was the sole reason that Chicago mayor Harold Washington abandoned plans to build a new stadium by the lake.

Baade concludes that sports might actually be a negative multiplier— that is, it might diminish spending on other urban activities that do more to create local economic strength. In seven of nine cities Baade studied, the city's share of regional income actually declined after the construction or renovation of a stadium or the adoption of a new team. Five of the cities in this study showed declines in their share of income in the standard metropolitan statistical areas (SMSAs), and the other four showed no statistically significant change.

A test of aggregate income levels of another set of nine cities showed that stadium construction had positive but insignificant effects. The presence of a baseball team had negative economic results, while football teams did not have a statistically significant effect on local economies (probably because they play one-tenth as many games as baseball teams).

Moreover, stadium construction and team adoption appear to divert economic development away from manufacturing and toward the service sector. Baade calls the shift an economic "realignment" rather than growth.[62]

The multiplier effect is likely to be greatest when a city acquires a team for the first time or constructs a stadium that has unique features. If a city builds a new stadium for a team already operating in the city, the gain is likely to be minimal or nonexistent. Unless the facility offers features that set it apart from the norm, as Toronto's SkyDome complex does, most of the fans attending the new stadium would also have attended the old stadium. Most sports economists agree that attendance is likely to increase for the first two or three years of a new stadium's operation, because of the interest in the new facility, and then settle close to old levels. The Toronto Blue Jays and the Baltimore Orioles set attendance records at their new facilities in the early 1990s, but attendance may fall off when the novelty of those stadiums diminishes or if the teams perform poorly.

Even if a stadium attracts fresh spending that the city would otherwise have no chance to enjoy, that spending does not necessarily redound to the benefit of the local economy. Most of a team's business and practice operations are conducted outside the city, and the player salaries that the fans pay do not usually end up in the city. Most professional athletes live outside the cities for which they play and even outside the state. Also, most vendors that operate at the stadium are based outside the city. Wilbur Thompson writes, "Local investment expenditures, moreover, do not have a local income-generating effect unless they are spent for locally produced capital goods."[63]

The wide variation in estimates of the local economic impact of sports would suggest that those estimates are unreliable. Around the time the NFL Eagles threatened to leave Philadelphia, a study conducted by a researcher at the Wharton School of Finance of the University of Pennsylvania estimated that sports teams contributed some $500 million to the Philadelphia economy in 1983 alone. Another analyst at the University of Pennsylvania argued that sports teams' contribution to the local economy was negligible. A study of the situation in Pittsburgh estimated that the Pirates baseball team produced $33 million for that city's economy. The Milwaukee Brewers estimated their direct impact on the local economy in 1987 to be $212 million. A study by the accounting firm Touche Ross the same year estimated the probable impact of a baseball team in northern New Jersey at $118 million. Estimates in Jacksonville, Florida, and Denver place the economic benefits of local sports franchises at $60 million to $70 million annually. On the lower end of the scale, the departure of the football's Colts cost the Baltimore economy just $200,000 per year, according to one researcher's estimate.[64] As for stadiums, the New Orleans Superdome has been estimated to add an average of $100 million to the local economy each year.

Major League Reputation

A third argument on behalf of sports franchises and stadiums is that the city enhances its reputation when it hosts a sports franchise and that this "major league" status helps the city attract business. An executive with American Appraisal Associates, which analyzes the values of companies, said: "I talked about what teams mean to cities to the chairman of the board of Westinghouse. He said it was very simple. He said, 'How can I bring people to Pittsburgh to work for Westinghouse if I can't tell them we have a major league community?' Now you want to translate that into dollars. It can't be done. But that's not the important thing. It's the desire, the image."[65]

Robert Baade and Richard Dye used a regression analysis to test the proposition that a sports franchise or new stadium attracts economic activity to the local economy and concluded that the effect was positive in only one of eight cities. The study assessed the level of manufacturing activity in Buffalo, Cincinnati, Denver, Miami, New Orleans, San Diego, Seattle, and Tampa Bay, between 1965 and 1978.[66] It used a dummy variable, in which the value of 0 was given to a city before it constructed a stadium, renovated a stadium, or attracted a baseball or football franchise, and the value of 1 was given to that city after the stadium or franchise action.

Manufacturing activity was measured in three ways—manufacturing employment, manufacturing value added, and new capital expenditures. The study controlled for the population of the metropolitan area and the secular, or long-term, changes in manufacturing activities. The study yielded thirty-six non-zero possibilities. At a 5-percent level of significance, thirty-one of them showed no significant change in manufacturing activity as a result of stadiums or franchises. Only four of the possibilities measured positive, and one measured negative. San Diego was the only city that appeared to have registered statistically significant economic gains as a result of stadium construction; both manufacturing employment and capital expenditures were correlated with the construction of Jack Murphy Stadium. Cincinnati showed a positive correlation between professional sports and manufacturing activity. It is difficult to determine why these cases were different from others; the increase in economic activity may have been merely coincidental.

Dean Baim argues that sports can have an important "advertising effect" for a city, especially an obscure or emerging city.[67] Kenneth Adams agrees: "The inescapable conclusion of the last ten years is that a professional sports franchise has more value to an Irwindale or a Sacramento than a Los Angeles or a San Francisco."[68] As both of the smaller cities discovered, however, the task of proving worthiness as a potential major league city is greater, and small cities must therefore be willing to spend more to attract a team in the first place.

Even assuming that sports can be an important instrument of economic development, competition for sports franchises has become so feverish that what once may have been sensible is now foolish. A stadium may be a valuable development tool for the cities that capture the disproportionate gains that come from being first. However, just as the first firm to offer a popular product enjoys windfall profits then gradually loses market shares, a stadium may provide an early boost and then lose its relative advantage as other cities offer similar facilities. Fred Hirsch uses the term "positional economy" to refer to the phenomenon of diminishing returns once a product or service becomes widespread. Overproduction is an inevitable consequence of an economy in which many competitors seek at the same time to benefit in a limited market.

The positional good's value lies in the amount of utility or prestige it affords the user beyond that which is available to others. The classic example of a positional good is a house at the seashore, which declines in value as more houses get built on the seashore. Another positional good might be a computer, which initially might offer a wide variety of competitive advantages to a company but, when other firms also obtain computers, becomes less of an advantage or none at all. When gains accrue because of only temporary advantage, they cannot be relied upon as the basis of economic development.

If just a few cities have modern stadiums, arenas, or convention centers, they will attract tenants at the expense of cities with less-sophisticated facilities; but once these structures proliferate, and present less-distinctive attractions, building new facilities only creates an oversupply. In that situation, attracting lucrative tenants gets difficult. As Hirsch writes, "when everyone stands on tiptoe, no one sees better."[69]

The Limits of Sports Development

States and cities always have competed with one another for economic development. The scramble for professional baseball and football teams, and the concommitant stadium construction boom, represent just one recent instance of cities seeking some kind of advantage over other cities.

The sports scramble may offer some important lessons about the limits of policies that seek to attract footloose economic forms.

In the years of nation building and industrialization, cities competed with each other for canals, railroad lines, and other internal improvements. In the 1860s, Kansas City used land grants, federal money, and bond issues to attract railroads and surpass Leavenworth in economic development. San Francisco topped San Diego economically by successfully lobbying to become the terminus of the transcontinental railway. Houston built a canal to the Gulf of Mexico and passed rival Galveston economically. Denver became the western crossroads in the 1950s when it obtained the highway routes its officials had sought. Because fiscal collapse has often resulted from local governments giving businesses excessive inducements to locate in their cities, many states have adopted constitutional limitations on development incentives, to avoid reckless intercity competition in the future.[70]

This intercity competition has become more intense in recent years. The development of sophisticated transportation and communications technologies, the restructuring of production processes, and the emergence of new markets have made industry more mobile than ever. Economic attachment to place has been weakened. Meanwhile, the economic condition of cities has worsened. As a result, states and cities now battle each other to attract increasingly footloose firms.

Firms have shown great willingness in recent years to break up and move their operations if the business climate is more favorable in another place. Although only 2 percent of all annual employment change in the 1970s in the U.S. private sector was the result of runaway shops (firms moving their entire operations to different sites), as many as 38 million jobs were lost as a result of other disinvestment.[71] It is not unusual for a firm to break up its operations and spin them out to distant territories.

In some situations, a stadium might offer a city a way to distinguish itself from competing cities. By establishing a city as unique, a stadium might attract businesses directly and indirectly. Cities with stadiums might enjoy an advantage in attracting lucrative businesses, as well as in advertising the city's name. But once other cities imitate a winning development strategy the advantage diminishes. And if the supply of stadiums exceeds the demand—clearly the case in the 1980s—their potential to spur growth declines. Striking examples of that overproduction are the stadium-building efforts of Tampa, St. Petersburg, Orlando, Jacksonville, and Miami. Florida may not receive more than one team in the next decade, but all five cities have scrambled to initiate projects anyway.[72]

Stadiums, of course, are not the only public projects overproduced as a result of intercity competition. Convention centers, office buildings, condominiums, mall-like retail strips, shopping centers, and amusement districts all represent urban development efforts in which construction continued long after such facilities set the city apart from competitors. Such facilities are so overproduced—supply and demand are so unbalanced—that the municipal operators must offer them to tenants at unprofitable rates. If convention business were distributed equally to all of the cities with at least 50,000 square feet of convention space, each would get fewer than six bookings annually, yet the boom in convention center building continues.[73]

Despite the questionable value of stadiums and other facilities to the local economy, cities often provide them and whatever other benefits the franchises demand. States and cities faced with constant threats of firm relocation, especially of symbolic entities like sports teams, lose the ability to make distinctions between beneficial and useless capital-attraction programs. They are swayed by consultants' studies promising extraordinary multiplier effects from various businesses. Opportunities arise in unpredictable ways, at different times, not all at once. Precisely because urban decision making takes place almost accidentally, policy makers cannot systematically compare the expected value of an array of development opportunities and have little ability to develop comprehensive approaches to development.

City governments are highly reactive. The demands from different firms reinforce each other, and public officials feel they have little choice but to respond. Virtually any firm doing business in the city has some grounds for seeking special benefits from the municipal government. Firms monitor what benefits other firms get, and act accordingly. The inability of mayors to resist such a fusillade of demands may be one sign of the diffuseness of power in cities. The practice of "me-tooism," in which the benefits accorded one group are demanded by another in the name of fairness, is especially prevalent in city government.

In addition, to demonstrate that they are successfully coping with local or regional economic problems, governors and mayors go all out to deal with the high-visibility issues among the many that confront them. Capital flight has hurt some cities so badly that public officials feel they must make visible, vigorous efforts to keep business, no matter what the ultimate cost in an individual case. The hope is that even small successes in retaining business can serve as a foundation for later, more significant successes. A sports franchise is one of the most visible enterprises in a city, even if it does not provide much boost for the economy. Other highly visible projects that can be said to benefit the whole community are performing arts organizations in central cities.[74]

Whatever the merits of sports-based development, those cities that most need an economic boost are least able to make major investments such as stadium construction. Studies have shown that economically struggling cities tend to pay more for expensive and ineffective projects for development because of a sense of desperation to show tangible improvement.[75] Stadiums and sports teams are luxuries that fiscally strapped cities can ill afford—yet have great difficulty bypassing because of the potency of symbolic notions like "renaissance" and "major league status."

Los Angeles: Raided and Raider

"It Would Be a Whole Lot Easier to Say Hello If You
Weren't Always Walking Out the Door"
—Working title of country-and-western song about the
Los Angeles Raiders

At the annual meetings of the National Football League owners in March 1990, Al Davis announced a decision that would have been considered absurd just a few years before. Davis, the managing general partner of the Los Angeles Raiders, said he would move the Raiders back to Oakland, the city that had hosted the franchise for twenty-two years after its founding in 1960. Davis had transferred the franchise to Southern California amidst a storm of public criticism and legal action involving the city of Oakland and other NFL clubs.

The lawsuits against the Raiders were among the most significant challenges ever made to the structure of professional sports. If an early court decision, in Oakland's eminent domain suit against the Raiders, had stood, Davis would have lost control of the franchise. In another case, the Raiders and the Los Angeles Memorial Coliseum Commission charged the NFL with violations of federal antitrust law because of its attempt to block the team's move to Los Angeles. Had the NFL won that case—quite possible, given the hung jury in the first trial of the case—Davis would have been forced to keep the franchise in Oakland and pay his fellow club owners millions of dollars. Davis won both cases, however, and took the team south.

Eight years after the 1982 shift of the team to the 90,000-seat Los Angeles Memorial Coliseum, Davis was declaring his intention to move the "Black and Silver" back to their original home. Less than a year before, the Raiders and Oakland officials had finally reached a financial settlement in the eminent domain suit, at a cost to the city of $27 million, yet the victor and the vanquished in perhaps the most bitter struggle in the history of U.S. sports were about to embark on a new marriage. While Oakland Mayor Lionel Wilson exulted at a press conference, Davis claimed he had made a mistake in moving to Los Angeles. "The greatness of the Raiders started in Oakland," he said. "I just wanted to get the Raiders settled. . . . We've had fights and feuds, but that's just part of the egos of men and that's part of life."[1]

Much of the Raiders case, like many sports stories, was indeed understood as a gigantic clash of egos and personalities. Davis had the reputation of a conniving and resourceful genius. The Raiders' success in Oakland was attributed to his personal will and his skill at assembling into a winning team ragtag players who had failed to excel for other teams. Davis's 1980 announcement of his intention to move the Raiders to Los Angeles raised the curtain on a morality play, in which he was regarded as the villain and the Oakland fans who had filled the stadium to capacity for ten years were regarded as the victims.

Important as the personalities sometimes were, the structure of the sports industry, of state and local government in California, and the legal process really shaped the politics of the Raiders. The fragmented nature of the California political system and culture channelled important issues to the courts in the first place. Once the cases were in the courts, the legal system's rules of admissibility of contestants, issues, and evidence narrowed the range of politics.

Ultimately, the Raiders stayed in Southern California. Mayor Wilson's generous financial guarantees to the Raiders were thought excessive by even the most die-hard Raiders fans in Oakland. Public reaction against the deal was partly responsible for Wilson's defeat in his reelection campaign in 1991. In response to Oakland's aborted offer, Los Angeles authorities committed as much as $200 million to build luxury suites and make other renovations at the L.A. Coliseum, as well as millions in other benefits for Davis and the Raiders. Until the renovations are completed, the deal is just an "agreement to agree." When renovations are finished, Davis will sign a twenty-year lease.

The Fragmented Politics of Southern California

The Raiders affair was typical of politics in California. Pluralist theories of urban politics might have predicted that the drama would mobilize a variety of urban interests—from the neighborhood of the sports facility to the city's authority over itinerant businesses. But even when the issue was personalized or involved large amounts of money or real estate, it failed to generate thorough debate. The political process broke it up into uncoordinated parts. As a result, the political outcomes were often bizarre, reflecting little of the power structure or even political skills of the main combatants.

The greater Los Angeles metropolitan area extends across 464 square miles of territory, five counties, and 157 separate cities. In addition, the area is divided into dozens of special districts for purposes ranging from organized sports to mosquito abatement.[2] It is a city of distances; even when traffic is light, it takes two hours to drive from one end of the city to the other. Its geographic expansiveness and institutional fragmentation make coherent action on any issue in Los Angeles difficult.

The politics of Los Angeles is individualistic and disjointed, like its geography, and is marked by long, drawn-out interaction among distinct groups. "Words like *city* and *suburb* are meaningless in Los Angeles," two experts write, "because they imply a metropolitan area that has followed the traditional development pattern, in which a dominant high-density business center is surrounded by a dependent and mostly residential low-density periphery." Southern California is more like a series of population "constellations" forming a "galaxy."[3] The galaxy's parts are related to each other, but it is difficult to pull them away from their usual courses to become part of a unified movement. Decentralization undermines the possibility of common political action. Citizens do not get a political education—and politics is not a meaningful activity to many. Joan Didion writes: "Maybe a hundred people in Los Angeles, besides the handful of reporters assigned to City Hall, actually follow city and county politics. A significant number of the hundred are lawyers at Mannatt [a prominent law firm]."[4]

The Los Angeles Memorial Coliseum Commission (LAMCC) is typical of the California's quasi-public agencies. Nine members compose the commission; the executives of the state, the county, and the city each appoint three members. The coliseum, constructed by private developers in 1923 to help Los Angeles attract the Olympic Games, reverted to public hands after the 1932 games. Its operation and finances are separate from general-purpose government. The LAMCC's quasi-public makeup seemed to work well for decades. During the 1970s, however, as other cities constructed modern facilities, the coliseum became out of date. With 92,000 seats, the stadium is larger than most other sports facilities, but it suffers serious disadvantages all the same. Half of the seats offer poor views of football games; the facility is also difficult to sell out, a distinct disadvantage in local public relations efforts, since sellouts are a condition for network telecasting of home games to local viewers. Finally, the coliseum lacks many amenities of newer facilities, particularly the luxury suites that have become a key funding source for NFL teams. (The LAMCC and the Raiders have sparred over failed plans to build the premium seating.) In the 1980s the coliseum lost four major tenants: the NFL Rams, the University of California at Los Angeles, the Clippers of the National Basketball Association, and the Kings of the National Hockey League. The University of Southern California was the coliseum's only full-time tenant besides the Raiders.

Since the coliseum operates as an independent corporation, without tax revenues, it needs payments from tenants to pay basic expenses; losses cannot be absorbed by a larger governmental body. As a result, the LAMCC is more aggressive than a typical public agency. The LAMCC is also the locus of a wide range of political scuffles. "It's certainly true that the Coliseum Commission is fragmented," noted Kenneth Reich, a reporter for the *Los Angeles Times*. "It has three appointees [each] from the state, county, and city. They often don't agree, and the membership changes rapidly and so nobody has control."[5] Also, because it is not tightly connected to the larger political systems, it does not have to conform to the norms of those systems.[6]

Despite public skirmishes played out in the daily press, stadium deliberations in Los Angeles had an eery quality of "un-politics."[7] At no time did the stadium issue—despite its involvement with professional football, the U.S. Olympics, and collegiate athletics—engage the community in any sustained way. Stadium negotiations were almost entirely a matter for bureaucratic and business elites. To be sure, Mayor Thomas Bradley and his appointee as head of the LAMCC, William Robertson, had political reasons for securing a coliseum tenant, but stadium politics did not engage ordinary Angelinos.

The Raiders Look South

The saga of the Raiders and the Los Angeles Memorial Coliseum began in 1978, when the NFL's Rams franchise announced plans to move to Anaheim Stadium in nearby Orange County. Because the coliseum commission needed a new tenant, it immediately started recruiting NFL franchises, with the lure of the nation's second largest market and promises to make the long-sought renovations to the facility.

The LAMCC had attempted to keep the Rams. Coliseum officials told Carroll Rosenbloom, the owner of the team, that they would address his demands for improvements to the coliseum as soon as the city learned whether its bid to host the 1984 Olympic Games was successful. If Los Angeles hosted the games, renovation for the Rams could be dovetailed with Olympics improvements. But before the International Olympic Committee picked Los Angeles, Rosenbloom announced the transfer of the Rams to Anaheim, a city famed for its Disneyland amusement park and made prosperous because of federally subsidized military and space research.

The root of the Rams' wanderlust, as always in American professional sports, was the undersupply of teams. Anaheim conducted a splashy public campaign to lure the Rams—capped by a full-page advertisement in the *Los Angeles Times*. Small cities like Inglewood and Carson City, also wanting to attract the Rams, developed proposals to build stadiums. Rosenbloom used these proposals to put pressure on both Los Angeles and Anaheim. The agreement that lured Rosenbloom and the Rams included expansion of the Anaheim Stadium from 43,250 to 70,000 seats, construction of new executive offices and 100 luxury boxes that would be owned by the Rams, and generally more favorable lease terms than the LAMCC offered. The deal also gave Rosenbloom the opportunity to develop part of a 95-acre parcel next to the stadium—a project worth $125 million over ten to fifteen years. It was, according to one observer, "the fattest deal in the history of sports."[8] Another motivation for the move was escape from the Watts ghetto, an isolated and depressed part of south-central Los Angeles. The comfort and safety of Anaheim was an important part of Anaheim's campaign all along.

With the Rams out, the Los Angeles Coliseum Commission moved quickly. Unless it found a replacement tenant, the coliseum would run a $750,000 annual deficit, and possibly go bankrupt.[9] Los Angeles was an attractive site: it could either make another NFL team wealthy or host an expansion team. With the Rams playing forty-five miles away in Anaheim, Los Angeles was open territory. Even though the NFL did not recognize the two cities as separate markets, Los Angeles offered a lucrative site for football, especially since LAMCC officials were desperate for a team and would offer favorable lease terms.

The NFL did not consider the Rams move an official transfer because it occurred within a seventy-five-mile radius ("home territory") of Los Angeles. Commissioner Pete Rozelle told LAMCC president William Robertson that an expansion team for Los Angeles was unlikely, so Robertson decided to look within the NFL ranks for a new tenant.[10] He contacted the owners of the Buffalo Bills, San Diego Chargers, and Minnesota Vikings about relocating. Negotiations between the Vikings' owner, Max Winter, and Robertson helped Winter to convince Minnesota legislators to approve construction of a new stadium.[11] With its lease in Oakland–Alameda County Coliseum due to expire in January 1980, the Raiders franchise entered the fray. At the time, the Raiders were negotiating with the Oakland Coliseum for a new lease. The Raiders quickly decided to pursue the Los Angeles option.

The Oakland-Raiders negotiations were characterized by indirectness on both sides. Neither side appeared willing to reveal to the other its complete list of demands, lest it undermine its chances to ratchet up those demands and get a more favorable deal. Early in the discussions, for example, the Oakland Coliseum Commission used a technicality to claim that the Raiders' lease had already expired, as a way of negotiating rent increases—an opening gambit that created an atmosphere of mistrust.[12] George Vukasin, a member of Oakland's negotiating team, remembers that Al Davis refused to commit lease proposals to paper: "He'd write on the blackboard, then as soon as we'd read it he'd erase it."[13]

The Raiders were probably more responsible for the willful lack of communication. Davis, for example, did not respond to one lease proposal until twenty-three months after it had been submitted. His response in March 1978 came, not coincidentally, at the same time the Rams announced their move to Anaheim. Later, while the Raiders conducted intensive negotiations with Los Angeles in 1979, they maintained only minimal contact with Oakland stadium officials. The Rams' move put pressure on Oakland because of the obvious possibility that the Raiders would fill the Rams' place. Not until the Los Angeles Coliseum became available did Davis take a definitive stand in negotiations with Oakland, rejecting two lease proposals outright in early 1979. With Los Angeles open, the Raiders could be more aggressive with Oakland. Robert T. Nahas, president of Oakland Coliseum, Incorporated until the fall of 1979, recalled that Raiders executive Al LoCasale "wrote us letters that were very vitriolic in nature and accused us of bad behavior. That had not been characteristic before" contacts with the Los Angeles Coliseum Commission began.[14]

An accumulation of grievances undermined the Oakland-Raiders negotiations. A series of slights, real and imagined, broke down trust. Unanswered memoranda and telephone calls, demands for higher or lower rents, demands for stadium improvement, struggles over the coliseum schedule, and personality clashes all destroyed the mutual respect essential for cooperation.

Mistrust was strong because both parties were convinced that they had made considerable and unappreciated sacrifices. In a sense, both sides were right about their sacrifices. The Raiders franchise could have negotiated more lucrative deals in other cities. On the other hand, Oakland had built its coliseum in 1965 specifically to house the Raiders and in 1979 and 1980 was willing to make concessions worth about $10 million; furthermore, Oakland fans had shown more enthusiasm for their franchise than the fans of almost any other city.

As the Raiders and Los Angeles continued talks to bring the Raiders south, the NFL remained skeptical. Commissioner Pete Rozelle and most club owners wanted to protect the league's control over matters such as franchise shifts. Owners worried that football's credibility would be undermined if the Raiders jilted Oakland fans, who were probably the sport's most loyal. Georgia Frontiere, who became the Rams' owner when her husband Carroll Rosenbloom died, opposed the move because of the competition that the team would create in Southern California. Finally, the Raiders' Al Davis had aroused great animosity in the league; most agreed that Davis was a football "genius" but that his acerbic and aloof manner had created bitter rivalries with Rozelle, Frontiere, and others.

After months of tense maneuvering, the Raiders declared that they would not be bound by the league requirement for approval of franchise shifts. Then, in January 1980, to preempt and challenge an expected league vote against the team transfer, the Raiders and the LAMCC sued the NFL, charging violation of the Sherman Antitrust Act. The Raiders and the LAMCC alleged that the league's Rule 4.3 prevented its franchises from conducting their affairs freely. The Raiders said the rule—which required a three-fourths majority of owners to approve franchise shifts, without any criteria guiding the decision—arbitrarily restrained trade.

Davis acknowledged that a move would damage the interests of Oakland fans but argued that the nature of the football industry dictated the move. The ability of other franchises to get more favorable leases undermined the Raiders' competitiveness. Each new lease agreement—such as the deals the Rams, Giants, and Vikings had recently obtained—set new standards for playing facilities. In particular, more and more teams reaped millions in luxury stadium seating, and Oakland's facility did not accommodate such seating. Davis was determined not to be a "sucker:"

> The environment forces people to act. I always believed I could beat it, I could make the environment work for me. But this time it's making me act in a way I never thought I would. . . . I will take into account the community, but I will also give myself an opportunity I never thought I would. I'm going to weigh the opportunity. I would hope you wouldn't treat this as an indictment of anybody, but this is where we ended up.[15]

Because of the pressures on both coliseum commissions, the Raiders won several millions of dollars more in concessions in a matter of months. Both cities risked financial losses greater than $1 million annually if they did not have professional football tenants. On January 19, 1980, Oakland submitted a bid committing itself to $8 million worth of facility improvements, mainly the construction of luxury suites. Davis responded that "certain things had to be changed." Two more Oakland offers followed, on January 22 and February 4, the second of which a Raiders executive angrily threw into the parking lot unread. Davis later testified that "we needed approximately $2 million more than what was in that deal. I don't see what's wrong with that." [16]

After weeks of negotiations with the LAMCC, the Raiders' demand to Oakland increased to $15 million in coliseum improvements—exceeding limits that Oakland had set earlier and the Raiders had implicitly accepted by continuing the talks. [17] Perhaps not coincidentally, that demand matched the latest Los Angeles offer. Clearly, Davis's arguments about what was "essential" depended upon the stage of negotiations, and, more specifically, on what concessions the other city had recently made. The more the deliberations continued, the more Davis could demand. [18]

Oakland's last, most desperate attempt to retain the Raiders came at this stage. Mayor Wilson and Cornell Maier, the chief executive of Kaiser Aluminum Company and an acknowledged community leader, put together a package that met Davis's demands. When other Oakland officials balked at signing on to the Wilson-Maier plan, Davis angrily quit the negotiations, arguing that politicians had fatally compromised the package. In their haste to devise a plan acceptable to the Raiders, Wilson and Maier had accepted obligations that the coliseum commission could not meet. Coliseum corporation president Nahas argued that Davis was unwilling to deal with the problems of public officials. "I understand how he felt. He likes to negotiate one-on-one in a quiet room with complete confidentiality. I do too." But, Nahas added, public arrangements require some accommodation of public authority. [19]

Los Angeles officials felt the same kinds of pressures and failed to work out details on their offer to the Raiders. That failure later undermined the deal. Because of the pace of negotiations, the LAMCC turned a blind eye to the potential dangers of the agreement's provision concerning construction of luxury boxes. LAMCC president Robertson has acknowledged that during the negotiations he was "extremely sensitive and didn't want anything out there that would jeopardize the package." [20] That "sensitivity" limited Los Angeles's options.

At the time of the 1982 agreement between Los Angeles and the Raiders, Robertson dismissed the possibility that the vagueness of the deal left room for later problems. "I've got no qualms about being burdened by the highly unlikely possibility of Davis moving out in ten years," he said. LAMCC member Peter Schabarum, the Los Angeles County Board of Supervisors chairman, was not so sure: "There are a lot of unanswered questions and a great volume of stated good intentions in this deal, but they're not in this document." One NFL stadium manager asked incredulously, "Do you know what a nonrecourse loan is? If I don't pay, tough. That's what it boils down to."[21] Stephen Reinhardt, a negotiator for Los Angeles, said later that his side had ignored complications that might arise out of promises to Davis. The city officials' desire for resolution led to a willing suspension of disbelief that the deal could work. "Skyboxes were the most important issue in the negotiations. Davis was always clear about what he wanted. When he didn't get something he asked for, he took it like a man. The problem was that the Commission promised the same things to different people—Davis and Ueberroth [1984 Olympic Games organizer]."[22]

On January 22, the Raiders announced an agreement to play at the Los Angeles Coliseum. The package included a $6.7-million loan, tax breaks, title to ninety-nine luxury suites, and the dominant share of revenues from ticket receipts, concessions, scoreboard advertising, and parking. The Raiders' title to the luxury suites was arranged to give the team an additional tax break, the federal depreciation allowance for physical capital.[23] But the Raiders' ownership of the suites would create trouble for the lease in just a few years. The Raiders franchise interpreted *ownership* to mean that it could charge rents to other users of the stadium, including the spectators of the 1984 Olympic Games.

Controversy over skybox ownership eventually unraveled the agreement. By 1987, the Raiders declared the LAMCC pact null and void and began searching for a new stadium. Because of the hurried negotiations between two overanxious and vulnerable parties, matters requiring clarity were allowed to remain muddy. And in the eventual scramble for the Raiders involving Los Angeles, Irwindale, Oakland, and Sacramento, the cost of hosting the Raiders increased from less than $20 million to as much as $600 million in a period of five years.

The Antitrust Suit

California's disjointed politics created a political vacuum and a crisis of authority that would be filled by the courts. Divisions among Los Angeles Coliseum Commission appointees from different political parties and levels of government created gridlock. The commission's tenuous fiscal status inevitably led to shaky arrangements with tenants, and that in turn led to judicial action. The Oakland–Alameda County Coliseum Commission confronted a similar dilemma. As governmental authorities and the Raiders veered toward court, citizens and interest groups failed to define clearly their interests and strategies regarding the Raiders' move. Interest groups did not mobilize, even when the outcome of the negotiations could have produced profound effects on them (particularly the neighborhoods in which the two stadiums were located). As a result, the controversy shifted to the courts.[24]

That legal contests narrow political discourse is a truism.[25] The U.S. legal system separates disputes from their contexts with rigid understandings of rules, evidence, court procedures, and justiciable claims. Court cases are treated as tightly constructed equations rather than social struggles with implications for all of society. "Once the issues are narrowed in this way," Lynn Mather and Barbara Yngvesson note, "there is no need to inquire into the general situation, the background, the relationships of the parties, and the like."[26]

When the legal process dealt with the Raiders' move, it did not confront the overall context of how power is distributed in the city and in the sports industry. Specifically, the process did not address the way the NFL's monopoly control gives teams an edge in bargaining with cities. The narrow focus of decision making excluded many groups whose interests might have been affected by the outcome, such as the Watts neighborhood, social workers working there, and even developers.

The Raiders controversy could be understood as variations on the theme of corporate law. One variation concerned the structure of the National Football League: whether it had the authority to control the movement of its member franchises and whether the NFL's attempt to restrict movement was a violation of antitrust law. A second variation concerned the legal power of cities: whether Oakland had the authority to seize the Raiders franchise with its powers of eminent domain in order to prevent it from moving to Los Angeles.

The antitrust suit against the NFL—filed in 1980 by the Los Angeles Coliseum Commission and joined by the Raiders—did the most to restrict complex social issues to narrow legal questions. The case delayed the Raiders' move for two years but, even more important, reduced the scope of the controversy. Rather than exploring a wide range of issues, the courts focused on technical standards of modern corporate law.

The suit's focus was whether the NFL should be considered a "single entity" or several independent businesses. If the league is a single entity, then cooperation among separate franchises is legitimate; if not, then cooperation may be considered a conspiracy to constrain trade. The Raiders and the LAMCC prevailed in the antitrust case, freeing the franchise to move to Los Angeles and winning $42 million in damages, to be split between them. After the first trial ended in a hung jury, a U.S. District Court jury in May 1982 found that the NFL constitution violated antitrust laws and that any attempt by other club owners to block the Raiders' transfer would illegally restrain competition in the Los Angeles market.

At a key stage in the first trial, on July 28, Judge Harry Pregerson of the Ninth Circuit Court of Appeals ruled that the NFL was really a loose alliance of separate businesses rather than a single entity. The franchises' separate bookkeeping, managements, player contracts, stadium leases, and ticket sales all indicated that the franchises were independent businesses in direct competition with each other, Pregerson concluded. Since the teams' financial success was at least partly determined by their field competition, the franchises should be considered competitors.

The antitrust suit put the issue of franchise relocation on a narrow footing. First, the drawn-out proceedings whittled down the issues that would be considered. Second, the very terminology and evidentiary requirements of the law prevented discussion of a wide range of related issues. Third, legal considerations restricted the scope of continuing negotiations among the parties. The combatants kept the discussion narrow, inside and outside of court.

The dispute over one minor incident illustrates the narrowness of the legal engagement. At a meeting of NFL owners in Chicago in October 1978, in a debate about changing the league rules for approving transfer shifts, Raiders owner Davis abstained and stated that he reserved his right to move the franchise. Davis claimed in court that his abstention was part of a deal with NFL Commissioner Pete Rozelle in which the commissioner personally granted approval to move the franchise. Owners present at the meeting later recalled a vague statement from Davis, but the statement was never discussed or considered important to league proceedings. An executive of the Washington Redskins franchise said, "It's very difficult to know what Al's saying. . . . He was equivocating. . . . He seemed to want to stay flexible and to reserve all his options, whatever they might be."[27]

Just what Davis said, and what status Rozelle and the owners gave to the statement, was a matter of intense dispute in court. Interpretation of this statement may have changed the course of the trial. Interestingly, one argument that the NFL did not make was that Davis's abstention claim may have actually indicated a general acceptance of the NFL's broad powers. Had the NFL made such an argument, the central part of the Raiders' case would have been undermined. The point was lost to the litigation, in all likelihood, because of the pressures of the trial.

The lawsuit's timing was crucial. Had the NFL first sued the Raiders for a breach of contract, the antitrust issue might have been secondary. The issue would have been framed in terms of the Raiders' acceptance of the web of obligations binding it to other clubs. (When the U.S. Congress approved the merger of the National and American football leagues in 1966, it insisted on assurances that franchises not be moved unless the locality was not supporting the franchise.) Instead, the Raiders acted first, with the suit alleging that the NFL had violated the Sherman Act by preventing the Raiders from competing for the Los Angeles market with the nearby Rams—one of the controversy's least important aspects.

The NFL was nervous and defensive about the possible long-term consequences of its fight with the Raiders. The league persisted in its claim to authority over franchise transfers but moderated its position in important ways. For example, in anticipation of a possible legal challenge, the league in 1979 eliminated its requirement that franchise moves be approved unanimously. The league then retreated from its 1980 threats to drop the Raiders from the league schedule. Such scrambling to change long-held policies served to delegitimize the league's operations.

As part of their court strategies, each side made preemptive strikes against the other in the form of injunctions and stays. On January 18, 1980, for example, the Raiders asked for an injunction in federal court on the basis that it would "be prevented from closing a deal" with Los Angeles unless the NFL were blocked from halting the move. That request was granted the next month, giving the Raiders the time needed to complete the deal with Los Angeles, and then the injunction was stayed in federal appeals court. Finally, in December, the appeals court reversed the lower court order that would have permitted the Raiders' move to Los Angeles, pending the outcome of the antitrust case. By then, the two sides had hardened their positions.

In another important development, Judge Pregerson cut the case in half in February 1982, allowing contestation of the antitrust dispute but not the question of whether Davis had an oral NFL agreement to the move. The judge's order narrowed the case further. Oakland's lawyer, Edwin Heafey, Jr., interpreted the judge's decision as a victory: "The Raiders had two legs in their suit. Now the judge has cut one off. I'd say that's significant."[28] The Raiders' attorney, Joseph Alioto, responded, "The judge may be doing us a favor by streamlining the case and just have the jury concentrate on one issue."[29] The more narrowly the Raiders could focus the case on particular evidence of NFL collusion, the better their chance to prevail.

One crucial and arcane battle concerned whether the business practice in question was to be decided on the basis of "per se" or "rule of reason" considerations. The per se standard requires a simple finding of collusion among businesses or a restriction of access to the industry. The rule of reason, on the other hand, takes into account a wide range of other considerations, such as prices, consumer interest, and the importance of the industry to society. This arcane debate separated legal proceedings from the context of sports industry and local politics—and in that sense depoliticized the matter.[30] Judge Pregerson used the rule of reason, but because the case had already been narrowed he did not apply that standard to the wide range of issues that might have been considered relevant to the controversy.

In the final analysis, the jury in the case concluded that the NFL's action to prevent the Raiders from moving into the Los Angeles market was an attempt to prevent competition with the Rams or to keep the market open for a later expansion team that would produce league-entry fees for all NFL clubs. The NFL unwittingly confirmed the conspiracy charge with its court testimony about the value of the Los Angeles market. Commissioner Pete Rozelle said on the stand that he considered Los Angeles to be a prime expansion site but that expansion into the area would not be possible with the Raiders playing there.

Absent from court testimony was analysis of the web of contracts to which the Raiders assented by joining the league. Other considerations were also neglected—the importance of franchise stability for all member clubs, the interests of the city of Oakland and the Oakland–Alameda County Coliseum Commission, and the reasonableness of Oakland's many stadium lease proposals, which the Raiders' management said was the reason for the decision to move the franchise.

The case hampered the ongoing talks between Oakland and the Raiders. Technically, Oakland mayor Lionel Wilson and the Raiders' Al Davis formally continued their negotiations, but in reality they did not meet for a period of eighteen months. The NFL also attempted to negotiate with Los Angeles and Oakland as well as the Raiders. The most frequently mentioned NFL proposal was to give one of the cities an expansion team. Commissioner Pete Rozelle had limited room for promoting a negotiated solution, since he was the case's leading defendant. One LAMCC statement during the trial showed that the possibility of fruitful negotiations was nil: "The Commission has authorized no one to negotiate any compromise short of its objective."[31] It was all or nothing once the controversy reached court.

The antitrust case narrowed the controversy over the potential move to a few technical concerns and excluded consideration of many important community concerns. Once the parties to the Raiders case got on the legal track, several issues and solutions to problems were simply foreclosed without debate. Unsubstantial factors, like vague statements at meetings and internal league rules concerning procedures for approving franchise transfers, had a greater effect on the outcome and direction of the disputes than they would have if the many complex issues had been deliberated comprehensively.

The Eminent Domain Suit

Oakland's most daring response to the Raiders' departure was its attempt to seize control of the franchise in an eminent domain suit. The suit, filed in February 1980, could have opened up the debate about sports and urban politics, because throughout the long process it was the only action in which broad public concerns played a prominent role. As others battled over narrow legal issues, one observer noted, Oakland "picked up on the community issue and showed that when mobilized effectively, it could produce startling results."[32] In the final analysis, however, this case also proceeded according to the narrow, adversarial terms of the judicial system.

Under the law of eminent domain, cities may take private property for a public use, without the owner's consent, if the owner is compensated for the full value of the property. The U.S. Constitution's Fifth and Fourteenth amendments set the limits of this power.[33] Eminent domain is usually used to clear space for public construction projects, such as highways, stadiums and convention centers, outdoor malls and development projects, and public housing projects. Governments have also used the power of eminent domain to acquire stock in railroads, utilities, cable television companies, bus systems, automobile plants, and even a laundry in pursuit of the "public good." Oakland argued that the Raiders franchise was an important part of the city's economic and social makeup and that the city had the right to seize the franchise to protect those public interests.[34]

Oakland's city attorney, David A. Self, filed the eminent domain action against the Raiders in February 1980 in Alameda County Superior Court. After a temporary restraining order and a preliminary injunction were issued, the case was transferred to Monterey County Superior Court. The superior court's ruling was against Oakland, which appealed the ruling to the California Court of Appeals, where the claim was also rejected. But in June 1982 the state supreme court ruled that Oakland had the authority to condemn private property, including the Raiders franchise, and ordered the lower courts to address the particulars of the case. After skirmishes concerning Oakland's right to hold the Raiders during the legal proceedings, a new trial began, in Monterey County Superior Court before Judge Nathan Agliano in May 1983.

The case turned into an all-out war that precluded other political options. Open public discussion was impossible before the city filed its suit, because if the Raiders had become aware of a possible eminent domain action they would have moved immediately. "The city of Oakland was carrying a concealed weapon," charged Raiders attorney Joseph Alioto. "Here is a man [Davis] who is subject to eminent domain and the first he hears about it is after the suit is filed."[35] Open discussion was also impossible during and after the suit, because resentment hardened the two sides' positions.

The suit ultimately failed. Seizure of the Raiders to preserve the vague sense of community engendered by the team did not fit the usual understanding of eminent domain, the court ruled. At first the suit was considered more a symbol of Oakland's abiding love for the Raiders than a serious policy initiative. The Oakland government, however, demonstrated its seriousness by pursuing the case through several stages of the judicial process, and legal scholars said the takeover of a football franchise by a municipality could be won.

Traditionally, courts allow localities great leeway in applying eminent domain, but the threat of "creeping eminent domain," though not properly a legal issue, hovered over the whole case. Even the liberal chief justice of the California Supreme Court, Rose Elizabeth Bird, while she voted with the court majority to allow an eminent domain claim to be pursued, expressed concern about the possibility of abuse. She said Oakland's use of eminent domain power was

> not only novel but virtually without limit. This is troubling because the potential for abuse of such a great power is boundless. . . . The rights both of the the owners of the Raiders and of its employees are threatened by the city's action. Thus, one unexplored aspect of the majority's decision is the ruling that contract rights can be taken by eminent domain. . . . It strikes me as dangerous and heavy-handed for a government to take over a business, including all of its intangible assets, for the sole purpose of preventing its relocation. The decisional

law appears to be silent as to this particular question [and therefore it should be] considered legislative, rather than judicial, in nature.[36]

Potentially, cities could use eminent domain as an instrument to protect their ties to a many mobile businesses.[37] Cities might even use eminent domain to redistribute wealth: a federal court determined that an agrarian reform law that condemned large estates for the purpose of transferring the land to small farmers was a valid public use.[38]

The Oakland case turned on three main legal issues, which had to be separated from other concerns in the Oakland-Raiders situation: the requirements for public use, the limits on local control of commerce, and antitrust limitations on city authority.

Oakland argued that the presence of the team served two valid and important public uses: promotion of economic and recreational activity, and utilization of the Oakland Coliseum, which was constructed principally for the Raiders in 1966. The Raiders said that the franchise was not essential to the city, that the taking would needlessly complicate management of the team, and that Oakland could not afford to pay the full market value for the team. The Raiders also said Oakland had violated their due-process rights, since they were served the eminent domain papers without any warning.

The courts ultimately agreed with the Raiders that the franchise was not important enough to the city to justify the novel application of the law. The California Court of Appeals stated that "eminent domain laws are strictly construed, and are to be strictly followed."[39] The court of appeals said Oakland's action was "the precise brand of parochial meddling with the national economy that the commerce clause was designed to prohibit." One opponent of Oakland's use of eminent domain argued that "even if keeping a business such as the Raiders within the state may increase the level of economic welfare, this effect would be 'too remote and indirect to justify obstructions to the normal flow of commerce.' "[40] Such narrow interpretation left little room to consider the broad implications of the Raiders' transfer to Southern California.

One of the Raiders' main arguments was that Oakland's seizure of the franchise would upset a "web" of contractual agreements that was required for the operation of businesses such as the National Football League. The California state supreme court, despite accepting Oakland's eminent domain claims, agreed with the Raiders' concerns with "the varied and complex business relationships involved" in the Raiders' operation and their status as intangible property as part of the NFL.[41] Interestingly, in contesting the eminent domain action on the grounds that it interfered with contracts, the Raiders directly contradicted their accusations towards the NFL in the antitrust case. In the case against Oakland, the Raiders argued that a wide range of mutually binding agreements was necessary for the league to do business. In the antitrust suit, the Raiders argued that NFL franchises enjoyed great leeway to run their own affairs and that the league's "unreasonable" provisions (such as a three-fourths vote of league owners on franchise transfer applications) could not be binding. Contracts, then, were considered sacred in the eminent domain suit but sometimes meaningless in the antitrust suit. This important contradiction could not be addressed in the separate legal deliberations, however. The consideration of antitrust and eminent domain issues in two different trials prevented the courts from placing the matters into context.

Throughout the trial, the Raiders stressed the inconveniences of a public takeover. They raised the specter of public operation of the franchise. Oakland officials stated repeatedly that they did not intend to operate the franchise but would immediately sell the team to investors. Those protests went unacknowledged. Judge Richard Silver of Monterey County Superior Court, in dismissing the eminent domain suit in 1980, declared that "a municipal corporation has no authority to engage in any independent business enterprise such as is usually pursued by private individuals."[42]

David Self, Oakland's attorney, later concluded that both the novelty and the narrowness of the legal conflict prevented its success. The public needed to explore the wider uses of eminent domain; the possibility that cities can claim control over vital private interests is not widely accepted in the United States. That exploration had to occur in an open public arena, rather than the restricted sphere of legal proceedings, if the community was to accept such innovation. Legal discourse prevented the city from using relevent social concerns, such as the responsibility of a corporation to a city, as evidence. Furthermore, the fear of a conspiracy suit prevented Oakland from allying with other interested parties, such as the NFL. Self said, "Public dialogue takes a long time. [Eminent domain] is so emotion-charged . . . you can't do it with one case. . . . Americans have always looked up to someone [like Al Davis] who achieved great success. If we'd taken some less flamboyant person's property, we would have been home free."[43] In other words, the incubation period for this policy never occurred. There was neither the time nor the public arena necessary to pursue the educational and public-relations efforts needed to legitimate such a novel policy approach. An innovative approach to the issue of franchise movement, which could have engaged a host of related issues that until then had been addressed only piecemeal, was stillborn.

Another Raider Raid?

Controversies concerning the Raiders were not likely to end just because the team had become ensconced in its new home in Los Angeles. The characteristics of the sports industry and of urban politics that drove the conflict in Oakland remained in effect as the franchise moved to Southern California. In addition, too many issues were inadequately settled during the frantic negotiations to bring the Raiders to Los Angeles. Misunderstandings were inevitable.

Soon after settling into Los Angeles, the Raiders' relations with the Los Angeles Memorial Coliseum Commission and other local authorities deteriorated. As always, two interpretations are given for the tensions— one pro-Davis and the other anti-Davis. "Al didn't have any idea what awaited him politically," said Melvin Durslag, the long-time sports writer who initiated the talks to bring the Raiders to Los Angeles. "The sports fans were ecstatic but [the LAMCC] was obstructionist from the start."[44] The anti-Davis position was that Davis cunningly used the complexity and vagueness of the lease to evade the Raiders' responsibilities. Whatever the case, bitter disputes arose about the terms of the agreement. By 1987, Davis had declared the pact null and void and began talks with other cities wishing to host the club.

The agreement that had brought the Raiders to Los Angeles included informal provisions for construction of luxury boxes, improvement of sight lines for fans, and a reduction of seating capacity (which would make sellouts more frequent and allow local television stations to carry network broadcasts of more games). The commitments were not set out in a detailed, public document, but vaguely outlined in a letter and some personal assurances given by William Robertson, the past president of the coliseum commission. In effect, both the Raiders and the commission were taking a leap of faith.

The LAMCC granted Davis a $6.75-million "loan" to construct the skyboxes, which could bring the team an additional $20 million in revenues annually. LAMCC officials acknowledged that the loan could be considered a gift, since the agreement contained a provision releasing the Raiders from the obligation if the team eventually decided to leave the coliseum. "In our mind, it's a small price to pay to get a professional football team for Los Angeles," Robertson said.[45]

Davis could have built the skyboxes at any time, but he delayed action.

Going ahead with the construction would have bound him tightly to the lease agreement. The delay kept stadium politics open and left Davis with room to maneuver. Construction began on February 1, 1987, but stopped three weeks later; the LAMCC, he said, had reneged on its unwritten agreement to make stadium improvements such as moving the seats closer to the field. Davis said the skybox construction could not be completed without other structural changes that the LAMCC had not undertaken.

In the spring of 1987, after weeks of public haggling with the coliseum commission, Davis announced an agreement with officials from Irwindale, population 1,000. The San Gabriel Valley town was committed to building a $115-million, 65,000-seat stadium in an abandoned gravel pit. Davis declared that he no longer had any legal obligations to Los Angeles, the LAMCC having failed to make the promised stadium improvements. Davis's unwillingness to develop a plan for building luxury suites at the Los Angeles Coliseum and his negotiations with Irwindale, however, suggest that Davis was using the breakdown of negotiations as a pretext for abrogating the agreement.

Throughout the Davis's disputes with Los Angeles, a number of cities offered themselves as possible new homes for the franchise. Oakland never dropped its interest in the Raiders. It pursued the eminent domain suit until 1989, when it agreed to drop the suit and pay the Raiders $27 million; yet even while the eminent domain controversy continued, the city made occasional overtures to the Raiders concerning refurbishment of the Oakland–Alameda County Coliseum or even construction of a brand new stadium. Other cities, including Sacramento, Hollywood Park, Carson City, and Santa Monica, also made overtures to the Raiders. The city most determined in its pursuit of the Raiders, however, was Irwindale, a small industrial town located on the eastern edge of Los Angeles County.

Irwindale was a product of the municipal incorporation movement that fragmented politics in Los Angeles County in the post–World War II era. During that movement, dozens of communities formed independent political jurisdictions dedicated to limited taxation and exclusion of populations that would drive up the costs of municipal government. The idea was to have Los Angeles County provide basic utilities and roads and then allow towns to promote development in a way that excluded so-called undesirables. The result was to divide Los Angeles County into hundreds of jurisdictions whose political action and resources could not be coordinated.[46]

In the absence of a wide political arena for decision making in the county, urban planning was privatized. The limited scale of local government operations left a political void, which was filled by private planners, financiers, and attorneys. These consultants formed a network throughout the San Gabriel Valley, working simultaneously with cities like Irwindale, Azusa, San Marino, South Pasadena, and Temple City— sometimes even advising cities that pursued competing development projects. City officials enjoyed a perpetual revolving-door arrangement, in which they held several municipal positions at a time and also worked for the private firms doing business with the cities. At one point, the city manager of Irwindale held fourteen official jobs in cities throughout the valley. One planner, even after agreeing in 1983 to do business with only one other city in return for a $75,000 salary as South Pasadena city manager, was discovered to be on retainer in three other cities. Besides retainers and salaries, private consultants also received a cut of profits from deals; one consultant earned fees in excess of $2 million on one development project. The consultants for the many cities often worked together on projects, and favoritism among friends was common.[47]

Like other cities that incorporated in the 1950s and 1960s, Irwindale aimed to limit the groups that could benefit from its rich tax base. Irwindale had no property tax; it received its minimal public services from the county or provided its own services with federal and state revenues. Unlike other cities, Irwindale used its wealth to promote long-range economic development, by levying taxes on the principal industry, gravel mining. According to political scientist Gary Miller,

> while the mining companies objected that they were already providing revenue through sales tax and property taxation to the county government and school district, the citizens of Irwindale felt that the extraction of their only resource required a special tax, to prepare for the day (estimated to arrive before the year 2000) when the resource would be exhausted and Irwindale would be left with twenty holes in the ground.[48]

Irwindale instituted a city property tax in 1970 to finance a variety of development projects. Administered by the Community Redevelopment Agency, those projects included a state-of-the-art $390-million brewery built on a 227-acre parcel and sold to the Miller Brewing Company for one dollar. In 1976, Irwindale turned all but a few of its streets into an industrial development zone. Other businesses attracted by the city included Toys R Us, Home Savings and Loan, and the Koll development company.

Irwindale's campaign to attract the Los Angeles Raiders was perhaps the city's boldest stroke. Raiders officials acknowledge that they had never heard of the city when it first began its lobbying efforts. The most important part of the deal was the city's $10-million "loan"—in reality, a straight cash payment to Davis. The money was meant to be part of an eventual loan of $110 million, $80 million of which was to be raised by revenue bonds, another $12 million by general obligation bonds. The loan was to be paid back with 50 percent of stadium revenues from the sale of concessions and scoreboard advertising. Irwindale also promised the Raiders 180 acres of land and all the gate receipts and television revenues.

Irwindale was able to provide the $10-million advance easily from its $36-million savings account. Less certain was the city's ability to raise the rest of the money required for stadium construction. The bond payment schedule rested on questionable assumptions, especially since the bond market was increasingly sluggish. The city's projections of revenues to be generated by the stadium's operations were considered wildly optimistic by most industry analysts.

To many observers, Irwindale's politicians were snookered, not only by the Raiders, but also by the private consultants who designed the arrangement. "Irwindale clearly has delusions of grandeur," the veteran sports writer Melvin Durslag said. "It's just a fleck on the map. They figured it would enhance a lot of real estate out there."[49] In its zeal to land the Raiders, Irwindale ignored its fiscal capacity. But the small city had a big effect on the process of sports politics; its efforts unleashed a new round of bidding by cities like Oakland and Sacramento.

Step by step, the Irwindale proposal unraveled. Political upheavals in Irwindale changed the composition of the city council and the city's development team. At one point, a recall movement resulted in a major overhaul of the local government. Controversies over the private consultants further eroded confidence in the project. California state and Los Angeles County officials were reluctant to allow Irwindale to undermine the LAMCC. Federal and state legislators opposed the use of tax-free bonds to enable Irwindale to take away L.A.'s team. Environmentalists and planners worried about the stadium's impact on traffic patterns. Neighboring cities, which had been persuaded by Irwindale officials and consultants to pledge $35 million to the project, objected to the congestion it would create. Taxpayers criticized the $10-million advance as an illegal gift of public funds. Homeowners expressed skepticism about the use of the Raiders as a development tool. State legislative hearings in 1988 also drew attention to the inadequate sources of revenue for construction of the Irwindale stadium.

Irwindale probably never had a real chance to pull off the stadium project. By any realistic standards, Davis should have ignored the small city all along, but he was able to use the long negotiations with Irwindale to drive up the benefits cities would offer franchises. In effect, Davis's behavior exploited a small band of overzealous planners, and it changed the relationship between cities and sports—perhaps even more than did the legendary move of the Brooklyn Dodgers to Los Angeles.

The (New) Oakland Option

As the 1990s began, the sports situation in Los Angeles headed toward a peculiar resolution. The Raiders, in Los Angeles, and Rams, in Anaheim, encountered difficulties at their stadiums, and both indicated an interest in returning to their original cities. This state of affairs could not have been predicted when the two franchises originally made their moves, or even as recently as the late 1980s.

Negotiations with Irwindale ground to a halt in the summer of 1989. At about the same time, Oakland civic leaders once more started to talk about the Raiders moving back to Oakland. Raider fanaticism in Oakland had remained strong during the seven years after the team's move south. A weekly newspaper in Oakland devoted to the Raiders had 40,000 paid subscribers, and Raiders games were broadcast in the bay area. Black and silver Raiders souvenirs remained ubiquitous in the city. A 1989 petition drive collected more than 30,000 signatures demanding that the city get the Raiders back. The same year, city officials offered to renovate the Oakland Coliseum and also give the Raiders a $32-million "franchise fee" (the prevailing euphemism for a cash grant) to get them to return to Oakland.

As the summer of 1989 drew to a close, Los Angeles, Oakland, Irwindale, and Sacramento all were battling for the Raiders. The competition was especially intense because of the proximity of Oakland to Sacramento and of Los Angeles to Irwindale. All sides considered their chances for an NFL team to be nil unless they landed the Raiders. Sacramento, which had long sought an expansion team, would have little chance if nearby Oakland got the Raiders—and vice versa. Likewise, Los Angeles would have little chance if Irwindale won the team.

In March 1990, Al Davis made his announcement that the franchise would move back to Oakland. The long sequence of city-against-city bidding had significantly increased the Raiders' price. "Davis is such a shrewd negotiator that he gets offers that can't be fulfilled," said one expert.[50] Oakland's final proposal could have cost the city $660 million over 15 years. Before agreeing to terms with the Raiders, Oakland provided the other coliseum tenant, the baseball's Athletics, with an escape clause. If sharing the coliseum created conflicts with the Raiders, the

Athletics would be free to break their lease and move. In other words, in its zeal to get the Raiders, Oakland set itself up for future difficulties with the Athletics.

The Rams, meanwhile, had grown disenchanted with their lease at Anaheim Stadium. The California Angels, the Rams' co-tenants at the "Big A," blocked the Rams' plans to use parking lots adjacent to the stadium for a lucrative development project. The plan to build four 12- to 17-story high-rise buildings on 68 acres of parking lots had been crucial in luring the Rams from Los Angeles. When a judge ruled that the Angels' need for parking space superseded the development agreement, the Rams hinted that they might extricate themselves from the lease and move back to Los Angeles.[51]

Even though the Raiders later backed out of the Oakland deal, after public anger undermined the agreement, it was still conceivable that the Raiders might return to Oakland and the Rams might return to Los Angeles—an everybody-marries-everybody conclusion worthy of Shakespeare's *A Midsummer Night's Dream*.

Whatever happens, the long sequence of Raiders politics wrought major changes in the relationships between cities and franchises. Oakland officials who had balked at spending $10 million to keep the Raiders were willing to commit themselves to as much as fifty times that amount just a few years later. As the politics of franchises and stadiums spread to other cities in both football and baseball, municipal officials made offers they never would have imagined just a few years before. The decade of maneuvering over the Raiders permanently altered the terms of sports politics in American cities.

Baltimore:
City of Defensive Renaissance

> You know what will happen if we lose the Colts? First
> there will be lawsuits filed and all kinds of frantic
> action in the legislature, none of which will bring back
> the Colts. Then there will be a drive to get 50,000
> season-ticket pledges for a new franchise. Finally,
> there will be a campaign to build a new $100-million
> stadium. That would not be ready for five years,
> maybe ten.
> —Bill Tanton, Baltimore *Evening Sun*, February 29, 1984

Baltimore in the 1980s was a city of conflicting images. Under Mayor
William Donald Schaefer, Baltimore developed a national reputation for
pragmatic energy. Using federal money and extensive tax abatement programs, the city ripped up seedy piers by the Inner Harbor and built an
outdoor mall that helped to make tourism one of the city's leading industries. Development of a vibrant financial-services district, rehabilitation of dilapidated rowhouses, and promotion of neighborhood identity
all contributed to Baltimore's reputation as a city on the rebound. Schaefer's flamboyant, gruff style attracted national media attention. Praise for
Baltimore's "renaissance" seemed unanimous. One observer saw in Baltimore "the town other cities unabashedly seek to copy to revive their
own decaying downtowns." From the standpoint of a number of groups—
developers, real estate speculators, financiers, suburban professionals,
tourists, and young urban professionals—Baltimore was indeed experi-
encing a renaissance.[1]

At the same time, however, the city suffered severe decay. In 1980 Baltimore ranked fifth among fifty-eight cities on a composite measure of urban distress that includes poverty rates, decline in per capita income, and unemployment. Some 25 percent of the city's 780,000 residents in 1980 lived below the federal poverty line. Of the city's 277 recognized neighborhoods, 210 had experienced increases in the percentage of residents living below the poverty line between 1970 and 1980. More than 30 percent of the city's housing stock was substandard, and more than 40,000 families filled the waiting lists for public housing.[2] Housing affordability, once a great Baltimore virtue, was declining: because of a shrinking capital base, property taxes increased as much as fivefold in some middle-class neighborhoods between 1980 and 1990, and the tax rates averaged twice those of neighboring Washington, D.C.[3] The city lost 13 percent of its population during the 1970s. More than 50,000 jobs disappeared during the same period, and another 20,000 between 1980 and 1983.[4] The city's new jobs favored outsiders: the percentage of downtown workers who were city residents declined from 57.6 to 46.2 in the 1970s.[5]

The political institutions of Maryland and Baltimore appeared powerless to address the city's major problems. The mayor, the Board of Estimates and City Council, the bureaucracy, the schools, political parties, and philanthropies all reacted to problems rather than confronting them in any fundamental or comprehensive way.

Reflecting the city's mixed fortunes were the fates of its two major league sports franchises. The Colts of the National Football League, once an emblem of blue-collar pride, left in 1984. Owner Robert Irsay moved the team to Indianapolis after protracted bickering and negotiating in Maryland and romancing and negotiating in Indiana and elsewhere. After the Colts' departure, Maryland approved construction of a new stadium to keep the Orioles baseball team in town.[6] The construction project promised a glittering addition to the city's downtown but did little if anything to help the city address its basic problems.

The sports franchises had the advantage in talks with the city because they could initiate action whenever and wherever they wanted in the long process of negotiations. Even under the leadership of its most powerful mayor in the century, Baltimore had limited negotiating leverage. The city's most important tool, the power of eminent domain, was not only questionable legally but also risked pushing the team out of the city.

The Manipulation of a City

When the National Football League's Colts franchise moved from Baltimore to Indianapolis on March 12, 1984, local fans reacted as though the move were a sudden and shocking act of treachery. That the physical move itself happened in the dead of night contributed to this reaction, but the departure actually took place over more than a dozen years. During that period, a long chain of events shaped the relationship between city and franchise. Baltimore's only major decision was to refuse to build a new stadium when the Colts asked for one, but innumerable smaller encounters, none of which had any great importance in and of itself, led the Colts in one direction—to the Hoosier Dome in Indianapolis.[7]

The threat of a Colts move surfaced as early as 1977, with disclosures that the mayor of Indianapolis, William Hudnut, and several business and philanthropic leaders there had met with Irsay.[8] That city had just begun planning a domed stadium as part of a downtown revitalization project. Two years later, Irsay presented Maryland governor Harry Hughes with demands for $25 million in renovations of Memorial Stadium. He also began talks with Los Angeles, Memphis, and Jacksonville.

When the Colts were still playing in Baltimore, Mayor Schaefer and others rejected the idea of building a new stadium, insisting that Memorial Stadium was one of the best in sports. Schaefer wanted to avoid the expensive debt service that other cities had incurred with new stadiums. A city parks official told the Board of Estimates, "Not building a new stadium but granting the teams more favorable leases is a far less expensive method of maintaining strong major league franchises."[9] But the Colts and Orioles refused to sign leases longer than two years, and the city's concessions to the two teams escalated. Increasingly, new facilities appeared to be the only way to keep the teams in Baltimore.

The city's relations with Robert Irsay typify the fragmented, step-by-step progression of controversies between sports franchises and cities. When Irsay acknowledged that he had met with representatives of Indianapolis and Phoenix in 1976, Baltimore officials scrambled to meet the immediate threat at the expense of coherent, long-term planning. Between 1979, when Irsay said the issue of moving had become a question of "when" rather than "if," and 1984, when Irsay stated unequivocally that he would not move, Baltimore officials vacillated between bold and timid approaches to the owner. For example, when Irsay held a bitter news conference at Baltimore-Washington International Airport in 1984, the city shifted from a posture of competition to one of conciliation. All the while, the city was kept off balance and the owner increased his demands.

Mayor Schaefer and Baltimore played a defensive game. The minutes of a December 19, 1983, meeting involving Schaefer, Irsay, and Edward Bennett Williams, owner of the Orioles, indicate that the sports executives' perspectives dominated the discussion. The deliberations showed little evidence of reciprocity. At issue was how much the city should give the teams. During the meeting, each team demanded different forms of parity with the other on issues such as concessions, rent, and length of lease. Schaefer's notes on the meeting betray the city's weak position in negotiations: "I had high hopes for meeting. Beginning was awkward and tense, and finally, I suggested we review possible areas of agreement. . . . Irsay will not sign the lease, and I am of the opinion he will move the Colts from Baltimore. . . . Results of the meeting from my standpoint—totally unsatisfactory, and there seems to be no possibility for continuation of negotiations."[10]

Later, after the Colts had left town, Mayor Schaefer recounted the frustrating negotiations: "It was a series of shifting demands, changing demands. . . . Every time [Irsay] said, 'This is the latest. I've got to have this,' everyone responded. The governor responded. The legislature responded. The community responded." After Irsay insisted on a change in the starting time of games to 1 P.M. to accommodate the needs of broadcasting, Schaefer convinced community leaders to drop their opposition, which was based on concern for church schedules. "So I called [Irsay] and said 'We got that.' We got the starting time. Well, then, that wasn't so important anymore. . . . [Irsay] took our offer and drove Indianapolis up. He caused me an awful lot of difficulty. I really tried awfully hard to understand him. . . . You really have to listen, because he says an awful lot of things and you have to cull out what he means."[11]

Baltimore's public and private leaders did not always present a united front. When the Colts demanded restructuring of a loan Irsay had received in 1972 to buy the Colts, Indianapolis quickly offered a loan at 3 percent below the 1984 prime lending rate. Baltimore did not match the offer. Mayor Schaefer expressed frustration at the failure of local financiers to help keep the Colts. "It's an amazing thing . . . I haven't heard from any banks in Baltimore," he said.[12] In addition, local media expressed reservations about the mayor's bidding war for the team, while the Indianapolis media and public almost unanimously supported that city's efforts.

Ironically, as the Colts case shows, teams with poor management can be tougher negotiating partners. The Colts—once the envy of the NFL, with fifty-one consecutive sellouts at the 60,714-seat Memorial Stadium—suffered from a series of questionable front-office decisions. Irsay, for example, fired General Manager Joe Thomas, who had assembled a young squad that won three straight playoff berths. Irsay also let go one of the league's most dynamic young quarterbacks, John Elway. In addition, Irsay committed a number of public relations blunders, such as ignominiously benching Johnny Unitas, a local hero. It was no accident that Irsay first demanded improvements in the Memorial Stadium lease in 1979 when the team was starting to perform poorly on the field.

Since the Colts controlled the pace of negotiations, the city had to exercise care in dealing with Irsay's mercurial personal moods. The slightest misunderstanding could have undermined negotiations. The most notorious of several public outbursts by Irsay came at the press conference in January 1984 at the airport, amid rumors that the Colts were headed to Arizona. Irsay argued with reporters, delivering personal barbs and even ethnic slurs. "I give you my word of honor, on my kids' life, I flew six hours to be here to tell you goddamn guys off. . . . If you love the Colts why don't you treat me right? . . . What do you hang me for?" Irsay was so angry that it fell to Mayor Schaefer to ask for reporters' questions. Schaefer pleaded with the media: "If we could just be a little more gentle, maybe it would work both ways. He would be a little more gentle with you, and you'd be a little more gentle with him." Irsay said he and Mayor Schaefer were close to terms on a new lease and "I have not any intention to move the goddamn team."[13] Days later, however, Irsay began final talks with Indianapolis.

The city was buffeted by a protracted game of "me-tooism" by the Colts and Orioles. The process began in 1973 when the Orioles owner, Jerold Hoffberger, put the team on the market but found no buyers; immediately afterward, he demanded and got a more favorable lease. The Colts responded by demanding a new lease based on dollar parity with the Orioles. They got the new lease, in which the Colts paid the same rent as the Orioles, in 1977, and it was made retroactive to 1975. When the 1980-81 lease talks came along, the Colts management again complained about its level of payments vis-à-vis the Orioles, and refused to sign. This time the Colts argued that they and the Orioles should not pay equal rent because the Orioles used the stadium for more games. The Colts asked for rent based on a formula rather than preset dollar amounts. The city agreed and the Colts promised to stay in Baltimore at least until 1984. In 1980 the state legislature approved a $22-million package for improvements at Memorial Stadium, contingent on the Colts and Orioles signing long-term leases, but negotiations foundered even after the extension of a two-year deadline. The Orioles, under new management starting in 1979, challenged proposed stadium improvements for football.

Starting in 1982, the Orioles refused to sign leases for periods longer than one year.

In February 1983, Mayor Schaefer attempted to end the game of metooism by conducting separate negotiations with the Colts and the Orioles. He asked the general assembly to approve $15 million for renovation of Memorial Stadium—$7.5 million to address complaints of each of the teams. The legislature approved the measure that spring, after intense lobbying by Schaefer. Following difficult negotiations, the city and the Orioles signed a three-year lease in January 1984. The "decoupling" of Orioles and Colts negotiations was a crucial moment in Baltimore sports history, because it tacitly acknowledged that the Colts would probably leave. Schaefer's objective was to do what he could to hold on to at least one major league franchise. The Colts, now isolated, were ripe for the picking by Indianapolis.

Timing shaped the relationship between the Colts and Baltimore. Irsay controlled the pace of deliberations over leases. As the Colts negotiations in 1984 proceeded, the mood at City Hall grew desperate. Mayor Schaefer, worried that he had cut himself off and lost influence with Irsay, decided to enlist businessmen to serve as intermediaries between the city and the team.[14] The hope was that the businessmen could open up the city-team relationship again—suggest new possibilities, including perhaps a new stadium, as well as ways of pursuing those possibilities. Perhaps the trust that had eroded in city-team negotiations could be restored by Irsay's fellow businessmen. That attempt came to naught.

Irsay's most frustrating tactic could be termed "plausible deniability."[15] He could take a step that seemed ominous for Baltimore, then plausibly deny intending any harm. For example, in February 1984, Irsay halted the mailing of the Colts season tickets. It was speculated that he was holding back tickets to gain leverage in stadium negotiations, but he said the delay was due to indecision on ticket prices. Whether or not Irsay was sincere, there is no question that halting ticket distribution had the effect of putting pressure on the city. In the constantly shifting set of issues, Irsay would turn the focus first to reports of negotiations with Phoenix and Indianapolis, then to complaints about Memorial Stadium, then to comparisons with the Orioles' lease, keeping city officials off balance.

Schaefer had concentrated on wooing rather than confronting Irsay, but in 1984 aides to the mayor started to consider a more aggressive approach. Mayoral aide Mark Wasserman proposed seizing control of the Colts through eminent domain. Wasserman's memo on the subject suggests just how difficult the city's position had been throughout the negotiations; the city could only respond to Irsay's consecutive demands. The handwritten memo, dated March 2, reads:

> I can't help but assume that Irsay has himself so boxed in that there is almost nothing left but for him to move the franchise. Even if the Indianapolis deal were to fall through this morning, the situation here is so badly deteriorated that it would be virtually impossible to think that he would or could [remain] here. I find it hard to believe that we are going to sit back and watch him go without so much as a whimper after the mistreatment we (you) have been subjected to. For my money (what little there is), we ought to take our best shot and complicate the move any way we can. I recommend that you consider seriously seeking Council passage of a condemnation ordinance today and couple that with seeking an injunction.[16]

The abuse that Baltimore officials felt finally led to such a challenge, but the Colts fled the city before it could be implemented.

After the Colts moved, one political ally of Mayor Schaefer suggested suing both the Colts and the National Football League—the only time the city considered addressing the real root of the problem, professional football's monopoly status. Noting that the NFL bylaws require consent of team owners for franchise shifts, attorney George W. Baker suggested, in a confidential memorandum dated March 30, that the city attack the league for failing to honor its own rules. The league, Baker suggested, might have an obligation to the city and authority over the Colts by dint of the league's definition of a franchise as the right "to operate a professional football club in a designated city."

> It has always been understood that the owners generally did not approve moving a franchise if the team has been properly supported. That has been the history in Baltimore. That again might put Baltimore City in the position of being a third-party beneficiary of that rule. The owners, knowing that Mr. Irsay was shopping the Baltimore franchise around, nevertheless refused to take action because they were concerned that Mr. Irsay might institute litigation similar to that brought by Al Davis. . . . The NFL owners are running so scared of a lawsuit that they abandoned the consent rule that is so essential for the honor and integrity of the League. In so doing, the League has caused Baltimore irreparable losses. . . . If an NFL franchise means 30 million dollars a year to Baltimore, as estimated by the State Comptroller, the amount of damages would be staggering were a judgement to be obtained against the NFL. Even if the NFL's attorneys considered Baltimore's

case to be weak, [the League] could well be induced to settle by way of an expansion franchise rather than run the gamble [of losing the case].[17]

Interestingly, Baltimore won the rights to the Colts franchise in 1952 as the result of a lawsuit against the NFL.[18] The litigation strategy might have had a chance in 1984; the mere threat of a suit against the NFL or Irsay might have induced them to seriously consider leaving the team in Baltimore. But, in the end, Schaefer decided to cooperate with, rather than challenge, the NFL. Schaefer wrote to Commissioner Pete Rozelle after the Colts move, informing him that Baltimore had formed a committee to seek a new franchise.

Baker later explained that he was "frustrated" by the mayor's inability to seize control of the problem's many aspects in a comprehensive way. Only a dramatic move could have advanced the city beyond its nickel-and-dime approach to the Colts.[19]

The Eminent Domain Suit

Employing the city's greatest power—eminent domain authority—required great delicacy, since the mere mention of that power would undoubtedly unsettle Irsay and hasten his flight from Baltimore. Ultimately, the city's attempt to seize the franchise failed.

The failure may have been a result of the city's cautious legal strategy. Under the state constitution, municipalities enjoy broad powers of eminent domain and probably do not need special authorization from the state legislature to use them. Mayor Schaefer and his aides were so busy managing the Colts crisis that they never defined their legal objectives or the city's legal relationship with the team. They were not sure how much authority they had, and so they decided to seek passage of special eminent domain legislation in Annapolis.

Before seeking the legislation, Baltimore officials had contacted David Self, the Oakland lawyer who had filed the legal action to condemn the Raiders franchise. Self privately advised Baltimore to avoid state legislative action because it would antagonize Irsay.[20] He claimed that the city already had sufficient authority to take the team. Baltimore officials never contacted him again.

Going to the general assembly did indeed alert the Colts. Rather than striking quickly and decisively, Baltimore had just given the Colts notice of impending legal war. The legislative process gave Irsay enough time to arrange the team transfer. Irsay later said that he moved the club as a direct result of the legislation. The city also probably undermined its legal case by seeking special legislation. The action reflected the city's lack of confidence in its authority—and gave the courts room to doubt the new legislation.

Even after filing the suit, Baltimore exhibited uncertainty about its legal relationship to the Colts. At one time, the city seemed to think physical property like uniforms and equipment constituted the Colts property: city officials gathered information about the team's workout complex just outside Baltimore. The emphasis on physical property appeared to betray a lack of confidence that intangible property, such as title to a league franchise, could be taken. And gathering such information about the training complex outside the Baltimore city jurisdiction was odd. That the search for property extended into suburban Baltimore County may indicate that the team's real home was outside the city limits.

For more than a year after the Colts' move, Baltimore fought Irsay in the courts. The case turned on whether Irsay had moved the franchise before Baltimore initiated condemnation procedures. At issue was whether the state still had jurisdiction over the franchise, or whether such a claim could be made by other involved states, like Delaware (site of the team's corporate headquarters), Indiana (where Irsay had reached an informal but firm agreement to move the team), or Illinois (the location of trucks carrying team equipment when the eminent domain case was filed).

The Colts argued that they were no longer a part of Baltimore at the time of Maryland's action. If the Colts were no longer part of Maryland, the state had no jurisdiction over the team, and the team could not be held by the state's laws. Some $100,000 worth of equipment, files, and furniture was safely ensconced in Indiana as the case moved through the courts. Significantly, the club did not challenge the notion that a team could be taken under eminent domain law.

Baltimore's attempt to take the Colts—for the market value of $40 million to $70 million—was more difficult than Oakland's suit, because the Colts claimed to be under another state's jurisdiction at the time of filing. Baltimore and Maryland argued that the team had established deep ties with the city. The removal of $100,000 worth of physical assets, the city argued, was not tantamount to separation from the state. As one NFL owner asked, "What difference does it make where the helmets are?"[21] At the time of the suit, the Colts had not signed a lease with Indiana officials or sold a ticket, mounted an advertising campaign, or held a practice there, much less staged one of the games that was the reason for the team's existence.

The legal theory at the center of the suit was *mobilia sequunter personam,* which literally means "movables follow the person." [22] If a person engages in some activity in a jurisdiction, that jurisdiction may regulate him even if he also conducts business elsewhere. In *People* v. *Graves,* the Supreme Court rejected a taxpayer's contention that New York Stock Exchange membership was taxable only in his home state: "That privilege of conducting business of buying and selling of securities on the floor of the Exchange is the dominant feature of the membership or 'seat.' Its very nature localizes it at the Exchange." But even with legal control over entities within its borders, the jurisdiction has limited authority. Persons and firms have the right to sever ties to a jurisdiction after fulfilling their formal obligations. A locality's authority is also limited by the dispersal of most company activities over several jurisdictions.

Federal Judge Walter E. Black, Jr., dismissed Baltimore's suit in December 1984. Judge Black ruled that Baltimore did not have jurisdiction over the club when the case was filed. "Under any of the workable tests for [the location] of the franchise, the Court concludes that the Colts were 'gone' on March 30." [23] Rather than appeal the case, which had already cost the city $500,000 in legal fees, Mayor Schaefer began a campaign to to attract a new football club and to build a new stadium to keep the Orioles. The city was signaling its willingness to play sports politics by league rules.

Baltimore's best legal gambit—one it did not attempt—might have been to argue that the Colts had failed to bargain fairly. Under the league's bylaws and the limited antitrust exemption that Congress had granted to the NFL in 1966, the Colts might have owed Baltimore the right of first refusal. [24] If Baltimore's lease proposals had addressed the team's objective needs, the city might have had a legitimate complaint under league bylaws. A city and the league have a long-term relationship based on the understanding that a team should stay in its city until that city no longer supports the team. Baltimore's lease terms were substantially on par with those of Indianapolis, and satisfied this requirement.

"It was a dark and stormy night"

On the night of March 12, 1984, moving vans arrived unannounced at the Baltimore Colts' training complex at Owings Mills, Maryland, to remove the club's property. Cold rain and sleet fell and a despondent mood hung in the air as neighbors and fans who had spotted the vans gathered to watch. By morning, all the team's possessions—helmets, shoulder pads, weights, video equipment—were in a caravan of eleven moving vans headed west on Interstate 70.

Mayor Schaefer heard about the move on the radio news. He called an emergency session of the city council to consider action. City Hall took on the aura of a center for crisis management. A mayoral aide said of Irsay, "He may finally have crossed the wrong man." Public reaction was fast and angry. Hundreds of telephone calls deluged City Hall in the days after the move, and the city began preparations for a lawsuit to bring the Colts back.[25]

The scene at the Owings Mills complex became more vivid in the public mind as time passed, and it was an important influence in the city's eventual decision to build a new stadium. The image of the departing moving vans became the symbol of the Robert Irsay's underhanded and cowardly ways. The name *Mayflower* took on sinister overtones, because that was the moving company that did the dirty deed. Irsay's action was dubbed the "midnight move" and "midnight raid," conjuring up images of furtiveness and deceit. Irsay was reviled as a coward, a carpetbagger; his physical attributes were the source of bitter local parody. Bumper stickers condensed the long and sorry episode: "Will Rogers Never Met Bob Irsay."

As is often the case in sports discourse, the situation was reduced to a simple opposition: Baltimore versus Irsay. Ignoring the larger question of how the structure of major league sports makes franchise shifts a constant possibility undermined Baltimore's ability to take a well-rounded, rational view of the problem at hand and of professional sports in general.[26] By focusing on Irsay's personality, the city eventually wasted millions of dollars, antagonized the NFL, and failed to confront the real meaning of the loss.

Baltimore's pursuit of Irsay in the courts gave the owner permanent villain status. As Murray Edelman has argued, the construction of a political enemy often involves production of a narrative—a story with a beginning, middle, and end—in order to gain the illusion of control over the complicated events that are in fact beyond the control of the community.[27] The story gains resonance as it is retold. Around the time of Irsay's exit, Baltimore newspapers exhumed Irsay's past and found patterns of deceit that made Irsay's betrayal appear to be the inevitable denouement in a modern tragedy. Upon his arrival in Baltimore, the local media had given Irsay an enthusiastic welcome. But with each day of crisis, the reports became more deeply personal. The Baltimore *Sun* wrote: "The Colts owner is an insecure man who deeply desires to be courted, a man given to royal tantrums when he doesn't get his way, a man prone to titanic swings in behavior. . . . There has been widespread speculation that Mr. Irsay drinks heavily. . . . [He is] a loud, brutish, erratic man who cannot be taken at his word . . . an interfering, miserly, incompetent manager . . . a man who thrives on turmoil whatever the cost.[28]

It is possible to imagine the foregoing characteristics cited approvingly under happier circumstances. Impulsiveness is often depicted as decisiveness, tantrums can be seen as signs of commanding presence, miserliness as prudence, and so on. The whole portrait could have been pulled together in a more sympathetic way by paying more attention to the tragedies in Irsay's life—the institutionalization of a retarded son and the death of a daughter in an automobile accident. The article and its extensive detective work on Irsay's educational, military, and family background, was an exercise in demonizing.

When, after the move to Indianapolis, Irsay's wife sued for divorce and demanded half the value of the Colts, Baltimore newspapers rejoiced as if the world was being made right again. To be sure, Irsay's personality played a part in the Colts saga; but Baltimore's loss of the team was more a result of a complicated industry's possessing monopoly powers with no safeguards for the community interest than a tale of a madman stealing a community treasure.

As Edelman observes, "enmity is a bond as well as a divider."[29] After a certain point Baltimore was helpless to do anything about the Colts, but its leadership became single-minded in its efforts to keep the Orioles in the city and to attract another football team. The obsession with landing a team would prevent the city and state from developing an imaginative response to the sports industry—and from dealing with the city's more entrenched problems.

With its demonizing of Irsay, Baltimore set itself up to be manipulated again—the next time by the NFL, which set rigid standards for cities seeking expansion teams, and by the Baltimore Orioles. Rather than addressing the many aspects of the sports-cities dynamic, Baltimore once again placed itself at the mercy of professional sports leagues. It accepted the idea that cities had to meet the demands of the leagues and franchises. Baltimore was only reactive during the next series of dealings with the professional sports industry.

Defensive Politics: The Twin Stadiums

Sports politics in Maryland changed dramatically when it became clear that Baltimore could not force the Colts to return. With the conversion of William Donald Schaefer to the cause, the drive for a new facility had irresistible momentum. State Senator George W. Della, Jr., remarked, "I have watched the stadium issue over the past year grow from eliminating a charter amendment which prohibited public funds from being spent anywhere except on Memorial Stadium to a political issue that truly has been allowed to get out of hand."[30]

Schaefer had always argued against a new stadium on the grounds that other municipal problems were too pressing and the city budget too limited. Schaefer called Memorial Stadium one of the best sports facilities in the country. Typical was his comment in 1983, when Baltimore was still competing with Indianapolis and its brand-new Hoosier Dome to host the Colts: "We're not going to build a new stadium. We don't have the bonding capacity. We don't have the voters or the taxpayers who can support a $60 million stadium. One-third of the people in Baltimore pay taxes. Unless private enterprise builds it, we won't build it."[31] But by the time Schaefer ran a successful campaign for governor in 1986, he was a vocal proponent of a new stadium—and perhaps even two new stadiums.

Schaefer wanted new facilities in Camden Yards, a warehouse district near Baltimore's revitalized business district and Inner Harbor tourist attractions. That site had the virtue of downtown location and proximity to the increasingly important Washington, D.C., market. It also abutted a warehouse recently bought by a group of investors that included Schaefer's leading fundraiser. Schaefer's opponent for the Democratic nomination for governor, Attorney General Stephen Sachs, proposed building a new baseball stadium between Baltimore and Washington. Schaefer's proposal, Sachs charged, was evidence of a bias toward the city and against the rest of the state. Schaefer handily defeated Sachs.

By March 1987, barely three months into his term, Governor Schaefer had secured state funding for "twin stadiums." The governor used his overwhelming election victory the previous November as political capital, and he threatened and cajoled opponents of stadium building across the state. Schaefer was not bashful about offering material rewards to the legislators who cooperated—and deprivation to those who resisted.[32]

The Orioles' negotiating strength clearly got a big boost from the Colts' departure. Being the only team in town is more significant than being one of two. The Colts had proved that a franchise could leave whenever it wanted; attention turned to a possible Orioles exit. When Edward Bennett Williams, a prominent Washington attorney, bought the team in 1979, it was feared that he would transfer the team to the capital's Robert F. Kennedy Stadium. Baltimore would have to respond or it would risk losing the team without any legal or political recourse.

Williams made vague and contradictory statements that gave him extraordinary leverage. Williams rarely talked about moving the team, and in fact vowed to stay in the city; but by refusing to sign a long-term lease, he assured that the team's departure was always a possibility. Williams was in the driver's seat. He could determine whether the city-franchise relationship was to be considered an immediate or a long-term concern, and when specific complaints would become public issues. It became clear that only a new stadium could entice Williams into a long-term relationship. Even when the city agreed to build a new stadium, the Orioles would agree to only a fifteen-year lease (the standard sports lease prior to the 1980s was twice that duration).

Starting in 1983, Williams was a constant presence in the lobbying for a new stadium. He said the city should build a facility "near the new harbor area and call it Babe Ruth Memorial Stadium—wouldn't that be perfect."[33] After the Colts' departure, Williams insisted on a baseball-only facility. During the 1987 legislative hearings, Williams testified that only a new stadium would guarantee a long association between Baltimore and the Orioles. He praised Governor Schaefer's efforts and "understanding" of the issue.

The Politics of Numbers

Reports filled with promises of economic benefits, backed by a steady stream of debatable numbers, paved the way for a new stadium. Reports were produced by a task force appointed by Mayor Schaefer and led by J. Henry Butta (report released in 1985), by consultants hired by Governor Harry Hughes (1985), and by another sports commission, appointed by Hughes and led by Bernard Manekin (1986).

The reports gave the campaign for a new facility an aura of scientific objectivity and legitimacy. Murray Edelman calls the official discourse "bureaucratic language as incantation."[34] Official reports use a number of strategies.[35] First, they emphasize the city as a whole, in order to submerge a project's impact on specific interests.[36] Second, the reports focus on statistics and technical concerns that drown out qualitative considerations. Statistics tend to reduce neighborhoods to undifferentiated parts rather than distinctive communities. Third, the appearance of officialness enables those who wield these report to depict even the most perfunctory encounters with citizens as serious deliberation.

The reports' major argument was that a new stadium would produce substantial economic benefits to the city and region. The Butta report, for example, maintained that a stadium at Camden Yards would have a larger economic impact than Memorial Stadium had, but it based this conclusion on the assumption that the Orioles would attract 20 percent more fans at the new site. The report did not submit the estimate to any analysis, but rather derived it from "information provided during discussions with local government officials, Baltimore Orioles management, and other community representatives"—that is, the promoters of the new facility. The report also projected a "new stadium bonus," an attendance increase of 400,000 in the first year and 200,000 in the sceond year due to the excitement of a new stadium. While the estimate turned out to be correct, it did not take into account other factors considered more crucial to attendance, like team performance and population base.[37]

The Butta report also understated the costs of building a new stadium, most notably by excluding the costs of financing (as much as $10 million a year for thirty years) and by ignoring property tax revenues lost to the tax-free stadium (as much as $16 million annually). Other miscalculations characterize the Butta report. The stadium authority, for example, budgeted $7.4 million for relocation of all the businesses and homes on the construction site—a low estimate, as events would eventually demonstrate. The authority also estimated that state lotteries would attract $12 million per year, but the state's legislative review of lotteries found the current lotteries to be "in trouble" from a lack of enthusiasm. The multiplier effect was often offered as a major justification for building the new stadium, even though a new Baltimore stadium would simply transfer an operation from one part of the city to another, and even push some businesses out of the city.

This quantitative blanket smothered the expression of intangible concerns, such as the fabric of neighborhoods and the need to balance sports with other urban concerns. The neutral-sounding words of planning officials reduced the ability of the affected parties to respond. Murray Edelman notes: "Like responsive readings in church, they dull the critical faculties of those who use them and those who hear them and at the same time give developments a reassuring meaning, thereby mollifying the fears everyone holds of arbitrary or malevolent administrative action."[38]

Stadium opponents had a difficult time overcoming the steady beat of arguments not only in consultant reports but also in the local news media. When these reports did not tout the economic gains for the whole city, they underscored the project's inevitability. Governor Schaefer, it was said, was too powerful a public figure to confront on the stadium issue. Community resistance to the stadium plans was practically impossible. There was no way to shift the issue from small-scale skirmishes fought

against overwhelming odds to a larger debate involving the priorities of
the city as a whole.

A City of Neighborhoods

Baltimore's reputation as a "city of neighborhoods" was central to its
national prominence as a renaissance city in the 1980s. Long a place
where neighborhood associations and political clubs carved out turf for
self-governance, Baltimore zealously advertised that fact under William
Donald Schaefer's mayoralty.[39] But the neighborhoods did not shape their
own destinies in the case of Baltimore's stadium politics. The sports
industry's ability to control the pace and tempo of the deliberations reduced neighborhood participation to a few quixotic battles mostly irrelevent to the decision-making process.

People in both the current and the proposed stadium neighborhoods
opposed the new stadium because of the way it would affect the fabric
of their communities, but they failed to involve a wide variety of community groups in a broad-based debate. The discussion, therefore, proceeded according to the logic and demands of the sports industry.

As is often the case with large public projects, some neighborhoods
felt they had to accept the basic premise that a new stadium was necessary.
When a new stadium appeared inevitable, neighborhoods organized to
protect their own parochial interests. For example, in 1985 Baltimore's
Otterbein Community Association expressed concern to the state's advisory commission on sports about locating a new stadium in Camden
Yards, but they did not question the need for a new park. The association
thus acceded to the exclusion of this basic question from the stadium
debate.[40]

Stadium advocates located the new facility in one of the choice areas
of the city. Geographer Sherry Olson argues that Baltimore is organized
in two ways—as rings and wedges—and that this organization affects
the movement of people and groups in and out of the city. The concentric-
ring model is a classic image of urban development: "Like other cities,
Baltimore grew ring by ring, a building boom every twenty years or so,
annexing territory, filling it up, spilling out."[41] The wedges, which re-
semble pieces of pie, extend from the central business district out to choice
urban and suburban communities. The wedges provide axes of movement
that avoid the core's disadvantaged and sometimes dangerous areas.

The new stadium site, Camden railroad yards, is on a choice wedge,
two blocks to the west of the Inner Harbor. The 85 acres included the
Parks Sausage Company, a CSX Railroad shop, a heavy-metal disco-

theque named Hammerjacks, a school, and a union local. The site is directly connected to the suburban and Washington markets by the Baltimore-Washington Expressway, the Baltimore Beltway, and a number of major downtown arteries. The near-by Inner Harbor development, which cost a total of $2 billion, covers 275 acres and includes a $45-million convention center, a $30-million shopping area, and the $18-million National Aquarium, as well as hotels and office buildings.

Public support for construction of new stadiums in Baltimore was doubtful, especially in the state at large. While 53 percent of persons surveyed in the Baltimore City area said they supported building a new stadium, 45 percent said it was not important whether Baltimore had a professional football team.[42] The survey did not include the opinions of residents of the rest of the state, which was overwhelmingly opposed to the stadium by most reports, and the poll was taken without the public debate that would precede a referendum. However imperfect they were, the data seemed to suggest that the stadium might fail if the question of its construction were opened up for public debate.

Despite the bitterness that lingered after the Colts' departure, many Marylanders saw little reason to believe that the Orioles would leave the city. The Orioles drew more fans than ever at Memorial Stadium, even when the team suffered bad seasons on the playing field. In 1987 and 1988, for example, the team finished in last place but still managed to draw close to 2 million paying customers; in 1988, the team set all-time records for ineptitude but still drew 1.6 million fans. The stadium was located in a charming part of town, the franchise's promotion efforts were successful inside and outside the city, and the team seemed to have won a place in the hearts and routines of the city.

Even though the public was lukewarm about the need to build a new stadium, Governor Schaefer decided to act, for three reasons. First, Schaefer did not want to be the public official held responsible for "losing" another major league franchise. Schaefer avoided blame for the Colts' departure because Irsay was the target of enmity, but losing a second team could be the municipal equivalent of "losing China." Schaefer also wanted to attract a new NFL team to restore the city's damaged pride. Second, big public works projects involve big contracts and public works jobs. Third, large projects provide visible signs of life for the state and city. Schaefer promoted a stadium for the same reasons he had, as mayor, championed the Harborplace development, downtown construction projects, and various gentrification schemes. They gave the city an image of renaissance and action.

Governor Schaefer put his proposal for a new stadium at the top of his legislative agenda. His resounding victory in the previous year's primary and general election campaigns, and his own energy, gave him that executive "power to persuade" that he needed to get stadium legislation through the general assembly. Some legislators from outside the Baltimore area—chiefly, from Montgomery County, Frederick County, and the Eastern Shore—resisted the legislation; but they eventually agreed, when legislative horse trading gave them some highway funds in exchange.

The mechanism that the state adopted to implement the plan for new stadiums was the quasi-public authority, with its politically advantageous quasi-accountability. The authority would coordinate the many aspects of stadium construction—from running the state lottery that would raise funds to evicting the residents of the neighborhood that would be the site of the new facility.[43] Such authorities have a long and storied history in state and local government. Authorities enable governments to undertake large projects without the inconvenience of public scrutiny. As Robert A. Caro has elaborated, a public authority, in addition to having "the powers of a large private corporation," possesses certain "powers of a sovereign state," such as the power of eminent domain and "the power to establish and enforce rules and regulations for the use of its facilities." Caro calls this "in reality nothing less than the power to govern its domain by its own laws."[44]

The Maryland Stadium Authority was designed to operate above the tangled politics of the Baltimore City. It had the power to select a stadium site and to condemn property in the area without negotiations. The authority did not consider renovation of the existing Memorial Stadium or a wide range of alternative sites for building a new stadium. Its extensive powers liberated it from the inconvenience of arguing with local interests.

The stadium authority was in character with the shadow government that Schaefer had established when he was mayor of Baltimore, to cut red tape and promote economic development. The central institution of Schaefer's shadow government, the City Trustees for Loans and Guarantees, was more powerful than the city council but held most of its important meetings in private. Until it folded in 1986, the board of trustees operated a publicly funded investment bank that provided loans for development initiatives. Other quasi-public corporations operate the city's Charles Center and Harborplace developments and the National Aquarium and fund efforts to recruit businesses. Quasi-governmental development efforts neutralize political opposition by masking the costs of development, separating the public from the decision-making process, preventing the systematic collection of useful information for public judgment of projects, and using such indirect means for financial development as tax breaks, bond authority, loans, influence with the federal government, and donated property, which appear to require no real government expenditures. The arrangements are, in the words of Robert P. Stoker, "public enough to garner resources yet private enough to limit popular participation."[45]

Opposing the stadium authority was difficult. The authority was an instrument of the state but also separate from the state. Its fund-raising capacity lay in the sale of tax-exempt bonds and the operation of lotteries. These devices avoided the direct coercion of taxes but were provided the state's fiscal backing. Because the public financial burden was indirect, challenges could be blunted. The state could claim that the authority did not impose a financial burden on the public; it could then turn around and claim the opposite, that the authority was a full-fledged part of the government, which is exactly what it did during the battle over the state referendum process. In short, the device of the authority could so blur the distinctions between public and private that a meaningful public discourse could not develop.

The nature of the legislation that authorized and funded Baltimore's stadium projects shaped the later battles over the referendum process. The Maryland legislature in 1987 passed three bills to authorize and finance a new stadium or stadiums. Chapter 122 authorized the Maryland Stadium Authority to acquire land for new stadiums and to contract to build the stadiums. Chapter 123 ensured that the stadium authority would be separate from the Maryland departments of General Services and of Housing and Economic Development, and gave it "quick take" powers of condemnation, which speed up property acquisition by eliminating negotiation over terms before the acquisition occurs. Chapter 124 provided financing power to the authority—$235 million in revenue bonds, two to four sports lotteries in each fiscal year to pay bond debt service, and $1 million annually from the city. Chapter 124 also set up an arrangement by which the state would lease the stadiums from the authority and then lease them back to teams.

On April 30, a community organization called Marylanders for Sports Sanity (MASS) began a petition campaign to put Chapters 122 and 124 to a statewide referendum. State officials gave MASS instructions on proper petitioning procedures. On May 27 and 28, MASS completed its drive, gathering more than twice the necessary signatures, but the state attorney general rejected the petitions. The attorney general argued that the legislation amounted to a state appropriation for the purpose of maintaining state government; the state constitution bans referendums for such programs. The state supreme court supported the attorney general's ruling.[46]

A referendum campaign could have created an open-ended debate about the role of professional sports in the city, subsidies to private interests, the role of neighborhoods in local politics, and other legislative and fiscal priorities for the state and city. The state's opposition to the referendum started, in essence, a discussion about whether full public discussion ought to be permitted.

Obscure legal issues determined the controversy's outcome. One issue was whether the stadium legislation ought to be considered as three separate statutes or one unified piece of legislation. If the bills were considered separate, the referendum proponents could put one of the two bills not relating to funding up for a public vote, since they could in no way be considered appropriations—and that would be sufficient to challenge the stadium. The state argued that the bills were really one piece of legislation.[47]

The two sides also debated whether sports and recreation constitute a "primary" or "valid" public purpose and whether stadium funds constituted "appropriations," and thus were immune from referendum challenge.[48] Referendum sponsors argued that funds deposited with a separate, temporary authority ought not to be regarded as appropriations.[49] Perhaps the most remarkable part of the debate was the state's assertion that the constitutional protection of health programs as essential protected the stadium project. "I don't believe the [stadium opponents] can separate the construction of a new sports stadium from the general governmental function for promoting recreation."[50]

The state prevailed in these disputes. It was able, in a sense, to dismember the stadium issue. The issue's many aspects were removed from public discussion—and even when they became part of the public discourse, it was in the form of minor issues involving small numbers of people.

Quixotic Resistance

Once the authority had the legal and financial wherewithal to condemn land and build stadiums, there was little room for public debate. Neighborhoods and other opponents could make claims for benefits from the stadium but could not question the project's validity. Given the existence of other urban problems needing state support, most decided that opposing a new stadium was not worth crossing the governor, especially since William Donald Schaefer is well known for his grudges and tit-for-tat style of politics. Working through the stadium authority enabled the state to avoid demands for democratic access, procedures, and debate. The public space was closed. Stadium politics was restricted to the course determined by the tightly controlled authority and the sports industry.

Without the referendum process, which San Francisco and New Jersey used to defeat major stadium projects the same year, opponents of the Baltimore stadiums had little recourse. The stadiums were not popular, but the issue of whether or not they should be built did not justify the kind of massive and concerted activism that would have been needed to defeat the proposal. Zan White, a Camden Yards community organizer, argued that opposition to the stadium failed because the project seemed both comparatively minor and predetermined:

> People are not going to die and spend a lot of money fighting. . . . We don't have the political weapons to fight it. The city is not going to fight the governor about it; they're going to try to make do with what they got. Most people think it's a ripoff. People feel like [the stadium project is like] the development of the waterfront: the [political campaign] contributors have more votes than the neighborhoods. There is a strong sense that things are not good, that major things are not working. We've got this showplace but what's this do for the lives we live? But unless you think about doing something major, you can't do much. Most people think we'll fight them as they come along. Most people think it's a foregone conclusion. You got to figure out what you can really do.[51]

The belief that the stadium controversy was not important enough to risk activism underscores the fragmentation of local politics. Even though the Camden Yards stadium had the potential to affect the makeup and even the existence of many neighborhoods, residents consciously decided to treat the stadium as an isolated matter. Urbanites are used to coping with numerous and difficult problems, and the kinds of problems that might result from the stadium—such as increasing traffic and driving out middle-income families and small businesses—were not immediate enough threats to prompt an all-out, coordinated fight.

State Senator Julian Lapides asserted that stadium development could cause a chain of events that might be disastrous for the city's neighborhoods and finances, that in both the old and the new stadium neighborhoods people's lives would be affect. "There is going to be a white elephant [in the old], and tremendous traffic problems at the new site. Coming in and out of the city is going to be virtually impossible. They're going to have to build new roads, and that's going to affect the neighborhoods that are left. It spirals."[52]

The residents of Ednor Gardens and Waverly, the site of the old stadium and the adjacent business and residential area, cooperated with Camden Yards activists during the legislative and petition processes, but the alliance did not endure. Attempts to show the damaging effects that a new stadium might have on the neighborhoods surrounding both old and new stadiums met with indifference and parochialism. Truckson Sykes of the Northeast Community Organization warned of major disruption to neighborhood patterns with the closing of Memorial Stadium and advised his neighbors that cooperation with the Camden Yards group was the only way to protect their own turf:

> I had a real feeling that since everything was concentrated in the harbor area—not only with the stadium, but also with the public housing units there coming up for sale soon—that the city would have to move the people somewhere. The only place they can move people is the [old] stadium area. The people in the projects are fighting to keep their housing, and we should help them. If you don't help them with their problems, the problems will end up in your lap. But people here feel it's in another part of the city. They don't realize that what happens in one part of the city affects all the other parts.[53]

The Waverly Improvement Association cut private deals with city administrators to protect their neighborhood interests—thereby cutting themselves out of the larger stadium debate. "We told them, 'We won't raise a wild protest anymore, but what are you going to give us in terms of public works?' " the association's John Bowman remembers. "Trying to cut a deal is all you can do. You just get burned out after a while."[54] The city agreed to increase its attention to streets, trees, and vacant buildings. With the deal, the city transformed complex concerns about the stadium to a concern for distribution of comparatively minor municipal benefits.

John Bowman described the fragmentation that prevented comprehensive public deliberation in Baltimore's stadium politics. "You just deal with little things at a time," he said. "If the city or state or team did something that [caused an uproar], they'd just pull it back until it quiets down. They use the timing element." The biggest neighborhood fear about the Orioles leaving Memorial Stadium, he said, was the prospect of piecemeal development. "We don't want piecemeal stuff. We want everything put on the table. If it's not, we lose control," he said. Unless the city developed a complete plan for the stadium site, there was a risk of disruptive events at the stadium. "We don't want any damn tractor pulls and rock shows. Too much has already happened piecemeal. They paved Eastern High School [adjacent to the stadium] without telling anyone. It made it harder to deal with the issue." The decision to close Eastern High School, a Baltimore landmark, was based as much on stadium considerations as on educational policy. Public meetings and regular assurances from city officials did little to calm residents.

One reason fragmented politics undermines local action is that it breeds uncertainty. "There are rumors all over," said Truckson Sykes. "You don't know where they pop up. Someone might say something in a meeting that causes unity in the community to dissipate. . . . It makes people very jittery." Rumors regularly swept Ednor Gardens and Waverly about what city planners would do with the real estate opened up with the demolition of Memorial Stadium and Eastern High School.

Mobilization in the Camden Yards neighborhood was too little too late. It was obvious to most people that Governor Schaefer wanted Camden Yards to be the site of the new stadiums. The only sustained movement against the stadium occurred in the small, cluttered apartment of William B. Marker, one of the founders of Marylanders for Sports Sanity and a local gadfly and aspirant to elective office. Marker, a lawyer, pursued a variety of strategies that might have linked and mobilized various interests, but he did not have the organizational skills or support of other activists necessary to mount a citywide effort. Marker was dismissed as a clumsy opportunist—someone determined to use the issue to attain public office but unskilled in political maneuvering.

MASS attempted to politicize the stadium issue by connecting it to a number of other relevant issues. The group developed an alternative proposal for economic development of Camden Yards that would take advantage of the site's rail links to Washington, D.C. MASS also filed a lawsuit challenging the legality of procedures used by the Maryland Stadium Authority and alleging conflicts of interest among public officials. Throughout, the quixotic organization attempted to develop links with other community groups by promoting local spending priorities, such as education and health care, and questioning the morality of the sports lottery.

MASS had to be versatile in its tactics. Sometimes it concentrated on the unglamorous work of letter writing and petition pushing, and at other times it attempted to make a splash in the local news media. The organization attempted to use a variety of legal and populist tactics at the state, local, and even national levels in an effort to connect the fate of Camden Yards with larger interests.

MASS raised both procedural concerns and substantive issues. It questioned the reliability of public statements by Governor Schaefer and stadium authority officials and demanded access to government agencies where policies were debated.[55] MASS forced itself upon the legislature's committees and state study commissions. Frequently, however, those organizations refused to hear public comment. The anti-stadium movement also charged that the commissions overstepped their legal authority. MASS questioned official estimates of the cost of stadium construction, which turned out to be wrong by at least 300 percent. The organization also tried to expose the charade of a public search for a stadium site. Governor Schaefer was known to have been a strong partisan of Camden Yards from the beginning. At various times, city officials acknowledged that the search was a formality. MASS also proposed taking the Orioles in an eminent domain action or buying the team, after the 1988 death of owner Edward Bennett Williams. MASS framed the issue most starkly when it proposed simply giving the Orioles franchise the $2 million per annum that the team said it needed to be competitive rather than incurring the costs of a new stadium.

Marker's organization did not faze the stadium juggernaut. Pitted against the city's power structure and Governor Schaefer's enormous power in Annapolis, MASS had little impact. It also failed to tie the issue to the broader historical picture. Chicago neighborhood activists, by contrast, argued that their displacement by a new stadium was just one event in a long series of policies that segregated the city.[56] Camden Yards stadium opponents might have argued that, combined with the earlier displacement of nearby residents and small businesses to make way for the Harborplace development, the stadium represented a complete takeover by commercial interests of a large part of the city.

In the final analysis, MASS and the neighborhoods failed to extend their battle beyond the immediate circumstances. The feeling of inevitability and the failure to see the linkages to other problems doomed the anti-stadium effort. Camden Yards was selected as the site of a new stadium, among other reasons, to minimize conflict. The area's isolation from more political neighborhood, and its proximity to the downtown area, made it a natural appendage to the already extensive downtown development. "Herbie has that in mind, I can tell you that," recounted one intimate of the stadium authority's director, Herbert Belgrad.[57]

After creation of the stadium authority, there was little that could be done to control it. The responses to the authority's early cost overruns indicate just how much the authority was in charge. State Senator Laurence Levitan said he was "shocked" by the cost overruns; "I'd say they did a lousy job" in estimating the costs of the project. But he added: "Overall we're stepping back, though we're not happy with what happened. The legislature is certainly uptight. The bottom line is we might have done things differently if we'd known about [cost inflation] to start with."[58] The legacy of the stadium has extended to Baltimore's attempt to lure a new football team. Because of the cost overruns on the baseball park, a football stadium probably will require private development. Public financing of the second facility may entail new state legislation—bound to be controversial.

Courting the Cardinals

The ability of a franchise owner to steer negotiations was again displayed in 1987, when the St. Louis Cardinals of the National Football League conducted negotiations with several cities about moving the team. After proposals to build a new stadium in Missouri faltered, Maryland actively sought to attract the franchise. Maryland never negotiated as an equal partner, however, because the team's owner skillfully orchestrated just what issues would be addressed at what stages of the sequence.

The Cardinals' owner, William V. Bidwell, announced in 1984 that he would move the franchise unless either the city or county of St. Louis constructed a new 70,000-seat stadium exclusively for football. The Cardinals negotiated with officials from Baltimore, Phoenix, Jacksonville, Columbus, and New York, as well as their own local governments, before finally announcing that they would move to Arizona in time for the 1988 season.

The courting of the Cardinals was conducted in a long procession of public and private bluster, cajolery, offers and counteroffers, demands, concessions, conciliation, and winks and nods. The terms of the negotiation changed with each new development, large or small. Approaching January 15, 1988, the deadline for the decision set by the NFL, Arizona and Maryland emerged as the principal competitors.

If the negotiations had been less fragmented, and if they adhered consistently to preestablished standards, St. Louis would have kept the team. In the end, St. Louis responded to Bidwell's most extravagent demands. Plans for a $170-million domed stadium fell through, but St. Louis officials managed to develop a proposal for a $117-million open-air facility, which Bidwell rejected. A week before the January 15 deadline, St. Louis officials offered a new $5-million practice facility and office complex, almost no rent, and a promise to pursue plans for a downtown domed stadium. Right before the NFL owners voted on Bidwell's request to move, a public-private consortium called Civic Progress made an offer of a 70,000-seat domed stadium with 65 skyboxes and a more lucrative concessions deal, but by then Arizona was a "done deal." Bidwell said the offer "was a very strong presentation," but he still asked for a move to Phoenix; the NFL owners voted 26-to-0 to approve the move.[59]

Bidwell employed tactics of delay and circumspection in the drawn-out negotiations. He insisted that competitors for the team limit public comments; he shielded the proposals from the competing cities and steadily notched up his demands. When Arizona made an offer, Bidwell would identify one or two deficiencies; he would then ask Baltimore and other cities to match the Arizona offer and enhance it in one or two additional specific ways. The different resources of the competing jurisdictions enabled Bidwell to get the competitors to ratchet up the offers. Rather than allowing the bidders to assess their competitors' offers as wholes, he broke them into pieces that he could then manipulate. Cardinals spokesmen would not say exactly what they sought, only that various "gaps" existed in the proposals of the suitors.[60] This strategy kept the negotiations fluid—and in Bidwell's control.

Bidwell's strategy spurred the competitors to improve their bids regularly. Arizona promised to build 60 skyboxes at Sun Devil Stadium in Tempe with annual revenues to Bidwell of $2.4 million.[61] Later, Arizona said it would construct a brand-new stadium in Phoenix.[62] By the time the Arizona package was complete, it reportedly added $20 million to $24 million in annual revenues to the Cardinals. Jacksonville offered a package that guaranteed profits of $115.2 million over a decade; later, renovation of the Gator Bowl was offered.[63] St. Louis made dozens of proposals in the four years after Bidwell expressed dissatisfaction with Busch Stadium. The final proposal, put together by a coalition of St. Louis and the surrounding county and incorporated communities, would have resulted in a downtown domed stadium that would have met Bidwell's seating, skybox, parking, and other revenue requirements. Earlier, Bidwell was promised the pivotal role in a development scheme in St. Louis County in the area surrounding the proposed stadium. Bidwell acknowledged that the differences between the dollar value of the packages were "essentially insignificant."[64]

Bidwell clearly relished his superior negotiating position. Negotiators from the competing cities could not say much publicly for fear that they would undermine their negotiating position. A spokesman said of Governor Schaefer, "He's using Mr. Bidwell's favorite quote: 'No comment.'"[65] Where Bidwell was mum as part of an offensive strategy, Schaefer was mum as part of a defensive strategy.[66] Bidwell controlled who spoke, and when.

The cities could only piece together scraps of information to inform their speculation, so insignificant developments acquired great importance. Surprise telephone calls or meetings were the stuff of banner headlines, even if they did not contain significant new information. Simple adjustments in Bidwell's schedule were taken as signs about Bidwell's mood. Concerning one such change, one participant said: "It shows there's a real surge of activity in each of the cities, and yet none of the cities has been told that it is out of the running."[67] In the end, participants did not even know whether Bidwell took them seriously.

Bidwell's comments in an interview with the Baltimore *Sun* illustrate his approach. Was Baltimore in the running, Bidwell was asked. "All we've ever said is we're looking at opportunities." Is the feverish competition for the franchise a surprise? "No." What exactly are the Cardinals demanding? "The opportunity to compete in an atmosphere conducive to winning." Is a domed stadium preferable? "I think whether a facility is domed or not is a community decision." Should St. Louis get serious consideration if it assembles an attractive proposal? "I have no comment on the St. Louis situation." Was the fan support in St. Louis adequate? "You've seen the last game. The fans we had here were good. They responded to the way the team performed." What have you learned from the business aspect of football? "The business aspect of it is something you try to put in a very private world. . . . I'm not prepared to talk about it." Can Baltimore do anything else to attract the club? "I can't comment on that." Any regrets? "I wouldn't comment on that." What about Bidwell's image problems? "No one said life is fair."[68]

NFL owners had no intention of undermining Bidwell. Before announcing his move, Bidwell spoke frequently about honoring the NFL's policy of requiring ownership approval for moves—music to the league's ears after the rancor of the Raiders' transfer. The Pittsburgh Steelers' president, Dan Rooney, said the fact that Bidwell had submitted his transfer proposal to the proper committee "would definitely weigh in the reaction of the league." Michael Lynn, general manager of the Minnesota Vikings, said: "He did it in a very measured way. It wasn't something that was done in haste."[69]

The other franchises, of course, had additional reasons for allowing the Bidwell escalation effect. One team's success in pitting cities against one another strengthens the bargaining position of other teams. Oakland Raiders owner Al Davis, for example, supported the efforts of Bidwell to get a new stadium, even though Bidwell is technically a competitor.

The Ripple Effect of Stadium Politics

As Maryland courted the Cardinals, Baltimore's professional indoor soccer team pressed the city for better lease terms. The Baltimore Blast of the Major Indoor Soccer League gained $245,000 worth of concessions in its lease with the Baltimore Arena and a possible $280,000 in guaranteed ticket sales. Negotiations proceeded according to the logic of me-tooism.

The Blast asked for a share of concessions equal to that of the Orioles (45 percent). It gained leverage from the city's desire to attract an NFL team. Mayor Kurt L. Schmoke said: "We don't want to get a reputation as an anti-sports town. . . . We're working hard to let people know this town will support professional sports."[70]

Baltimore's pursuit of a new NFL team may have been hurt by construction of the new baseball stadium. The stadium cost overruns were so severe that funding for a "twin" football stadium was threatened. Other cities' interests were affected as well. In Washington, D.C., efforts to attract a new major league baseball team were undermined by having the formidable Orioles franchise close by.[71] The efforts of the NFL's Washington Redskins to get either the D.C. or the Virginia government to erect a new facility could also affect Baltimore's expansion hopes, by increasing the minimum standards for a stadium and by occupying the time and resources of the area's leading sports boosters.

As Oriole Park at Camden Yards neared completion in the spring of 1992, some of the doubts about the project faded. The team spent $175,000 to celebrate the previously derided Memorial Stadium on its final day in 1991, tapping emotional springs and helping to ease the transition to the new facility. Breaking with the standard "cookie-cutter" approach to stadium design of the 1970s and 1980s, the stadium authority selected an architectural design that recalled the sport's traditional neighborhood parks. An irregular field shape, fewer seats, the use of a historic warehouse as a back drop to the right field fence, and art deco ornamentation made the park feel lived-in before it even opened. One wag commented that he had heard so much about the park's old-fashioned atmosphere that he "expected to see Harry Truman throw out the first pitch." Complaints about cost overruns, favoritism, and political pressure tactics did not seem to matter amidst the national and local media celebrations of the new facility.

The Baltimore elite's constant concern about professional sports can be attributed to a desire to counter the image of decline in the city. Such a concern is reactive, so it was predictable that the monopolistic sports industry would control the way issues were deliberated. With issues discussed in a narrow, sequential style, an open, public dialogue was prevented. The public may have financed the show, but it never managed to land a significant speaking part.

6

Chicago: Whither the White Sox?

> Can you imagine—the Hoosier dome? If there is
> anything that marks a town as being a genuine
> hicksville, it is the innocent belief that a domed
> stadium is the height of progress.
> —Mike Royko, Chicago *Sun-Times*, June 3, 1982

In the summer of 1989, the neighborhood known as South Armour Square was destroyed to make space for a new stadium for the Chicago White Sox. The new stadium would replace another in the neighborhood—Comiskey Park, the oldest facility in the major leagues. By opening day of the 1991 baseball season, scarcely a trace remained of the old neighborhood or the struggles it inspired.

The battle over South Armour Square appears to be a textbook example of the effects of the unequal distribution and use of power in American cities. Replacement of an existing stadium with a new stadium was successfully promoted by a privately owned baseball franchise, itself part of an entertainment cartel called a league, by local development interests, such as bankers, lawyers, bond writers, construction firms, and by political elites, mainly the governor and mayor but also local agencies and a state authority. A few marginal groups—poor residents who lost homes, a few quixotic planners, social workers, and assorted good-government types who argued that public money could be better spent—opposed the stadium.

South Armour Square was a politically weak and isolated community. To the east of the neighborhood was the Dan Ryan Expressway, the Chicago's busiest thoroughfare. The Dan Ryan cuts off the neighborhood from the Illinois Institute of Technology. Comiskey Park marked the community's northern border. Farther north was a city park and the conservative, white, mostly Irish bedroom community of Bridgeport, the lifelong home of the city's late machine boss and mayor, Richard J. Daley, and his son, the current Mayor Richard M. Daley. To the west were railyards.

The Eleventh Ward, which contained both Bridgeport and South Armour Square, has undergone major changes in recent years. Hispanics now compose about a quarter of the ward's population, and blacks make up another quarter. Also living in the ward are Chinese, Lithuanians, Poles, Italians, as well as Irish. In the minds of the White Sox management, such demographic characteristics in the surrounding neighborhood undermined Comiskey Park's attractiveness. The areas east and south of the stadium were almost completely black. The residents were not targets of White Sox marketing efforts. Their low incomes limited their attractiveness as fans, and club officials said the low-income neighborhood made whites nervous and kept them from coming to ballgames.

South Armour Square lost its struggle against the new stadium, but it demonstrated more influence than most political insiders had expected. One city advisor dismissed the neighborhood in the early stages of the struggle: "Those people have never been organized, they have no groups. They are not important in city or even ward politics."[1] But the activists confronted the immediate threat with sophisticated strategies. Even though they lost their homes, the residents got more benefits from the city than most experts predicted—and shaped the political debate in important ways.

White Sox Wanderlust

The approval of plans for a new stadium across the street from the historic Comiskey Park was the culmination of years of agitation by the White Sox. The team twice came close to moving to sites outside Chicago—the town of Addison, in suburban DuPage County, in 1986, and St. Petersburg, Florida, in 1988.

The White Sox owners, Jerry Reinsdorf and Edward M. Einhorn, maintained that Comiskey Park was structurally unsound and needed to be replaced. Renovation, they said, would not adequately address the stadium's dangers or unattractiveness. When the team threatened to move, the state and city came up with the financing and authority to build a new stadium. Reinsdorf acknowledged the strategy. "We had to make threats to get the new deal," he said. "If we didn't have the threat of moving, we wouldn't have gotten the deal."[2]

Although Reinsdorf and Einhorn discussed the possibility of moving the team with a number of other cities, their preferred site was suburban Addison, where they could continue to take advantage of the nation's third largest metropolitcan market. The White Sox also initiated discussions with officials from Denver, Washington, D.C., Phoenix, Jacksonville, and Tampa, as well as St. Petersburg.

The decision to move out of Comiskey Park, the team's home since 1910, can be traced to the sale of the team in 1981. After one of the most colorful and controversial careers in the sports industry, Sox owner Bill Veeck sold the franchise to a partnership headed by Reinsdorf and Einhorn. At the time of the sale, the new owners pledged to keep the team in Chicago throughout their tenure. In 1982 the Chicago City Council approved a $5-million tax-exempt industrial revenue bond to finance twenty-seven luxury suites at Comiskey Park, in return for another pledge to stay in Chicago.[3] Soon afterwards, however, the new management commissioned a market analysis that fundamentally changed the team's approach to the city.

The market analysis advised the White Sox to develop a base of suburban fans. Chicago's outlying areas had not only a greater population than Chicago but also significantly higher income levels. The strongest White Sox support was found to be in the western suburbs, areas of substantial economic growth. Comiskey Park, by constrast, was located in one of the most depressed neighborhoods of Chicago. Between 1972 and 1984, the ZIP code area that includes Comiskey Park lost nearly half its jobs. Suburban incomes and employment, meanwhile, rose during the same period. In suburban Addison, to which the White Sox attempted to move in 1986, employment doubled during the same period.[4]

Another factor entered the White Sox' decision to suburbanize. During the preceding couple of decades, the Cubs had become more popular than the White Sox within the city limits. The number of Cubs games broadcast over WGN-TV—about 140 out of 162 in a season—gave the North Side franchise greater visibility. In addition, the Cubs developed a nationwide following with its cable television "superstation." The Cubs marketed themselves well, stressing the historic and unique qualities of the "friendly confines" of Wrigley Field. The White Sox suffered in comparison, with a less prominent television presence and unstable management.

The first development in the White Sox suburbanization strategy was a broadcasting shift. In 1986 the franchise signed a lucrative contract to broadcast most of its games on cable television. The five-year contract more than doubled the team's annual television revenues, from $4 million to $8.3 million in its first year. It also put regular broadcasts of the games out of the reach some of the franchise's traditional working-class clientele.

The White Sox also started to look beyond South Armour Square. The location suffered from two significant disadvantages—inaccessibility to suburban fans and crime. The neighborhood's racial makeup accentuated the fears of crime. A 1974 report of the Brookings Institution concluded that ballparks in predominantly black neighborhoods had lower white attendance.[5] Marketing surveys regularly showed that middle-class fans, particularly white suburbanites, were afraid of crime in the Comiskey Park area.

The White Sox' decision to market to the suburbs paralleled a more general extension of Chicago's local identity from the inner city outward, underscored by the growing use in public discourse of terms like *Chicagoland*. The expression is a perfect example of the delocalization of identity, identification with a place without rootedness in that place. The term implicitly states that one can have access to the economic, cultural, and ethnic excitement of the city without having to confront the danger and blight associated with the city. *Chicagoland* blurs the boundaries between city and suburb, obscuring the real division of fortunes created by the lines drawn between Chicago, Cook County, and the surrounding five counties. Those lines, in fact, are of great importance in distributing urban fortunes. The levels of income, homeownership, poverty, segregation, transportation mobility, and so on, change markedly when crossing the city limits. But a boundary blurred is a boundary that does not have to be politically justified or addressed.

The Economics of the White Sox

The White Sox' decision to seek a new stadium—if not in Chicagoland, then elsewhere—stemmed in part from a peculiar dynamic of the sports industry. Oddly, the worst teams in professional sports often exert the most influence over stadium politics. Because they tend to have the greatest difficulty turning an acceptable profit, they seek more lucrative stadium leases. A state of long-term crisis leads them to make a series of demands on their host cities. They claim that their stadiums prevent them from attracting big crowds, even though research suggests that a team's field performance is the key determinant of attendance.[6] Meanwhile, because of a shortage of teams, other cities are willing to bid for the franchise.

This oddity of baseball economics creates a intermittent states of "crisis" that lead to a spiraling of stadium demands.[7] Franchises regularly move up and down in profitability. When they are down, they trim payrolls and bargain for better terms for stadium leases and other public amenities. When they are more successful, their bargaining power for broadcasting contracts improves. In other words, in both feast and famine, franchises are able to improve the terms of their relationships with the states and cities in which they play ball.

The White Sox used their momentary poor standing to gain higher profits and a more favorable lease with the Chicago government, and, eventually, a new stadium. By stripping the team of top players, the owners in three years (1985-88) reduced its payroll from $9.1 to $5.8 million, barely half of the major league average of $11 million. With revenues of about $30 million annually, the team increased its short-term profits substantially. And, of course, the club's management used short-term failure not only to initiate cost-cutting measures but to press for a more lucrative long-term relationship with the city.

In 1988, the White Sox' performance was so bad that their local broadcaster, WFLD (Channel 32), sued for breach of contract. The suit alleged that the White Sox management willfully destroyed the team's quality in order to reap immediate financial gains, and that the station lost advertisers and revenue that it had a right to expect from its baseball broadcasts. The WFLD contract, the suit argued, provided "an implied promise to act in good faith and to deal fairly, . . . by so managing the White Sox as not to destroy or impair unreasonably the team's appeal."[8] Poor personnel decisions and a string of threats to leave Chicago showed a lack of good faith, harming the television station. Between 1985 and 1988, the station's ratings fell from 5.1 to 1.7 points (each point represents 30,000 viewers), causing advertising rates to plummet; WFLD had earned a $1.5 million profit in 1985 but lost about the same amount in 1988.[9]

The White Sox were in a good position to make demands on public authorities because of their lack of success on the playing field. The franchise could claim that it could not build a competitive team because an inadequate stadium and a burdensome lease restricted its resources. As is often the case in negotiations over sports facilities, nothing succeeded like failure.

The Chain of White Sox Politics

Chicago's three major sports franchises are politically linked to one another. What happens to one club affects the others. The markets for fans overlap, proposed stadium projects have involved two or three teams at a time, and separate stadium proposals produce demands for parity and restrict the options for the other teams. The placement of a stadium in one part of town restricts the options for other stadium projects. The White Sox and Cubs and the Bears football team have all threatened to move away from Chicago if their stadium demands were not met. The actions of each of the major teams rippled throughout the system, producing a constantly changing set of options and alliances.

The most important stadium linkages concerned the Cubs and Bears. The Bears' plans to build a privately financed stadium always took into account those of the White Sox, because of the competition for appropriate plots of land for stadiums. In addition, the Bears and White Sox at one time considered sharing a stadium; the football team ultimately rejected that possibility. The public role in financing of sports facilities was another connection between the teams. Even if the football stadium could be privately constructed and operated, it would still require millions of public dollars for the provision of roads and other infrastructure.

The Cubs' success undermined the White Sox' position and spurred them to look outside the city. But the controversy about whether to install lights at the Cubs' Wrigley Field had a more direct impact on the White Sox. In the late 1980s, Major League Baseball put pressure on the Cubs to install lights, which would permit night games at Wrigley Field. Since the sport had become increasingly dependent on broadcasting revenues, the absence of Cubs games from prime time had annoyed the hierarchies of both Major League Baseball and television. Commissioner Peter V. Ueberroth threatened to bar playoff games at Wrigley Field unless lights were installed. The Cubs' management had long wanted to install lights but had deferred to the day-game tradition until it could claim to have no other choice because of pressure from the leagues.

Inspired by a romantic attachment to day baseball and concern about the potential effects of night games on the neighborhood, neighbors of Wrigley Field organized a movement against night games. The issue turned into a symbolic battle between "people trying to keep their neighborhood safe and healthy and a large corporation trying to make more money."[10] Local taverns and homeowners gathered signatures for a petition that declared opposition to lights. The Illinois General Assembly passed a law in 1982 that set noise pollution standards for facilities where night games were not played before 1982. The Chicago City Council passed legislation in 1983 that banned night contests in unenclosed stadiums located in residential neighborhoods.[11] As the battle over lights progressed, the Tribune Company put pressure on public officials who opposed lights.[12] The Tribune's interest stemmed primarily from its desire to increase ratings—and advertising revenues—on its national broadcasts of Cubs games over its WGN cable superstation. After protracted bargaining, lights were installed in 1988—upsetting White Sox officials, who were concerned about the games' effects on their own television ratings.

If lights had not been installed, the Cubs might have left the city. Although a successful club financially, the Cubs were always interested in enhancing their business potential. The team publicly threatened to move to suburban Schaumburg Township in 1985 and discussed plans to build a new facility in Arlington Heights. In the same year, the Cubs and Bears considered building a domed sports facility. If the Cubs had left, the White Sox might have been stuck, since the major leagues would never have allowed two teams to leave the nation's third largest market. The White Sox might therefore have had less bargaining power—or more, since local resources would have been concentrated on one team and the team would have been more important to the city. If the Cubs had built a domed stadium in the city, the White Sox might have been so outmatched in the local market that they would have moved.[13]

Once it was determined in 1986 that the White Sox would pursue construction of a new stadium in South Armour Square, linkage to other teams was reduced. The issue was simplified to a battle between the neighborhood and stadium proponents.

Governor James Thompson expressed willingness to support any proposal for keeping the White Sox in Illinois. Thompson did not favor Chicago; in fact, his feud with Chicago's Mayor Harold Washington could have given the suburbs the edge. At one point, at a Republican Party picnic, DuPage County Board president Jack T. Kneupfer presented the governor with a White Sox hat. Thompson observed that the hat said only "Sox." He exulted: "It doesn't say Brighton Park White Sox. It doesn't say Blue Island White Sox. It doesn't say Addison White Sox. This is a perfect hat!"[14]

Thompson initially favored a White Sox move to suburban Addison, but when that option failed in a November 1986 referendum, he became a champion of Chicago. The suburban option's failure may have reduced the franchise's leverage. Rather than finding assurance in this outcome, however, city politicians felt greater pressure to respond to White Sox demands. Former mayor Jane Byrne was reported to have prepared commercials for the 1987 mayoral campaign that charged Mayor Washington with losing the team. One city planner said, "I think that what happened was that the White Sox needed to save face after losing that Addison referendum and Washington needed to defuse Jane Byrne's charge that he was the Mayor who lost the White Sox."[15]

The state legislature actually passed two packages for a new baseball stadium. According to the first agreement—the "memorandum of understanding" that Mayor Washington and White Sox owner Reinsdorf signed December 1, 1986—the team would pay a base annual rent of $4 million for twenty years, then $2 million after construction bonds were paid off. But a feud delayed implementation of the plan. A standoff between Republican governor Thompson and Democratic mayor Washington lasted a year. The dispute centered on the membership of the authority and its control of construction contracts and professional fees.

The Thompson-Washington battle dominated stadium politics for ten months after the creation of the stadium authority in December 1986. Again, rather than a wide-ranging public debate, the discussion on this sports-related issue was dominated by the struggle between two strong personalities. Thompson, the white Republican governor, epitomized downstate Illinois's resentment of Chicago; Washington, the black Democratic mayor, represented the upstart forces of reform and liberalism in the city.

The governor and mayor each had three appointments to the Illinois Sports Facilities Authority; the governor was to name a seventh member, the chairman, with the consent of the mayor. When Thompson named Thomas Reynolds, Jr., a long-time political associate, as chairman, Washington withheld his consent until he got control over another major public works project, the McCormick Place Convention Center. Washington also sought assurances that the stadium authority would be independent of the White Sox and would limit displacement in South Armour Square.

In October 1987 Thompson and Washington finally compromised on all the major appointments. Compromise came because both men became embarrassed over continuing to inhibit the stadium authority's work by their bickering, and because their feud was affecting other significant issues, like redevelopment of the Navy Pier, development of the Chicago Avenue Armory—and a new stadium for the Bears.

Mayor Washington also feuded with U.S. Representative Dan Rostenkowski, a long-time nemesis. The dispute arose over Rostenkowski's reluctance to help secure federal tax exemptions for the bonds to finance the stadium. The tax exemptions could have cut $30 million to $40 million from the overall cost of stadium construction. Rostenkowski, the ultimate Washington insider, disingenuously claimed that his influence as chairman of the House Ways and Means Committee was exaggerated. When Rostenkowski balked at seeking a federal exemption for stadium bonds, Washington retaliated by removing from the city's powerful zoning committee a certain Rostenkowski ally—and Rostenkowski's sister lost a $33,000 job.[16] The two eventually patched things up and Rostenkowski arranged the tax exemptions for the stadium project.

Fifteen months after its creation the stadium authority finally met. While the governor and mayor had been feuding, St. Petersburg had begun construction of its own new stadium and had emerged as a possible landlord for the White Sox. The White Sox reopened the question of location. The team argued that the 1986 agreement was obsolete, and they negotiated a new agreement requiring an additional $30 million in subsidies from the state. Among the issues resurrected was the $4-million annual rent that the club had agreed to pay the sports facilities authority.

The Illinois legislature took up the new stadium package in 1988, just as St. Petersburg was completing construction of a domed stadium. Florida and St. Petersburg officials shuttled back and forth to Illinois in an attempt to lure the franchise south. The White Sox eventually signed a contingency agreement with Florida, agreeing to move the team to St. Petersburg if the Illinois legislature did not meet the White Sox' demands.

Even after the White Sox had secured their legislative demands in Springfield, the team refused to make a binding commitment to stay in Chicago. The franchise signed a "backup" deal with St. Petersburg in July and issued statements indicating that the team might still move. One statement read: "The problem's just gone into hibernation; we still could be gone. . . . people are thinking the Sox are in Chicago to stay. That's not final either. No one should believe anything until the first home game in the new stadium, if it's built. There are too many things that could go wrong." [17]

Local Resistance

Dislike of South Armour Square and a desire to attract suburban fans were the major reasons behind the White Sox' demand for a new stadium, but as residents in other potential sites rejected a new stadium, the old neighborhood inevitably became the site. The biggest reason for its eventual selection, oddly enough, may have been that the White Sox and the planners considered it so undesirable. The White Sox' lack of enthusiasm for the neighborhood kept it out of consideration at the early stages, when it might have had a greater chance to play the not-in-my-backyard game. The residents in the other potential stadium sites exercised what has been called "decision-making by objection." [18] They blocked location of the stadium in their neighborhoods during the long process of debate over the project. When South Armour Square finally was confronted with the issue, there were no other viable sites for the stadium. Other sites had greater power than South Armour Square, in part because they reacted sooner, when the consequences of site rejection were not as serious for the project. As the debate evolved, the reasons to build the stadium changed; by the end of the process, getting out of a poor inner-city neighborhood was no longer the White Sox' prime objective.

Four Chicago-area locations were considered as sites for Bears and White Sox stadiums—next to Lake Michigan, near the central business district called the Loop, on the west side, and in suburban Addison. Other sites, such as northwest Indiana, were mentioned but never seriously considered.

The Lakefront Site

Building a stadium by Lake Michigan was one of the first proposals made when site hunting began in 1986. Mayor Washington proposed putting a football and baseball stadium there, and Bears president Michael McCaskey endorsed the site. But opposition came quickly from the city's art museums, preservationists, and downtown business firms. The biggest problem was traffic. Each time adjustments were made in the plan to deal with traffic, new objections arose. Mayor Washington finally withdrew his support for the site after Governor Thompson, three opposing mayoral candidates, and preservationists all said they would fight it.

A coalition of groups headed by Friends of the Parks—including the League of Women Voters, Metropolitan Planning Council, South Side Planning Board, and the Lake Michigan Fund—suggested a number of alternative sites, such as Soldier Field, the Near West Side, and the South Loop. Governor Thompson announced his opposition to the lakefront site in 1987, saying he preferred a location on the West Side. Because the lakefront site was considered early, opponents could kill it without also appearing to kill the idea of a stadium in general.

It is not clear that the White Sox would have played at the lakefront site even if the stadium had been built. The Bears management always expressed reservations about sharing a facility, and the Bears would have controlled the facility, since they would have been supplying most of the funding. The city's only leverage with the Bears was its financing of the extensive infrastructural additions that would be required and its interest in the downtown area as a whole. Had the stadium been constructed for the Bears only, other sites that the Bears later pursued, like the West Side, might have been available for the White Sox.

The Loop Site

In the spring of 1986, Mayor Washington unveiled a plan to construct a $255-million stadium in the moribund Roosevelt Road railroad yards south of Chicago's Loop business district. Under the early version of this plan, the stadium would house both the Bears and White Sox; movable grandstands would allow the stadium's design to fit both baseball and football. Financing would come from industrial revenue bonds and revenues from 240 skyboxes.[19] Later, after objections to the idea of two teams sharing a facility were aired, the proposal changed to a baseball-only facility.

The Loop proposal sparked the immediate ire of the new residents who were part of a gentrification movement in the area. Development had been spurred by expansion of Chinatown to the south and west, construction of a school, and construction of two residential developments (River City and Dearborn Park).[20] The value of the real estate was enhanced when the city government moved a commuter rail line terminal to the area, opening land worth millions of dollars to commercial and residential development.[21] Franklin Cole, vice president of the Chicago Central Area Committee, opposed the site on the grounds that it would erect a wall between the South Loop and the rest of the South Side. Other objections were based on fears of traffic conjestion, noise, the cost of building a connecting road from the Dan Ryan Expressway to the 18th Street site, and, most important, the threat to residential development.

Residents quickly drew congressional, state legislative, and local officials to their side. The opposition of Alderman Frank B. Roti of the First District was crucial, because of the city council's "aldermanic courtesy," which allows council members to veto projects in their wards. Roti's opposition may also have been influenced by his opposition to Mayor Washington in the city's notorious "Council Wars."

Stadium opponents had a number of political options at their disposal besides lobbying their elected representatives and demonstrating in public places. At one point, the Citizens Against the Stadium (CATS) began a petition drive to get a referendum to make the district "dry"—that is, ban the sale of alcoholic beverages—a change that would have removed the site from consideration. Opponents also made issues of Mayor Washington's receipt of campaign contributions from key backers of the project and of the "exorbitant" tax and other benefits given the White Sox.[22]

State and local laws passed to protect residents of the Wrigley Field neighborhood on the North Side may have helped the South Loop residents. Illinois state law imposes noise pollution standards on professional sporting events in any facility in which night games were not played before 1982. That regulation, designed to prevent the installation of lights at Wrigley Field, could have prevented the erection of any new stadium in the city. Loop residents craftily exploited the law, thereby linking their fortunes to the more politically connected Wrigley Field neighborhood.

Robert Winslow, a principal developer of the project, began to back away, not just because of residential opposition but also because of difficulty putting together a development scheme for the entire area.[23]

The White Sox pulled out of the South Loop plan in July 1987 after the general assembly failed to appropriate the subsidies that would have been required to satisfy the team. Excessive White Sox demands may have killed that state subsidy appropriation. The team was demanding all revenues from tickets, parking, concessions, and stadium advertising, as well as a complete waiver of local taxes, and threatening to move to DuPage County if they were denied.

South Loop residents succeeded in their opposition partly because other sites were still open. At the time of the Loop's consideration, Addison officials were lobbying the White Sox and state officials to locate the team in their community.[24] Chicago officials appeared to accept the idea that the city might lose the White Sox. Under these circumstances it hardly seemed worth the trouble to beat South Loop residents into submission.

The West Side Site

A White Sox stadium on the West Side would have been shared with the Bears football team. After years of political wrangling, which included threats to move to the suburbs or another state, the Bears in 1987 had accepted a plan to build a new stadium on the city's West Side. The 75,000-seat open-air stadium, along with development of the surrounding area, would be operated by the Metropolitan Structures Corporation; the Bears' sole responsibility would be to play games there, for which the franchise would reap half of all revenues. After maneuvering by various parties over other Bears stadium proposals for the Lakeside, the South Loop, and the Roosevelt Road railroad yards, Mayor Washington endorsed the West Side site. Governor Thompson and legislators called for Bears–White Sox cooperation.

White Sox involvement in the project was killed by the financing proposal. The plan included an agreement to minimize displacement and disruptions in the neighborhood. The Bears' president, Michael Mc-Caskey, rejected calls to bring the baseball team into the venture, either as cotenants or as part of a twin-stadiums development, arguing that White Sox tenancy at the West Side site would break faith with neighborhood residents of a nearby model community.[25] For the White Sox, the Bears' blocking was as decisive as the neighborhood opposition in other sites.

The Addison Site

In 1986 the White Sox announced plans to move to a new domed stadium in suburban DuPage County, but after buying about 150 acres of land in the village of Addison, hiring architects to design a new facility, and winning approval to sell $100 million worth of bonds, the White Sox withdrew from the project. The opposition of a key state legislator, the narrow defeat of the stadium proposal in a nonbinding referendum in Addison in November 1986, and the opposition of homeowners and environmentalists set the White Sox scampering for another site.

DuPage County officials also talked about luring the Bears and the Bulls basketball team as well to a major sports complex. Large-scale development including a new convention center was considered necessary to recoup the costs of infrastructural improvements. Governor Thompson backed the multi-sports proposals, but State Senator James ("Pate") Philip backed an alternate site near Roselle and Hanover Park, also in DuPage County, since the Bears held an option to purchase more than 500 acres there. Philip acknowledged that putting a financial package through the legislature would be difficult: "The Chicago guys will be angry because they think we stole their team, which isn't true."[26]

The Addison proposal never had the backing of groups active in local or state politics. Whereas in Chicago the local government was unified and the opposition fractured, in Addison the opposite was the case. DuPage County Board president Jack Kneupfer argued that promotion of a stadium required strong executive leadership to overcome the opposition of local groups. "Otherwise you get involved in all kinds of petty wrangling: 'We want this' or 'We'll go along only if we get that.' . . . There wasn't anybody that was absolutely determined to have a stadium here. There were mixed views out here—not overwhelming support for them."[27]

It was homeowners and environmentalists who ultimately beat the stadium. Homeowners feared the stadium would undermine their placid way of life in the town thirty-five miles outside Chicago. Addison residents played hardball on the question of land sales. "If somebody wants to buy they have to pay the price," one homeowner said, intimating that the cost of buying the land would increase dramatically.[28] Environmentalists, meanwhile, argued that the stadium would endanger federally protected wetlands. David Sanders of Glendale Heights, adjacent to the stadium site, made preservation of the area's wetlands a personal crusade. "It's a one in a thousand piece of land."[29] The Army Corps of Engineers indicated that it would block stadium construction if the land were determined to be valuable wildlife habitat. The corps also expressed concern about the effect of roads and other infrastructure on the environment in surrounding communities.

The stadium opposition movement in Addison coordinated its campaign with Chicago's Save Our Sox organization. (That organization would later oppose South Armour Square activists.) Both lobbied state and local officials to keep the team in Chicago. They vowed to put pressure on baseball commissioner Peter Ueberroth. Said one Chicago organizer, "The Chicago community is begging the Sox to stay there. Ueberroth has got to react to that." DuPage County Board member Jane N. Spurgel, arguing against the stadium's location in the suburbs, linked the concerns of Addison with the concerns of nearby towns: "How do we take into account the appropriate concerns raised by Bloomingdale—the whole question of who pays and who benefits?"[30]

The White Sox spent close to $100,000 on its referendum campaign to locate in Addison, while opponents spent only $3,000; but in the referendum, Addison voters defeated the stadium proposal, albeit by a small margin (3,787 to 3,744—50.3 to 49.7 percent). Voters in the wider area of DuPage County did not appear willing to foreclose future development, however. A referendum to create an "open space" district, which would foreclose development, failed by a 12,306 to 5,888 vote (68 to 32 percent).

With nowhere else to go, at least in the Chicago area, the White Sox considered leaving the state—1,000 miles southeast, to Florida. They eventually turned back to South Armour Square. The irony of the situation was that the White Sox desperately wanted to get out of their neighborhood, but the long-running negotiations eventually ensconced them there.

From Chisox to Flosox?

In the summer of 1988, St. Petersburg attempted to lure the White Sox. Legislators in Florida and Illinois countered each other's offers, regularly raising the stakes. The packages addressed not only the team's stadium needs and related matters like parking, concessions, and rent, but also land development, taxes, and broadcasting possibilities. At various points, unconfirmed reports surfaced that the White Sox had already decided to move. Toward the end of the Illinois legislative session, the White Sox laid down a final challenge: if Illinois did not approve the appropriations, the franchise was committed to moving south.

Florida officials had sought major league baseball for decades before the White Sox option arose. Most speculation about sites centered on Tampa, Jacksonville, and Miami. However, in 1985, the St. Petersburg and Pinellas County governments agreed to erect a $50-million domed stadium. As the Suncoast Dome neared completion in 1988, the White Sox found themselves in need of a bargaining chip to play in their negotiations with Illinois—and St. Petersburg served that purpose. The White Sox entered into intensive negotiations to move the team south.

The White Sox' strategy in 1988 was a high-risk gamble. It could succeed only if political leaders in Chicago and Springfield were so scared of a move that they would give in to the White Sox. To keep pressure on Illinois, the White Sox publicly embraced the St. Petersburg site. White Sox owners ostentatiously toured the site of the Suncoast Dome and spoke enthusiastically about the broadcast riches of the open Florida market. To exploit the Florida card fully, however, the White Sox management had to provide proof that it was sincere in considering St. Petersburg. Toward the end of the 1988 Illinois legislative session, the team signed a provisional agreement to move to Florida.

The gambit might have backfired. The White Sox were committed to move if the Illinois legislature did not meet their demands. The White Sox offensive occurred at a time when Chicago was reluctant to grant further financial benefits and concessions and the state was so fiscally strapped that the Republican governor had called for a major tax increase to finance basic services such as education and health care. The White Sox' demands coincided with a campaign by the NFL's Chicago Bears for state backing of bonds to finance the West Side stadium complex. If the Illinois legislators had failed to approve the Sox' 1988 package, the owners might have found themselves caught between their legal commitment to St. Petersburg and the opposition of other major league team owners, who were not anxious to approve a franchise move from the biggest midwestern sports market.

But the White Sox succeeded, playing the two states and cities off each other during the protracted negotiations. After getting a $10-million loan offer from a Florida financier in April 1988, for example, the White Sox spurned Illinois officials for weeks while holding regular talks with St. Petersburg officials both in Florida and Illinois. This prompted Illinois officials to renegotiate the $4 million annual rent that both sides had previously accepted. Eventually the rent was cut in half, and no rent at all was to be paid if attendance fell below 1.2 million. It was estimated that the White Sox could receive a windfall of $60 million from the agreement.

Florida's big advantage was its television market. St. Petersburg officials put together a broadcast arrangement that would unofficially make the White Sox the state's team, with a commercial television contract in twelve cities, a radio network on fifty-five stations (plus the possibility of adding eight Spanish-language stations and of extending into the Bahamas and the Carribbean), and a cable television network reaching 2.5 million homes. Gross annual broadcast revenues in the first year of operation would be $14.9 million, with the White Sox' share being $10.3 million— several million dollars more than they finally got in their Chicago agreement. The revenues would rise in subsequent years. Cable broadcasts could have been the biggest boon, since more than 50 percent of all Florida homes are wired for cable compared with 30 percent of all Chicago homes. One member of the St. Petersburg negotiating team acknowledged the advantage of being the first to reach the market. "The first team to hit Florida will have a gold mine forever," the official said.[31] Florida offered the kind of open market opportunity that the Dodgers had seized when they moved to Los Angeles in the late 1950s.

Some experts predicted that organized baseball would reject a move of the White Sox from the third largest market in the nation, but at no time did the baseball hierarchy intercede to restrain the bidding. In fact, the American League president injected himself into the process, only to strengthen the White Sox' bargaining position, when he argued that Comiskey Park was inadequate.[32]

Bidding escalated, in part, because of the precarious political condition of government officials in Florida. Since St. Petersburg began construction of the Suncoast Dome before getting any assurance that it would get a major league team, local officials had put themselves at great risk. As the battle with Chicago commenced, grassroots movements for the dismissal of those officials were emerging. The dome was becoming a symbol of rash speculation and political hubris. A former mayor, Charles Shuh, Jr., dismissed the stadium boosters: "We've always had a group of what I call SBLE's—small brains, large egos—that wanted to be the city of Tampa."[33]

St. Petersburg's efforts might have succeeded if not for a long-running feud with Tampa, which had been attempting to snare a baseball franchise for decades. The Tampa Bay Baseball Group vowed to undermine the neighboring city's efforts to lure a team.[34] Politicians and the media in Tampa conducted a campaign to sully St. Petersburg's image. That campaign may have planted enough doubt in the minds of the White Sox management to incline them toward Chicago's offers. Some St. Petersburg officials suggested that Tampa was in collusion with Chicago to prevent the team's move south. No evidence supporting that charge surfaced, but the rumor was an indication of the bad feelings between the two Florida cities.

Ostensibly, the major dispute between Tampa and St. Petersburg was the relative merits of transportation serving their stadium sites. Tampa officials claimed that St. Petersburg was inaccessible to the rest of the state and too far from the area's population center; St. Petersburg countered that its site and the one in Tampa were equally accessible. Eventually, the Tampans acknowledged that they had never formally studied the issue and that a site in St. Petersburg was probably as viable as one in Tampa.[35]

Boosters in both cities were aware that the area would get at most one franchise, and they attacked each other's efforts relentlessly. The battle between the two cities was a game of chicken, with a major league club as the possible prize and a $130-million white elephant of a stadium as the possible booby prize. The competition was reflected in their major daily newspapers, which were fighting a local war for readership and advertising lines. Typical of the battle was this editorial salvo in the Tampa *Tribune*:

> What St. Pete has going for it is a baseball stadium now under construction, although at enormous public cost for a medium-sized city tucked away in a lower corner of a little peninsula. . . . The most recent figures suggest that even with a team in residence the stadium is unlikely to break even—thus saddling the people of St. Petersburg, and their children's children, with an even greater debt load than originally calculated. And, we believe, it would be a dark day for the White Sox, because many fans would think twice about setting forth on Pinellas County's clogged roadways to take in a night game in an impoverished neighborhood.[36]

The cities would eventually end their bitter competition and form an alliance, but to do it they had to accept each other as equal partners. First, St. Petersburg needed credibility as a potential major league city— which it got with its attempts to lure the White Sox in the summer of 1988. Second, efforts to get a team had to shift toward an expansion team. Tampa organizers were interested as much in ownership as in getting a team for the bay area, so they would work with St. Petersburg only if they could assemble an ownership group. If the White Sox came, the team would bring its owners as well, precluding proprietorship for Tampa's entrepreneurs.

In December 1988, the Tampa Bay Baseball Group initiated negotiations that quickly brought together Tampa and St. Petersburg in the quest for major league baseball. The rapprochement came as both sides realized that their competition might doom the area's chance to get a team. The alliance would not have been possible if St. Petersburg had not come so close to luring the White Sox. "The White Sox changed the entire transaction," one Tampa organizer said. "You can talk about theory, but you don't know until it gets going. . . . There was a basic disbelief in the St. Petersburg site until the White Sox."[37] St. Petersburg's bid for the Sox had also helped improve the terms of the team's new lease and stadium in Chicago. By way of thanks, White Sox co-owner Jerry Reinsdorf became an advocate for St. Petersburg with the major leagues. With his influence increasing in the sport, Reinsdorf's friendship was invaluable.

Ironcially, St. Petersburg's attractiveness may have been illusory. According to many participants, ranging from the commissioner's office to the White Sox management itself, St. Petersburg was just a tool for the White Sox to use against Illinois legislators—a suitor to be teased and then cast aside when the Illinois deal was concluded. Even if that was the case, the process still gave St. Petersburg legitimacy in the baseball sweepstakes.

The Battle of South Armour Square

By the time of the competition with St. Petersburg, the only remaining obstacle within Chicago was the neighborhood of South Armour Square. Under state legislation passed in December 1986, the Illinois Sports Facilities Authority had the power, starting July 1, 1987, to take over private property on the proposed stadium site. South Armour Square residents opposed construction of a new stadium for a simple reason: it threatened to destroy their homes and neighborhood. The plan to build a stadium across the street from the existing park would displace some 1,000 residents, mostly black, living in 85 houses and 420 low-rise Chicago Housing Authority units. The area was economically depressed but offered affordable housing and access to public transit. Houses were old and in need of repair but generally well-maintained. Many residents had lived in the neighborhood for decades.

The neighborhood organized like never before. The area previously had failed in their resistance to projects that had threatened black businesses and homes, but the stadium issue galvanized the residents. They hired a social worker to organize the resistance and a lawyer to handle negotiations with government and White Sox officials. Residents of South Armour Square demonstrated, met with government officials, and threatened legal action to prevent displacement. In the end, the South Armour Square residents were forced out, but the activists negotiated a settlement that provided greater compensation than was necessary, given the authority's power of eminent domain.

South Armour Square faced a number of political disadvantages. Residents could not offer alternative sites to shift the focus from their own neighborhood, because other potential locales had taken themselves out of contention. More important was the area's poverty and isolation. Most residents had little political experience. When they did pull together, they had few resources for public relations and legal representation. The coalition had to scrape to pay for the bus that took residents to Springfield to lobby against the 1988 stadium legislation.[38] Jacqueline Grimshaw, who served on mayoral committees dealing with the stadium issue, predicted that South Armour Square would not be able to mobilize. "The larger picture is not that important there because of the Dan Ryan [Expressway], the Illinois Institute of Technology, and the Chicago Housing Authority units—the community is already boxed off enough."[39]

The neighborhood's population was a small minority of the Eleventh Ward. Local politicians could win elections without the support of South Armour Square, so there was little political leverage available. The clout of another neighborhood in stadium politics—Wrigleyville—provides an instructive comparison. Until 1988, neighborhood pressures had prevented the Cubs from installing lights at Wrigley Field because of concerns about traffic, crowds, and rowdiness. The "symbolic fight between a community and a giant corporation," as one anti-lights activist called it, attracted more media attention than the potential destruction of the entire community of South Armour Square.[40]

Attempts to forge ties with nearby communities elicited brusque rebuffs. Mary Milano, the neighborhood's lawyer, said building a coalition with the predominantly white Bridgeport area was impossible. "I personally am in favor of building all kinds of alliances, but the historic tensions between Bridgeport and South Armour Square made it illogical. There wasn't the ability to see the common interest." One resident said: "We don't have much contact with the folks to the west and to the north, and that's a shame. We're sort of a taboo over in North Armour. You never cross 35th Street to go over there. It's just something that you don't do."[41] A neighborhood activist said he had attempted to develop ties with the conservative, white Bridgeport neighborhood north of Comiskey Park but that his overtures had been deflected. "They asked if I had talked to the ward party leader. They were not interested in [movement] politics."[42]

Building ties to Bridgeport—whatever the possible impact of the project on that neighborhood—would have been nearly impossible. The areas to the north and west of South Armour Square have over the past forty-five years been off-limits to blacks. An informal but severe system of segregation keeps blacks out of Bridgeport. Blacks venturing into the area have regularly been abused verbally and physically; the few black families that have attempted to move into the area have been similarly rejected. Armour Square Park, directly north of Comiskey Park and south of Bridgeport, "belongs" to whites. Violence against blacks has required police action on several occasions.

Ironically, the destruction of the black neighborhood of South Armour Square could devastate Bridgeport. Attorney James Chapman has argued:

> The victims of the stadium will be the people of Bridgeport. [Residents on the western edge of Bridgeport] are going to be ten feet from the new stadium. They'll be priced out of their community. It's always the case with stadiums and other development that it enhances certain kinds of residential and commercial development. It's gentrification. The whites to the north and west [of the new stadium] are going to be the ones to be hurt by this. Now several people from Bridgeport realize that maybe they're the endangered ones.[43]

Sheila Radford-Hill, the organizer hired by the residents, made the link between the black and white neighborhoods: "I think we could get more response from local politicians if we ally with white residents. We have to show how displacement and economic dislocation affect people of all races. Today it's South Armour, well, Bridgeport could be next."[44]

South Armour Square had a long history of displacement. The neighborhood's once-thriving shopping district was detroyed by the construction of the Dan Ryan Expressway in 1957. Other small businesses were destroyed to make way for a senior citizen center. Dozens of lots in the area became vacant in the middle to late 1980s.

The construction of the Dan Ryan was perhaps the greatest cause of the economic and social isolation of South Armour Square. The north-south highway originally was to have been located several blocks to the east of the parallel Wentworth Avenue, which would have kept a thriving business district accessible to residents. That location would have allowed the area to develop, and the black population might have advanced into Bridgeport. City planners, however, moved the highway west, to a strip immediately east of Wentworth Avenue, destroying black housing and the business district on Wentworth. According to the legal brief in a suit filed on behalf of the neighborhood by attorney James Chapman in 1989, the intent of the City in relocating the Dan Ryan was to create a buffer area and artificial barrier to [limit black residence to] South Armour Square. By restricting the black population primarily to the east of the Dan Ryan Expresssway, the black residents of South Armour Square were effectively isolated. This isolation, in combination with the associated destruction of Wentworth Avenue as a major arterial street, effectively eliminated the pressure and opportunity to further expand the areas populated by black persons to the north (beyond Comiskey Park) or to the west (beyond the railroad tracks) into Bridgeport.[45]

The highway shift cut off blacks politically as well as socially and economically. The way district lines were drawn made blacks a consistent minority in federal, state, and local electoral districts. Forming political coalitions, became almost impossible.

Activism and Settlement

South Armour Square residents were not consulted before their neighborhood was selected for the new stadium, but they became a force. The neighborhood coalition searched for pressure points at which to stage its anti-stadium battles. The organization wanted to implicate a wide range of institutions in its campaign, but specific tactics were never certain. While some wanted to negotiate through formal channels such as the mayor's office, others wanted merely to tie up the system and create so many delays that the project would eventually be canceled—or moved. Because of the neighborhood's reactive posture, however, it could never develop a coherent assessment of the situation, much less a comprehensive strategy.

The activists were further controlled by the legislative timetable at the state capital. As the legislation to fund a new stadium reached the critical stage in Springfield, the coalition debated tactics and demands.[46] Looking ahead to a meeting with Acting Mayor Eugene Sawyer, one community leader, Curly Cohen, the lone representative of Bridgeport, urged a "bleed and die" statement: "We should . . . get a mayoral statement saying no housing displacement is acceptable." Another suggested developing public pressure by somehow provoking arrests at the meeting. Several said the coalition should only attempt to change the site. "The rest is irrelevent," said another. "The West Side is a good site. Who cares what neighborhood gets the stadium, as long as we don't have it here?" One suggested that pushing the pressure elsewhere, like the West Side, would not only rid South Armour Square of the problem but also change the dynamics of the citywide debate. Radford-Hill suggested a legal strategy to complicate the sale of bonds necessary to finance the stadium. Cohen promoted coalitions with other neighborhood groups, even though the South Armour group had repeatedly been rebuffed by Bridgeport community and local political figures. Members also disagreed about whether to concentrate pressure on Governor Thompson and Acting Mayor Sawyer or to contact all the city's political leaders in the city council and state legislature. Eventually, they concentrated on Sawyer, who faced a difficult election to hold on to the position to which he had been appointed after the death of Mayor Washington.

The neighborhood managed to force a negotiated settlement. The settlement did not prevent the neighborhood's destruction, but at least it provided the displaced residents more generous terms than were legally required. With a $10-million compensation package, the stadium authority obtained the consent to move of some forty homeowners. The package paid residents market prices for their homes, plus $25,000 cash bonus, moving expenses, and legal costs. Renters agreeing to the package received moving expenses plus $4,500 bonuses and a $250 monthly rent differential for one year for rent in new areas. Homeowners could have new homes built for free if their mortgages were paid off, or could receive mortgage payments identical to their South Armour Square payments. Renters who did not voluntarily sign on to the deal were cut out.

The prospects for the area as a whole may have worsened. Mary Milano maintained that she negotiated the best possible deal for the people directly affected by the new stadium. She argued that she could not be expected to negotiate for the whole area—to link the neighborhood struggle with larger forces in the metropolis.

> I approached this project the way I approach a commercial real estate deal, which is my usual line of work. I tried to get the best deal possible for the people affected by the development. When I went in I thought our chances were remote. I think these people got the best condemnation deal in the history of the state. The thing to do was to get people involved with a collective mechanism [the coalition] until such time as the individual contracts were signed.[47]

Others disagreed. They maintained that the neighborhood organization was split in half by the stadium authority and Milano. At the meeting where Milano announced the settlement, the people from adjoining areas charged that they had been betrayed. The coalition, an incorporated body requiring votes on policy decisions, never formally adopted the terms of the pact. Without some kind of formal vote, the coalition legally could not enter into an agreement with the authority. As the suit filed by James Chapman notes, the coalition's board "did not authorize execution of the relocation agreement, has never ratified the agreement, and immediately explicitly disavowed the agreement."[48]

Once the agreement was accepted by individual beneficiaries, residents no longer had group bargaining power.[49] The neighborhood representatives on the relocation oversight committee, outnumbered four-to-three, had little influence on issues regarding the agreement's implementation. Individuals had to fend for themselves. The authority conducted relocation by breaking the neighborhood into blocks and individuals. The stadium authority controlled appraisals of the houses; challengers could only introduce evidence not included in the appraiser's report. Whatever the evidence gathered by the homeowner, "the request should be made in a timely manner as the schedule for quick take proceeding will not change." Renters who failed to reach an agreement by the October 15 deadline, for whatever reason, faced eviction without any compensation. Renters also lost rights if they failed to settle accounts with the landlord before settling with the stadium authority and if they posed an unspecified "nuisance" to the authority.

The authority controlled all the stages of the pact's implementation. The negotiation of property sales and residential relocation, complete with appeals, was to take barely more than two months—even though the authority did not need the land for construction purposes for another five months. The agreement specified a number of deadlines and placed the burden of meeting the deadlines on the residents; failure to meet the deadlines damaged the residents' interests, regardless of which party was responsible for the delay and whether the delay was reasonable. Such time constraints, combined with the fragmentation of the neighborhood after the agreement's conclusion, reduced the possibility of dialogue. More important was the fact that residents entering the relocation process outlined in the agreement gave up all rights to "any litigation against ISFA (including but not limited to any litigation related to any condemnation proceeding undertaken by ISFA) other than as a result of a breach by ISFA of this agreement." In one respect, the agreement gave the residents an important tool for negotiations: the opportunity to consult the coalition's lawyer, who negotiated the agreement (or $1,000 for attorney's fees if the resident chose to hire an independent attorney). But, since the major issues were closed and the timeline restrictive, such assistance was likely to provide only minor help.

The agreement was a pseudo-transaction, since the coalition's attorney did not have the coalition's official backing. The settlement divided the

important groups in the neighborhood. The isolation of the groups remaining in the area may hinder their ability to confront the continuing
forces of economic and real estate speculation.

The Dream of Small-Scale Development

One alternative plan for a new White Sox stadium, created by an interested independent architect, Philip Bess,[50] could have satisfied virtually
all of the objections to other plans. Bess's plan would have produced a
new ballpark, displaced only a handful of residents, promoted residential
and small-business development, integrated automobile traffic and public
transportation systems, and maintained the historic integrity of the old
stadium. But the proposal never received serious consideration by the
city government or the franchise. The plan's fatal flaw was that it would
remove the buffer zone between the area's blacks and whites. The group
that wanted to maintain that buffer—Bridgeporters—was among the
least communicative and the best politically connected neighborhoods of
the city.

Bess designed a stadium that would retain the historic qualities of
Comiskey Park and its neighborhood and also appeal to fans' desire for
an idiosyncratic ballpark. Under the proposal, a new 40,200-seat stadium
would be built immediately to the north of the existing stadium, and a
general-purpose city park would occupy the old stadium site. The new
stadium would be modeled after the old-fashioned inner-city ballparks,
built when the tight grid of city streets that nestled the parks resulted in
odd field dimensions.

The proposal was an attempt to retrieve the traditional city-sports
relationship that had been undermined by suburban-style stadiums. Architects of modern facilities like Royals Stadium, Three Rivers Stadium,
and Riverfront Stadium, Bess argues, have built symmetrical and detached stadiums. Baseball parks once linked the team and community,
but suburbanization and the automobile have given rise to stadiums with
no connection to residential areas. The result has been a disaster for both
the game and the neighborhoods. Designers of such stadiums, Bess points
out, are "concerned with erecting long-span, column-free decks with good
sight lines. They also want easy motor-vehicle access. In other words,
the game of baseball is not their department."[51] The stadium's sterility
extends to the larger environs—a legitimate urban planning issue.

Under Philip Bess's plan, Armour Square Park's function as a buffer
between the black neighborhood and Bridgeport would have been threatened. Access to the community park would shift from Bridgeport to South

Armour Square, from the white ethnics to the blacks, and Bridgeport would be bounded on its east by the stadium rather than the park. The park would be transformed from a place almost exclusively for white Bridgeport residents to a citywide park used by both blacks and whites. Bridgeport would be accessible to blacks.

Bess's proposal was a master plan for the whole economically depressed area. "The assumption here is that what makes cities vital is the proximity to a wide number of diverse activities," Bess said. "[Careful plannning] does not cause vitality, but it facilitates it."[52] To induce outside investment, create a wide mix of uses in the area, and enable diverse groups to cross paths on a regular basis, Bess allocated three blocks facing the stadium for both commercial and residential development. The six-story multipurpose structures to be built there would be zoned for retail space on the first floor, offices and studios on the second floor, and residences on the top four floors. Residents with a view of the field would pay slightly more for their apartments. In total, 480 housing units and half a million square feet of business and studio space would be available for development. Automobile traffic would be funneled from the Dan Ryan Expressway into parking garages located behind the rowhouses, and therefore would not overrun pedestrian traffic. The area could take advantage of two usually antagonistic forms of transportation—public rails and high-speed freeways—since both would feed into the area without going through it. The cost of implementing the plan was estimated at $80 million to $100 million.

The Bess proposal would obey all of planning critic Jane Jacobs's rules for tightknit development and interactive neighborhoods: extensive use of sidewalks, to keep residents' "eyes on the street," thus deterring crime and encouraging neighborliness; limited automobile traffic, to keep public interactions on a human scale; small blocks, to do the same; a mixture of residential, business, and cultural activities, to create a steady stream of different people in public spaces; use of aged as well as new buildings, to protect long-time residents and lessen the heavy costs of totally new development; concentration of groups; the use of "gradual money" (spending that reinforces rather than overwhelms current neighborhood economic activity) and limits on "cataclysmic" money, to keep development as natural as possible and prevent big economic actors from dominating the area; effective use of parks, to encourage neighborhood mixing and a steady stream of strangers; and elimination of vacuums of space that can be overtaken by disruptive groups.[53]

The proposal at the same time consciously fulfilled the planning requirements of Peter Berger. According to Berger, every community needs "mediating structures" that link its smallest parts with its large structures.[54] If individuals and groups are to play a meaningful role in the larger society, they must have direct access to comprehensible structures. Individuals should become part of groups, associations, neighborhoods, different-sized businesses, and structures of local, regional, and national government. Bess explains: "We need civilizing institutions, [which] exist for reasons other than purely economic ones. Pre-twentieth-century architecture embodied civic intentions, but that's been lost."[55]

Bess failed to get allies for his proposal. He attracted only fleeting consideration by some professional planners and neighborhood groups. Had Bess or other neighborhood advocates tried to promote the plan widely, it is likely he would have failed anyway. The White Sox steered the stadium negotiations, and they clearly favored a suburban-style facility.

The White Sox management's choice of a suburban-style stadium was in accord with its efforts to attract more upscale fans from the outlying areas of the city. The team owners privately expressed dislike for the old-fashioned neighborhood stadiums. Bess sent architectural drawings of the stadium and neighborhood proposal to the club's management but received only a perfunctory response. The management, which had a contract with the designer of the Kansas City Royals ballpark, chastised Bess for working on the design and making it public after the team had already developed a plan. "It would seem to me," one official said, "that someone genuinely interested in putting forth a proposal for anything other than publicity purposes would talk to the prime tenant".[56]

The city government also opposed Bess. For City Hall even more than for the White Sox, the proposal raised too many issues. The city was desperately trying to keep up with the rush of events, and Bess's plan was a distraction. Mayor Harold Washington and his successor, Eugene Sawyer, were interested more in retaining the franchise than in elaborate planning schemes—and that required responding to the franchise's demands rather than framing the issue in a larger urban context. In addition, the scheme went against the "edifice complex" of city planners, the desire to build grand structures. State Senator William A. Marovitz, for example, argued for a large stadium in order to maintain Chicago as a "world-class city."

Was Something Better Possible?

Could South Armour Square and other opponents of a new stadium have promoted their interests better? Could the coalition have expanded its strategy to make more connections between its own interests and the interests of others in the city? Could the coalition have used its local understandings and organization to pick apart the demands and claims of the White Sox?

Labor lawyer Thomas H. Geoghegan argued that the city government should confront the structure of the sports industry. Geoghegan lobbied the state and local governments to confront the White Sox with claims of violating informal contracts. "This is clearly a case of unjust enrichment—the city lavished millions on the team, and they turn around and threaten to move," Geoghegan recalled. "There were lots of ways to go. There were reports that some of the partners were anxious about a move. Why not get the city to use them?"[57]

James Chapman, the attorney who filed one of the lawsuits to block the stadium, maintains that the stadium could have been stopped if the coalition had stayed together. "The Authority handled it cleverly," he said. "At a certain point it could have been defeated. The Sox at a certain point didn't have the heart for a fight. . . . The separate agreement with the homeowners left the people without a coalition."[58] Radford-Hill, the neighborhood organizer, argued that the Milano agreement narrowed the process but also could have spurred a new round of organizing. "There are tremendous opportunities if people can hang together. Involvement helps us to define our interests better. This whole process has helped the neighborhood to develop an identity and define a broad economic development program. It's an upside-down situation because we are turning losses into gains."[59]

Chapman and Radford-Hill agree that activists could have shaped events to a degree greater than their numbers and political resources would suggest. The problem is that it is difficult for the smaller players in political contests to know the moments, the stages in the process, when stubbornness and pressure can be used to their advantage. In the case of stadium politics, the franchises steer the process, shaping the specific issues and the timing of interactions.

7

Sports and the Dependent City

> I think it's sad that it's over here, but you can't stop
> progress. . . . I was looking around wondering,
> "What's wrong with this place?"
> —Former Orioles pitcher Dave McNally, after last game at
> Memorial Stadium

On October 6, 1991, Hall-of-Famer Brooks Robinson assumed his former position as Baltimore Orioles third baseman for the last time at Memorial Stadium. The 50,700 fans in attendance roared as Robinson tipped his cap. Then another great old-timer, Frank Robinson, trotted out to right field. The roars continued. Boog Powell took up his old post at first base, then Jim Palmer went to the pitcher's mound. Before long, the most talented players to work for one of baseball's most professional organizations were crowding around their old positions on the playing field. The players wore the uniforms that they had worn as players years before. Many of the players and their fans cried. This was the famous final scene at the stadium where the Orioles had played baseball for thirty-eight years.

Moments before, the Orioles had concluded their last game at Memorial Stadium, a miserable 7-1 loss to the Detroit Tigers. The Orioles finished the season in next-to-last place in the American League's eastern division. For days, the Orioles team management had promised fans a special finale to Memorial Stadium, and they had set aside $175,000 to pay for the festivities. The team was scheduled to begin play in a new facility, Oriole Park at Camden Yards, the next season.

Like the Chicago White Sox one year before, the Orioles were celebrating the memories of an old stadium in preparation for moving to a new facility. Not long before, team officials had criticized the stadium as an anachronism, a drain on the team's chances for success in the league; now the facility was feted as a landmark to the glories of professional sports in Baltimore. On hand at the stadium that day were not only the city's old baseball heroes but also its old football heroes. Johnny Unitas, the legendary quarterback for the Colts during the National Football League championship years of the 1960s, came to throw out a ceremonial "first ball" to Mayor Kurt L. Schmoke. Other luminaries—the vice president, members of Congress, corporate tycoons, and assorted celebrities—also attended the ceremonial finale.

The fans in attendance expressed regret at the impending move to a stadium under construction near the city's glittering Harborplace tourist pavilions. When the public address announcer told the crowd that home plate would be dug up and moved to the new facility, boos filled the stadium. But the bad feelings about the team's decision to leave Memorial Stadium paled next to the sentimentality of the moment. It was a day of memory for the fans. "There's a real touch of sadness in the air," one fan told the Baltimore *Sun*. "The weather is appropriate, no sun, kind of sad. But so many people are here to celebrate the joy of the memories they've got. So how do you feel? I'm not sure."[1]

The final game at Memorial Stadium underscored the contradictions of the professional sports industry and the place of sports in the community. The stadium finale tapped a wellspring of civic identity and sentiment. Real tears over real memories were shed. The baseball team had an undeniable place in the city's culture. But outside the stadium—away from the the choreographed reminiscences of municipal and corporate leaders, old sports heroes, and fans—many Baltimoreans did not seem to care. Some one hundred thousand people ignored baseball and attended Baltimore's twenty-fifth Fells Point Fun Festival. Others simply followed their daily rounds without a thought of the baseball event.

Among those who did care there was also bitterness about the decision to move and hopelessness about the political system that had made the decision. For years, residents of Baltimore and Maryland had expressed deep reservations about the plans to construct a new stadium. Polls showed that a state referendum on whether to build a new stadium might have failed. For most opponents, the objection to the project was the cost—more than $200 million—at a time when the city was in constant fiscal crisis and was deteriorating economically. For others, the concern was the move's effect on two neighborhoods—the old stadium's area and the new stadium's Camden Yards. For still others, the resentment concerned the political corruption and corporate greed that they perceived to be at the heart of the team owners' desire and the state's decision to build a new facility. The mounting cost overruns were resented, as were the sweetheart deals given to the friends and supporters of Governor William Donald Schaefer.

In the final analysis, the Orioles' departure from Memorial Stadium was not the result of community consensus or any demonstrated need for a new facility. The move resulted from the franchise's understated but repeated threats to leave unless the city met its demands for a facility with lucrative skybox seating and a location two miles closer to the profitable Washington, D.C., market. The team's ownership skillfully exploited the Orioles' emotional hold on the city at a time when civic leaders and citizens felt most vulnerable about the deteriorating condition of the city. The franchise struck at opportune moments and got a $203-million facility at public expense.

Cities and Mobile Firms

The politics that surrounded the Baltimore Orioles' move to a new facility has become commonplace in professional sports. In the 1970s and 1980s, virtually every major professional franchise at one point threatened to move if state and municipal officials did not meet demands for new stadiums and other benefits. Several teams—such as football's Los Angeles Rams, Oakland Raiders, Baltimore Colts, St. Louis Cardinals, New York Giants and Jets, and Detroit Lions—left their old cities for the more attractive facilities and public subsidies offered by other localities. Others—like baseball's Orioles, Chicago White Sox, Detroit Tigers, Cleveland Indians, and Texas Rangers—used the threat of departure as leverage to get a new facility in the old city. Franchises were able to play cities against each other to increase their profits at public expense. The game continued into the 1990s, the Seattle Mariners and San Francisco Giants being the most notable cases of wanderlust.

Professional sports, like other businesses, has in recent years experienced a process of "delocalization." As populations—including the nation's most affluent consumers—and economic activities have moved from the inner city to the suburbs and other less-settled regions of the country, leagues and franchises have intensely marketed their product to these new locales. Teams have moved either to stadiums in these outlying areas or to urban locales close to the network of highways serving the exurban areas. Broadcasting has extended its dominion, as well, enabling organized sports to feast on multibillion-dollar television contracts. As the broadcasting industry changes, with an increase in cable television and pay-per-view transmission of sporting events, sports will probably gain access to even greater financial opportunities. The next logical step, so far approached tentatively by the major sports leagues, is internationalization. Football has expanded its operations into Europe, and baseball is planning market inroads into Latin America and Europe.

When baseball awarded an expansion franchise to Miami in 1991, it was immediately apparent that the team's identity would be based more on the region than the city. The team planned to become the team of all Latin America, not merely Florida, with an extensive broadcasting network. In 1992, the Japanese firm that produces Nintendo video games bought the Seattle Mariners franchise to develop a new niche in the American entertainment industry and solidify its place in the economy and culture of the American Northwest. With the sale's controversial approval, the Mariners could develop a wide Pacific Rim following, just as the Los Angeles Dodgers gained domination of the California market a generation before.

Under such conditions, a team's specific location in the urban matrix is not as important as it was in the first century of professional team sports. A team will not lose its important markets by moving from an innercity site to a location on the edge of the city or in the suburbs. Broadcasting markets remain steady as long as the team remains in the same region. Fans with the most attractive characteristic—high disposable income—are located outside the city or in elite wedges of the city that extend from downtown business districts and gentrified neighborhoods out to the suburbs. Old fan bases may suffer, but the industry as a whole gains a more upscale audience in the process. "There's a revolution on in pro sports," says Robert A. Baade, an expert on the sports industry and local economic development. "Sports spectating is become more and more an elite activity."[2]

Even the loyalty of fans to teams has begun to delocalize. A number of teams with national cable "superstations"—like the Atlanta Braves, Chicago Cubs, New York Mets, and Boston Red Sox—attract national followings. The aggressive promotion of team merchandise, such as caps, apparel, and videos, outside the home territory expands the home crowd of a team even further. Football teams like the Los Angeles Raiders and the Chicago Bears have followings based more on ethnicity and group identity than allegiance to a specific place. In collegiate athletics, Notre Dame's exclusive broadcasting deal with NBC allowed it to solidify its already impressive national appeal; one sign of the school's widespread appeal is its $1 million annual revenues for licensed merchandise. U.S. broadcasting has penetrated world markets in odd ways that extend the "community" of a team even further. The Central American nation of Belize has many Cubs fans, because the nation's television station picks up programming from Chicago's WGN station.

Further loosening the ties that bind city and team are changes in teams' corporate orientation. Many franchises are not even the central concerns of their owners, but instead part of a diverse portfolio of economic interests. The Toronto Blue Jays, St. Louis Cardinals, and Colorado Rockies baseball teams, for example, are at least partly owned by breweries that use their franchises as marketing tools. The Montreal Expos used to be held by a distillery. Media outlets own the Atlanta Braves and Chicago Cubs and use the teams to provide free programming and expand corporate visibility. The Florida Marlins are owned by a new media conglomerate, Blockbuster Video, which was searching for ways to respond to a projected decline in demand for its product.

While sports is in many ways a unique industry—local teams are symbols of their home cities, and the monopolistic league organization limits the supply of franchises—it is far from the only industry that threatens relocation to extract benefits from localities. Playing the field, flirting with a number of cities, is a routine strategy in a number of businesses. In fact, the tension caused by mobile economic firms has been the defining characteristic of urban politics in the latter part of the twentieth century.

In industry after industry—automobiles, rubber, steel, clothes manufacturing, broadcasting, stocks and bonds, retail sales, education, computers, and the arts—the operators of private firms threaten to leave their cities. As John Logan and Harvey Molotch point out, "capital . . . comes much closer to the 'shopper model' of a consumer ever alert to the best deal."[3] As the price of staying, these enterprises demand new facilities, land, infrastructure, favorable labor policies, tax benefits, and special municipal services like police and sanitation from state and municipal governments. Many firms relocate their operations overseas. Between 1970 and 1983, for example, U.S. assets abroad tripled to a level of $226 billion.[4] One result is that the nation's economy experienced a dramatic shift from manufacturing to the service sector. Between 1945 and 1982, the percentage of total employment in the manufacturing sector declined from 38.4 to 21, while the service sector share rose from 10.4 to 21.2.[5] This mobility is not automatic or frictionless; often, negotiation with labor unions and restructuring of the corporate hierarchy and shop floor are also necessary.[6]

In recent decades, municipal governments faced a devastating Catch 22. On the one hand, city leaders did not want to watch idly as important companies and civic symbols moved to the suburbs or more distant venues. These companies not only spur the economy with production and distribution activities that spill over to the whole metropolis, but also help to create a distinctive urban identity. On the other hand, the cities that were most desperate to keep the firms were least capable of doing so.[7] Chronic fiscal crisis and other social problems undermined the cities' attempts to retain the mobile or "gypsy" firms. Firm relocation threatened to tear the guts out of America's cities—especially the old industrial cities that defined the American urban experience for more than a century.

The structures of American federalism necessitate contests among jurisdictions for economic development; states and localities must fend for themselves, since they have primary responsibility for providing direct public services and therefore need a steady stream of local revenue. Centralized systems, like those of France and Great Britain, do not encourage intercity competition, because responsibility for urban policy rests with the national government. Local officials "do not have to experience great popular pressure to take actions in the face of plant closures and high unemployment in their cities."[8] Pressure is applied at the center of the system instead. Even protest politics in those other nations is aimed at developing new national policies rather than spurring local reactions to deindustrialization.

The fundamental cause of mobility among firms, from factories to franchises, is a revolution in transportation and communications. This revolution has shortened the time required to move people and products from one place to another and has enabled the transmission of information across vast territories. Ann Markusen writes, "The new conglomerate form of the corporation and the increasing internationalization of the capital market permit both capital and goods greater ease in traversing national boundaries by lowering transaction costs and decreasing risks."[9] Producers can break up their management, production, distribution, and sales operations into numerous decentralized parts and still operate as a coherent unit. Companies can obtain information and capital almost instantly through a worldwide network of electronic communications. Factories can get inputs for their production processes with just days' notice, and then they deliver the manufactured products or parts just as quickly. Customers are linked in huge metropolitan areas.

Other factors have contributed to mobility as well. The development of new materials, such as plastics and synthetics, has allowed production plants to be smaller. Being lighter, these materials cost less to transport. Modern sources of power, such as electricity, expand access to energy and free plants from geographic restraints, such as the need to be near waterways and sites of raw energy materials. The reorganization of corporate structure has contributed to the dispersal of production; most large companies are now organized with a central headquarters and many geographically dispersed plants. Paul Kantor writes, "In effect, this multidivisional structure insulates the central staff from daily management while providing the organizational capability that enables the enterprise to engage in highly enlarged and diversified business interests."[10]

With these breakthroughs, location in specific kinds of territories is not the dominant factor it once was.[11] Distance is almost inconsequential in the transfer of financial assets such as money, stocks, and bonds. Managers do not need physical proximity to suppliers, sales corps, lawyers, or accountants—information is just a telephone call, a facsimile transmission, or at most a jet trip away. Companies also do not need to be so close to their markets, because the extensive transportation network can send the products out and bring the customers in. Corporations have gradually decentralized their major operations to the point where even the corporations that maintain downtown offices are "hollowed out"—not only production processes, but also middle-level management and support, have been moved out of the central location. The geographer David Harvey has written that technology has produced a "victory of time over space and place."[12]

Paradoxically, this dispersal of extraction, production, and distribution activities has been aided by a concentration of economic power. Large firms have the access to financial resources and political elites, not to mention the organizational sophistication, that enables them to conduct business on a global scale. Between 1955 and 1973, Fortune 500 companies increased their percentage shares of worldwide sales from 58 to 66, industrial assets from 64 to 83, employees from 49 to 66, and net income from 77 to 79. The fifteen hundred companies listed on the New York Stock Exchange—one-tenth of one percent of all corporations in the United States—accounted for 94 percent of total corporate earnings in 1970.[13] The concentration is even greater today, after the wave of mergers and the corporate restructuring in the 1970s and 1980s.

Economic delocalization and restructuring present a dilemma to cities. While different sectors of capital have varying degrees of mobility, the cities and many of their businesses and citizens are almost completely immobile. The city is like a boxer with his shoes nailed to the ground. While the opposing boxer dances around, establishing advantage by relative position, the immobile boxer must fight a defensive and reactive bout. Defense becomes both means and end. Also like a desperate boxer, wildly swinging for any kind of direct hit, the modern city often attempts to change unfavorable odds with dramatic efforts. The defense is at best a temporary survival tactic, and the wild swings often waste the fighter's meager strength. The chances of success in such circumstances are slim.

Symbolism and Monopoly

Cities are saturated with symbols. A symbol is a simplification of a complex reality. All symbols heighten the attention paid to one aspect of a complex reality while understating or ignoring the larger context. Symbols are necessary, because they help people find their way through a confusing world. Georg Simmel notes that, without mental screening and simplification, city dwellers would suffer an "unimaginable psychic state."[14] The symbols that make city life understandable concern race, ethnicity, neighborhoods, cultural institutions, political figures, organizations and groups, celebrities. One notable symbol of a city is its sports team, which often is thought to personify the civic spirit.

Just a small portion of a given city identifies regularly with a local team, but this portion may be decisive when sports issues reach the public arena. Sports boosters can be passionate enough about sports franchises, for material and ideological reasons, to steer the discussion of sports proposals in the community. These urbanites are active at every stage of debate over sports politics, while the indifferent masses are, logically enough, usually inert.

Even though most of the community is usually indifferent to sports, almost everyone gets carried away with the mystification of sports from time to time. Richard Lipsky writes that sports involvement can be

> a counterpoint to the decline of political effect and the widespread nostalgia for community in America. . . . The language of sports is the symbolic glue that holds the entire social lifeworld. It is the common idiom that links (heretofore male) Americans in the taverns, the living rooms, car pools and offices. . . . The team acts in many ways as the symbolic community that unites belief systems and authority structures with people's everyday lives.[15]

Even the most cynical urbanites are capable of occasionally accepting the wild claims of sports as a form of community. This "willing suspension of disbelief" often gives the sports franchise the leverage it needs over cities at crucial stages of their negotiations.[16]

Sports is symbolically potent because of the community identification with the team, and the resulting "we" orientation. Gerald Suttles argues that communities develop identity and an understanding of boundaries through their "foreign relations," or interactions with outsiders.[17] Sports provides one convenient way for their foreign relations to be conducted and understood. A city's confrontation of another city through sports can develop powerful identities. Famous sports rivalries—such as the Yankees and the Red Sox, the Dodgers and Giants (on both coasts), Raiders and Forty-Niners, Redskins and Cowboys, to name just a few—help members of those communities sharpen their images of themselves as well as others.

Sports politics can be riveting also, because of the vivid conflicts and personalities of key management figures, given saturation coverage by newspapers, magazines, radio and television, film and video, and even music. Throughout the political battles over stadiums and other franchise benefits, personalities like Al Davis, Robert Irsay, and Jerry Reinsdorf and Eddie Einhorn were the focus of attention. This focus on personalities and dramatic events—like the "midnight raid" that spirited the Colts from Baltimore to Indianapolis—obscures any attempts at a more thorough, deliberate, and sober discussion of the role of professional sports in the city.

The cultural uniqueness of sports gives teams leverage over cities. If the benefits of sports could be replaced by other forms of entertainment, public officials would have more negotiating leverage. For politicians, sports provides a convenient way to promote the image of the city as a community with unitary interests. For fans, sports provides both excitement and a pleasing daily routine. "Unlike the isolated entertainment of 'escapist' movies and much more like the effect of a religious celebration, sport fosters a sense of identification with the others who shared the experience," Janet Lever writes in a study of Brazilian soccer. "Where else do we meet with 50,000 others?"[18]

Professional sports benefits from its status as a positional good; it is, in other words, a commodity that derives its value from its exclusivity. Whereas a material good can be enjoyed for its intrinsic qualities—a salad for its nutritional value, for example—a positional good is valued because it is not enjoyed by many others. Roger Benjamin comments, "Enjoyment of one's villa on the French Riviera depends on limiting the rights of others to own similar villas in close proximity."[19] If every major city had a major league baseball team, the prestige of being a "big league city" would decline. The value of a team depends on only a few cities actually getting a team. Proposals to satisfy demand for major league sports by significantly expanding the number of teams would elicit protest from current host cities as well as the leagues.

The symbolic potency of sports can be decisive in political conflict. If a sporting event or institution is considered an essential part of the community, a contrary politician or activist group can be seen as anti-community. As Michael Peter Smith notes, the development of a contrived community "serves to delegitimize social conflict situations a priori, without carefully examining particular historical conflicts or their justifications."[20] Civic boosterism surrounding a sports team may undermine movements to deal with important social problems such as race relations, poverty, and capital flight. It is difficult for city officials and citizens to confront the two strengths of professional sports—cultural distinctiveness and monopoly power.

Industries that actually help to define the identities of their cities—like automobiles in Detroit, steel in Pittsburgh, and the stock exchange in New York—use appeals similar to those of sports franchises. Most businesses that seek benefits from cities, however, do not have the symbolic appeal of sports teams or companies in single-industry towns. Only occasionally do businesses manage to develop a case for public subsidization of their activities as symbolic parts of the city. At the same time that the Orioles were demanding a new facility as the price of staying in Baltimore, the Esskay Meats Company was also pressing state and municipal officials for a variety of subsidies. Even though Esskay had a long history in the city, the possibility of its departure did not create an obsession among editorial writers, shadow governments, or community groups to ensure that production conditions were beneficial for Esskay. The people who were activated by the Esskay issue were, for the most part, just the ones directly involved. Dramatizing the movement of even large firms can be difficult, especially since conventional economics teaches that such constant movement is a natural part of market systems.

One Carter administration official argued that cultural activities can improve the economic attractiveness of the community to a greater extent than raw economic data can capture. Arts, the official claimed, "provide a climate that attracts people, tourists, and businesses."[21] Researchers at the Johns Hopkins University suggest that "quality-of-life factors have become more important to firms and households, especially firms employing highly trained and mobile personnel."[22] In order to attract people with higher-order skills who have the potential for building local economies, it is argued, these elites must be amused with symphonies, museums, and ball clubs, as well as being served by reliable schools, police, and utilities.

Such arguments may be more leaps of faith than reasoned economic policy. Research suggests a kind of "groupthink" among state and local officials about the benefits from economic development packages.[23] The Johns Hopkins researchers reported being "struck by the unanimity of the views of these knowledgeable individuals."[24] Officials from state and local governments belong to many of the same "issue networks," the common professional affiliations and activities that cause people to speak about issues in similar ways.[25]

The Tactics of Domination

The mayor of a midwestern city once characterized the aggressive tactics by which businesses negotiate with municipalities as "the purple horse approach." The idea is for the business to make an unreasonable demand—"Bring me a purple horse in twenty-four hours, and I'll give you $100"—with the expectation that the demand cannot be met. The rejected demand gives the business a rationale for moving to a new city and establishes a standard by which future negotiations will be conducted.[26]

The purple horse approach is a central part of the negotiating repertoire of professional sports franchises, but the tactic would not be effective if it were not part of a larger, dynamic process. Because franchises shape so much of the negotiation process, they can select the moments when the purple horse tactic will be potent. Negotiations between a city and a team—or, for that matter, a city and any business—take place over a long period of time. Different issues move in and out of the deliberations depending on which groups are able to inject themselves into the process. The balance of power between the two principal bargainers shifts from issue to issue, but the team has an extraordinary advantage throughout because of its mobility.

The "exit" option—the ability to pick up operations and move to another locale—of teams and other mobile economic entities, and the immobility of the local polity, usually give business the advantage over public actors. The exit threat gives greater resonance to the "voice" of mobile firms, as Albert O. Hirschman notes: "The decision whether to exit will often be taken *in the light of the prospects for the effective use of voice.*"[27] This advantage, of course, does not always lead to business hegemony over city politics. There are many issues with which business has no concern, and other issues where skillful political action on the part of mayors and others can ameliorate the business advantage. To suggest otherwise would be deterministic and would leave little room for human agency in the political process.

Control over timing is perhaps the most important advantage that professional sports franchises enjoy. The teams can decide when and how to raise issues and demands in talks with municipal officials. Timing was an important part of the Oakland Raiders' move to Los Angeles in 1980 and the bidding war between Chicago and St. Petersburg for the White Sox in 1988. Both franchises gained the upper hand by carefully choosing when to act. The White Sox were especially adept at the timing game, setting arbitrary deadlines and responding only to the arguments and events that were bound to improve their bargaining position. Illinois officials had to either respond aggressively to White Sox' demands or risk losing the team to Florida—especially toward the end of a special state legislative session in 1988, when the White Sox signed a provisional agreement to move to St. Petersburg if Illinois did not meet the team's demands. The White Sox' boldest stroke was their unilateral announcement that delays in construction of a new facility had nullified the 1986 agreement between the Sox and Illinois and that more appropriations would be necessary to revise the deal. Constant reminders of the team's cultural uniqueness in Chicago reinforced the team's leverage during these negotiations.

In a different wrinkle on the matter of timing, the Baltimore Orioles waited until the departure of the Colts to begin pressing for a new stadium. The city was vulnerable because of its sense of betrayal and was desperate to maintain at least some of its major league status. It is also typical for a team to make demands on its host city when other teams have recently concluded lucrative agreements with their municipalities. When conditions for bargaining are not as good—for example, when the city's fiscal condition prohibits major construction projects—the team can lay back.

Oddly, sports, a minor industry, may have tactical advantages similar to those of major industries. Public support for sports development is limited, but that support is so intense in some quarters that the opponents, who are usually in the majority, do not find it worthwhile to contest: other issues are more important for them. *For many people,* a sports franchise is a symbolic embodiment of the city as a whole. Even if a majority of urban residents care not a whit about the local sports team, a significant cluster of mostly elite groups do care. The local media tend to be especially "boosterish" toward the local team because of the glow of major league status they receive through their association with the team. Other elites, like bankers and real estate developers, promote sports development for the same reasons they would support any major construction job. Political elites find the city-as-team analogy useful in giving definition and legitimacy to their necessarily biased administration of the city. Thousands of fans get caught up in the team both as a matter of habit and as a form of vicarious excitement, like that experienced by followers of Hollywood celebrities.

For city residents who are not caught up in the whirl of activities surrounding the sports franchise, political action against the franchise often seems a waste of time and motion. City officials and residents would rather save their energies for other political battles. "Trying to cut a deal is all you can do," one Baltimore organizer said. "You just get burned out after a while." [28] In Baltimore, the Waverly Improvement Association agreed to drop opposition to a new stadium in return for better city maintenance of their area. In Chicago, stadium foes agreed in their relocation settlement to drop their fight. Paul Kantor notes that many municipalities attempt to offer patronage benefits to neighborhoods to limit discussion of the larger aspects of the issue: "Neighborhood demands regarding development may be concerted to distributive issues that channel public involvement into nondevelopmental matters [thereby] discouraging formation of citywide coalitions." [29]

A city's ability to respond rationally to the demands of industries, from sports to tire manufacturing, usually depends on its perception of the industry's importance to the overall urban economy. Industries of overwhelming importance to the city are able to extract lucrative concessions from the municipal government. Especially with respect to the export sector, city officials accept the idea that as the industry goes, so goes the city. In the case of economic activities in which both production and consumption occur within city limits, urbanites are "simply taking in each other's laundry," but export industries enable the city to expand its economic reach. "Whatever helps them prosper redounds to the benefit of the community as a whole—perhaps four and five times over." [30] When that export industry involves a large share of the overall population, either directly or indirectly, the city's stake in the industry's continued operations increases.

The classic example of municipalities being dependent on large export sectors is the automobile industry in the Detroit area. In a study of the industry in the cities of Detroit, Flint, and Pontiac, Bryan D. Jones and Lynn W. Bachelor conclude: "The threat of moving out of state is almost always enough to gain the acquiescence of the community that would be losing the facility, even if the company might have to tolerate some posturing on the part of the city council." [31] The auto industry had spurred local governments to increase services—and trapped them into a position of dependence on the industry's revenues. [32] In the 1980s, major automobile-manufacturing capital investments overseas and in other U.S. cities increased the Detroit area's stake in the industry. [33] When General Motors encountered community opposition to its selection of Central Industrial Park for a new plant, the corporation was able to sweep away the objections by pointing to its other options. "The reasoning of the corporate planners was clear enough: as long as adequate sites outside the city could still be found, there was no reason to compromise plant design."[34]

Other cities in which a few industries are vitally important to the local government include Los Angeles (electronics, aerospace, entertainment), Pittsburgh and Birmingham (steel), New Orleans (oil and tourism), and Orlando (tourism). Those cities have been more vulnerable to corporate wanderlust, with the possible exception of Orlando, which is now practically a company town for Disney World and related tourist attractions.

By contrast, in cities with relatively diverse and stable economic bases, municipal officials find it easier to resist the blackmail of itinerant firms. Minneapolis and Milwaukee, for example, have escaped the decay of other heartland cities because they are home to a mix of corporate headquarters, manufacturing, and educational complexes.[35] New York's diverse export base, Robert Pecorella notes, "has largely insulated its government from the often-decisive political pressures that industrial concerns wield in more dependent cities."[36] Manhattan's business district, however, is dependent on financial interests such as banks, stock traders, insurance companies, accountants, lawyers, and so on. A city's vulnerability, therefore, varies from sector to sector and time to time.

Cities in decline are usually more urgently in search of development—and, of course, they are the cities with fewer resources and less maneuverability when negotiating with gypsy firms. Economic crises in Atlanta and Houston, for example, spurred civic leaders to develop expensive campaigns to lure capital from elsewhere in the United States and the world. Houston created an economic development corporation, a quasipublic body with great leeway in developing and implementing development strategies. A quantitative study of urban development programs by Irene S. Rubin and Herbert J. Rubin found that the more vulnerable cities—those with high rates of poverty and unemployment—spend the most on development incentives, such as programs for tax abatements, loans, and the establishment of tax-increment financing. More prosperous communities, the Rubins found, are not interested in such strategies. Regardless of the nature of a city's ills, and the evidence about the effects of these aggressive efforts, politicians are desperate to act.

The politics of urban business, whatever the size of the industry, has been increasingly marked by a tendency toward me-tooism. The executives of one firm demand that the government match the benefits given other firms. Of course, parity of benefits can be only rough, and city officials discriminate between the demands of different companies, but fairness always looms as an issue in the allocation of municipal benefits to the private sector. The premier example of me-tooism is the demand for stadiums with luxury seating that followed the construction of corporate suites at Texas Stadium. Nowadays if a stadium does not have luxury seating, it is considered fundamentally inadequate. Another example is the proliferation of more generous terms for team shares of parking and concessions revenues. Yet another example is the ratcheting up of lease terms by teams within a city, such as the Colts and Orioles in Baltimore in the late 1970s.

League officials do their best to make sure that the more favorable lease terms serve as the minimum standard for future negotiations of other teams. League pronouncements about minimum standards increase the minimum requirements for city participation in sports. Football Commissioner Pete Rozelle, for example, encouraged teams to seek the amenities that could only be obtained with suburban stadiums, such as wide-open spaces for parking. Recent baseball commissioners have demanded that cities not allow other sports teams to share stadiums used by major league teams. League management of minimum standards for stadiums, broadcasting, and labor relations has extended to the minor leagues and, indirectly, to collegiate sports.

City Limits

"In America," the French aristocrat Alexis de Tocqueville wrote after his 1831 visit, "the legislature of each state is supreme; nothing can impede its authority,—neither privileges, nor local immunities, nor personal influence, nor even the empire of reason. . . . Its own determination is, therefore, the only limit to its action."[37]

Much has changed in local governance since Tocqueville's day. Cities and towns exercise little of the authority over their jurisdictions that they did in the nineteenth century. The growth of federal fiscal and regulatory power, the rise of the national and the international economy, and a withdrawal of citizens from local politics have severely undermined the authority of state and local governments. Dependence, more than anything else, characterizes municipal politics in the United States as the country begins its third century.

Local governments have limited strategies for stimulating economic growth. National governments can boost both supply and demand with monetary policy, stimulate consumer demand through fiscal policies, and encourage investment by improving infrastructure.[38] Monetary policy at the local level is but a pipedream of a few odd visionaries.[39] State and local prohibitions against deficit spending prevent pursuit of Keynesian policies, although budgetary trickery has in the past offered some stimulative potential.[40] For all practical purposes, however, local governments are limited to the third option: pursuit of growth by investment in transportation, health services, public facility construction, education, and the like.

A number of indicators show the lack of policy autonomy of cities. In 1986, municipalities depended on the federal and state governments for close to 40 percent of their operating revenues.[41] Although, as a percentage of gross national product and as a percentage of local government spending, federal aid to cities has dropped significantly over the past twenty-five years,[42] in 1987, the federal government operated 435 different grant programs—up from 132 in 1960.[43] In return for these funds from higher levels of government, cities must adhere to mandates in policy areas such as welfare, housing, the environment, and employment practices. A recent study of federalism found that the most burdensome mandates are "cross-cutting regulations," rules which cities must enforce on a wide range of programs even though the programs were not designed for municipalities.[44] Former New York mayor Edward I. Koch estimates that in 1980, federal regulations cost that city $711 million in capital expenses, $6.25 billion in the city's operating budget, and $1.66 in lost revenues.[45] Federal grant regulations in the 1980s were so burdensome that many cities eschewed grant money to avoid the added costs of administration.

The logic of municipal government, as Yates and Crenson suggest, entails both survival within a system of "street-fighting pluralism" and the development of links with important elites in the city. The interaction of neighborhood and other advocacy groups, bureaucrats, federal and state governments, businesses and the media produces this street-fighting pluralism.[46] Pressures on the local government from local interest groups and media contribute to the improvisational nature of local governance. In such a context of uncertainty, it is impossible to develop any comprehensive strategy for dealing with the city's entrenched problems.

Political actors at all levels must "satisfice," to use the expression of Herbert Simon.[47] That is, they must settle for a combination of satisfaction and sacrifice in their pursuit of political goals. Rather than actually governing a city, mayors and department commissioners settle for achieving modest influence over a few selected areas of policy. They stake their reputations on the mediation of a neighborhood dispute, the rescue of a civic institution like a newspaper, the development of a new management system, the decentralization of the school system, or the development of a new style of police patroling. Contrary to the argument of Douglas Yates, such "position-taking"[48] is not just symbolic; it has substance. But it cannot be called governing in any meaningful sense of that word.

In a volatile environment, city officials attempt to carve out a few policy areas in which they can make an impact on the local political economy—and line up the political support they need to advance their careers. Mayors, by developing a core of supporters that they can reward with government contracts and influential positions, can develop a political base to see them through election campaigns, controversies over bureaucratic and development policy, and interest-group and street-level conflicts. Mayors can separate themselves from the rough-and-tumble world of the city by developing a public relations approach that stands above the conflict and alliances to circumvent the vested interests. Promoting major development projects and taking a position on controversial issues, like race relations or municipal unions, do not always provide broad-based support, but they do enable a mayor to develop regular support from the public-private governing structure. This strategy is similar to the machine-building techniques of municipal parties during the heyday of boss rule.

Major development projects constitute the most ambitious of the local officials' repertoire. Often cities will simultaneously promote several of these attractions, to project an image of a city on the rebound. Along with sports stadiums and arenas, such projects include convention centers, concert halls, museums, office buildings, condominium complexes, aquariums, shopping and tourist malls, and halls of fame. This urban image is designed to appeal to current residents and businesses, who might be tempted to leave the city, as well as to outsiders who might consider visiting or moving to the city. Tourism is in fact the biggest industry in San Francisco and one of the major industries in Phoenix, New Orleans, and Miami.[49] Many mayors, like Richard Lee of New Haven and William Donald Schaefer of Baltimore, have made national reputations with their vivid efforts to revive their downtowns and other strategic neighborhoods.

Other initiatives may be categorized along with development under the rubric of position-taking, or the "politics of announcement."[50] Hirings of more police, fire fighters, or sanitation workers are intended to dramatize the city's determination to recover public order. Well-publicized raids on red-light districts and drug-infested neighborhoods provide the same message, with a greater sense of urgency.

Cities are often driven to sports development out of a desire to achieve something tangible, even if it does not improve the city in any significant way. Insecurity about their ability to maintain their industry, image, and tax base spurs civic leaders to promote any policy that holds out some hope of revitalization. "Politicians supported tax abatements [in the 1980s] not because it was effective but because it was a remarkably easy path to follow," writes Todd Swanstrom. "Nothing is more tempting for a politician than to take a bow for causing some massive private project. With tax abatement, politicians can point to towering skyscrapers and say, 'Without my help, these never would have come about.' "[51] The edifice complex is one way to turn a politician's overall inefficacy into political gain.

Government officials may be eager to serve business constituents, but government does not simply mirror the desires of businesses or other constituents. As John Mollenkopf has noted, "government intervention follows its own logic rather than that of private interests."[52] Municipal officials try to use their close relationships with business to gain a modicum of resources, independence, and security for themselves. City leaders must operate within both political and economic "systems of constraint," to use Kantor's term.[53] Within those constraints they have some freedom of movement. Imaginative and skilled politicians with public support are able to strike better deals than more ordinary politicians.[54]

Groups that oppose the governing structure in its approach to the demands of sports franchises—for example, neighborhood associations in areas affected by stadium construction—find it difficult to form coalitions. The uncertainty of the benefits to be gained from collective action, the temporal distance of those rewards, the pressures and constraints of everyday life, the lack of organizational resources, and the formidability of the governing structure combine to make it difficult for a neighborhood to organize. As Matthew A. Crenson notes, "benefits that are diffuse or that can be captured by no one in particular do not promise to gratify anyone in particular."[55] In addition, as Crenson also notes, antagonistic relationships develop between street-level actors and the government, hampering collective efforts.

City officials can undermine coalition politics in general by taking opportunities to offer rewards to the groups that go along with projects that are depicted as foregone conclusions. By offering benefits to parts of the city, political officials transform issues from matters of broad community relevance to the fragmented politics of distribution. Baltimore officials impeded a potential alliance between Camden Yards and Waverly, both of which favored keeping the Orioles in their former neighborhood. Waverly activists acknowledge that they agreed to "keep quiet" about the stadium in return for increased funds for neighborhood rehabilitation and enforcement of housing codes to drive out slumlords. Likewise, Chicago officials drove a wedge into the anti-stadium coalition by apportioning contracts and job promises, as well as relocation allowances, to the compliant groups in the South Side. The governing structure can also defuse dissidence by co-opting the opposition with positions on government advisory boards and the like.[56]

A city's economic and social stability can have a major impact on its relations with businesses and the public. Robert C. Pecorella has found that times of fiscal stability enable government officials to be more open to the interests of non-elites but that during periods of fiscal stress, "a clear division develops between financial interests that are concerned with economic and political stability, on the one hand, and, on the other hand, attentive non-elites who are seeking to protect past political gains that would be threatened by retrenchment."[57] In order to promote political values of openness and representation, it is necessary to create a stable economy. The community is perhaps more capable of exercising judgment in the public interest, and less susceptible to the blandishments and threats of corporate interests, when it has a stable economy. Extremes of boom and bust unsettle the political equation.

Toward Collective Public Action

The major weakness of cities in negotiations with professional sports franchises stems from the mutually destructive competition for a commodity in limited supply. Teams manipulate cities by setting them against each other in a scramble for the limited number of major league teams. While the cities fight each other, the teams sit back and wait for the best conditions and terms.

If they expect to develop any economic stability, cities must figure out ways to confront challenges by sports teams, and by other itinerant firms. Municipal strategies toward sports teams may be applicable to other industries. The most important lesson is that a reactive approach to an industry's demands puts local government at a disadvantage. Rather than building up infrastructure, education, and public services, and dealing with the destructive conflicts between interest groups, the city becomes obsessed with the bidding process with the firm or industry. Certainly, local governments must deal with mobile firms, but obsession with the immediate demands rather than long-term conditions can be paralyzing.

Cooperation among states and among cities could prevent gypsy franchises from extorting greater and greater public benefits. If bidding wars did not drive up the costs of hosting major league teams, cities might not have to build new stadiums to replace adequate old stadiums, or offer real estate and tax deals to teams in return for signing a stadium lease. But such inter-jurisdictional cooperation is unlikely to occur. If jurisdictions agreed to a moritorium on bidding for teams, one or more cities would no doubt find advantage in breaking ranks and becoming sole bidders for teams. Even if cooperation were somehow enshrined into law, it is likely that some renegade jurisdictions would find loopholes in the law and a way to make attractive offers to itinerant teams.

Agreements among states and cities—what might be termed a treaty approach—is one collective approach to the problem of gypsy franchises. The National Governors Association in 1984 passed a resolution calling for safeguards against franchise movement when host cities have a record of supporting the franchise. In that spirit, Maryland Governor William Donald Schaefer pledged not to use the same predatory tactics that Indiana officials used to woo the Colts from Baltimore. But when the Cardinals football franchise announced that it might leave St. Louis if other states or cities could provide a better package of stadium and other benefits, Schaefer aggressively entered the fray for the franchise. The courtship of the Cardinals underscores the fundamental flaw of voluntary cooperation: enough states and cities want teams badly enough to break ranks from collective action and put their own interests ahead of the group. Some kind of legal power is necessary to enforce the cooperation.

National legislation could impose control over leagues and their host cities. For years, sports commentator Howard Cosell advocated creation of a federal agency to establish basic standards for professional, collegiate, and scholastic sports. More recently, bills before Congress would have established universal standards for franchise transfers, forced the leagues to compensate cities that have lost teams to the major leagues, and compelled the leagues to expand. None of these bills has come even close to passing, but a crisis such as a major strike or a sizable controversy over broadcasting or franchise transfers could improve the chances of such legislation. Moves to force league expansion amount to little more than pork barrel politics. The proposed standards for franchise transfers are the most interesting remedies from a policy standpoint. Universal team-transfer standards are based on the same principles as the plant-closing legislation that Congress passed in 1988. Plant-closing legislation is designed to give workers of failing companies a "window of opportunity" to seek new jobs or even develop a plan for taking over the failed company. Twenty-five states have passed laws that allow workers to buy the factories of failing companies via employee stock ownership plans.[58]

Congressmembers from areas spurned by the leagues have usually spearheaded these legislative efforts. Senators Barbara Mikulski and Paul Sarbanes of Maryland, John Danforth of Missouri, Albert Gore of Tennessee, and Brock Adams of Washington have been the major advocates of sports legislation. The thinly veiled threat behind this legislation is to eliminate the antitrust privileges that the leagues enjoy, unless the leagues can show responsibility by meeting the demands of potential major league host cities. The threat of legislation might have been the major factor behind Major League Baseball's decision to add two new teams by the 1993 season.

Another cooperative strategy is to form a rival league. As a response to the transfer of the Brooklyn Dodgers and New York Giants to California, New York civic leaders created an alliance with other cities to create the Continental League in 1960. If the major leagues had not responded to the threat by expanding by four teams, it is conceivable that the Continental League could have become a serious rival to the major leagues. Other upstart leagues have come and gone, most notably the American Football League, which forced the dominant National Football League to merge with it in 1969. Other upstart leagues have included the All-American Conference, World Football League, and United States Football League. These leagues were all the efforts of private entrepreneurs, but it is possible to imagine states and localities starting leagues of their own based on the model of European and Latin American leagues.

State and public officials avoid confrontation with the sports industry. In 1984, after the departure of the Colts franchise, a friend of then Mayor William Donald Schaefer proposed suing the National Football League, but Schaefer avoided the high-risk strategy with the hopes of building a constructive relationship for the future. Such an action would have branded Baltimore and Schaefer as troublemakers, and an informal blackballing of the city would surely have resulted. The league's collective action would have been able to enforce its informal sanctions against the city. Because of the high demand among cities for NFL teams, Baltimore would have experienced great difficulty recruiting other cities to join in its legal challenge.

Within cities, coalition building to confront the sports cartels may be effective in fighting specific projects. The legal strategies of activist lawyers like Thomas Geoghegan and James Chapman of Chicago aim to confront leagues and teams by addressing the issues comprehensively. Geoghegan attempted to connect the South Armour Square neighborhood's struggle against a new baseball stadium with instances of past government discrimination against the neighborhood. Chapman tried to forge legal linkages with the Bridgeport neighborhood—and in the process challenge the dominant understandings of Bridgeport's self-interest. In the end, Chapman could not convince Bridgeport's white ethnics that their neighborhood shared a common threat with the poor blacks of South

Armour Square. But at least Chapman made an attempt to speak to the suspicious neighborhood on its own terms. The politics of confrontation, necessary as it is, has limits and can only be a starting point for a democratic politics.

None of these collective approaches is likely to go very far. The only weapon that cities can use, on their own, to confront the sports industry is eminent domain. Taking property from private owners for the public good is perhaps the most controversial public-policy option that local governments have at their disposal. If the eminent domain suits filed by Oakland and Baltimore had succeeded, a wide range of other industries might have been exposed to similar community control. That is what the California judiciary feared when it rejected the legal gambit in the Raiders case.

Absent a "magic bullet" like eminent domain, cities and their citizens will need to develop a strategy of collective action to confront runaway firms. The prospects for such coordinated action appear slim, but some of the protagonists in sports politics have sketched out some approaches to developing this coordinated action. Perhaps more important, cities need to develop strategies for developing the kind of local economic system that minimizes their vulnerability in an age of mobility and rapid change.

The Urban Dilemma and the Future

American cities will never again have the kind of independence and autonomy that they enjoyed in the early days of the republic. Cities and towns will henceforth be caught up in powerful economic, political, and social systems, both nationally and internationally. This interdependence need not always be a curse to cities. Although it makes cities dependent on outsiders, it also offers access to more resources and knowledge than would have been considered possible just a generation ago.

The proper concern of the American city is not independence but the ability to steer its own course in the international systems. Cities need to develop policies that enhance stability in fundamental services and activities such as energy, transportation, housing, health care, and education. Such services and activities are the foundation of political, social, and economic life. At the same time, cities must promote innovation and flexibility in other policy areas that are on the cutting edge of the national and international systems. As Paul E. Peterson maintains, the city must enhance its position in the larger system. But the city's position will be enhanced not by scrambling to meet the demands of itinerant firms but by developing a foundation for all firms and encouraging a few industries for which the city's labor force, resources, and technology are well suited.

Mayor Harold Washington's reform administration in Chicago outlined an approach to economic development based on strategic planning.[59] Washington's plan emphasized the advantages that the city already had, consensus building, coordination of different projects, and the need to make hard decisions about which sectoral and neighborhood projects should take precedence.

The Washington team identified fourteen broad approaches to long-term development. Foremost, the planners determined that the city had to target its limited funds strategically to businesses that had a potential for longterm growth and that fit the city's resources, labor market, and education system. This local version of national industrial policy does not attempt to project an overly grand vision of the city. "Unlike comprehensive plans, which attempt to provide something for everyone, the development plan specified high-priority beneficiaries and focused on a few programs designed to benefit them."[60] In the creation of such policy, planners attempt to identify future growth industries, such as environmental technology, that they might help incubate and integrate with the city's economic and social web.

Along with this emphasis on sectoral development, the city needs to improve its overall base for economic growth. Indigenous firms and groups need the resources and opportunity to grow. Local preference in buying and hiring, a strengthened tax base, labor skill development, improvement of the infrastructure, public-private cooperation, and balanced growth between the downtown and other neighborhoods are policies intended to make the city a more reliable and attractive place for businesses. Still other policies address equity issues. Affirmative action, tax fairness, neighborhood-level planning, expanded housing, linkage between private development and public goals, and citizen access and involvement all aim to ensure that no groups gain at the expense of others.

Such principles are difficult to implement—as witnessed by the Washington administration's own desperation in dealings with the Chicago White Sox. One of the architects of the community development principles applied in Chicago was also the city's point man in the White Sox negotiations. Robert Mier, commissioner of economic development, was more successful in applying the principles to the Navy Pier development than to the White Sox franchise fracas.

The scramble of cities for professional sports franchises is symptomatic of the reactive nature of city politics today. Attracting teams is so time-consuming and expensive—costing hundreds of millions of dollars, directly and indirectly—that even the "winning" cities stand to lose. Zealous pursuit of gypsy franchises distracts city leaders from the more important job of building a viable political and economic base. Substituting a vicarious community for a more sturdy community promotes the illusion of progress while the city as a whole declines.

Nations such as Great Britain, France, and Sweden have developed coordinated strategies for dealing wth the inequalities and ingrained problems of localities. The fates of cities are understood to be related to each other and to the fate of the nation. In the United States, a tradition of decentralization has worked against formation of a national urban strategy, and the huge federal budget deficits of the Reagan and Bush administrations will handicap implementation if one is created. Even after riots in south-central Los Angeles alerted the nation to the urban crisis, the 1992 presidential campaign did not present any major initiatives for addressing the decline of cities.

At the end of the Carter administration, a presidential commission declared that the national government should not intervene in the "immutable" decline of cities. The rise and decline of cities, said the McGill Commission, is part of a natural economic cycle. The report urged the government to focus its attention on people, not places. But that is a false distinction. Education, housing, transportation, health care, and economic development, which might be considered people-oriented issues, all depend on the places in which they occur.[61]

A national urban policy would assure that the foundations for delivering these services are in place in communities across the nation. Each community should be assured of the resources it needs to provide for basic human necessities. A degree of intercity competition can be healthy; it can help cities determine the functions for which they are best suited in the larger scheme of things. But the intercity competition typified by the cannibalistic struggles for sports franchises undermines the prospects for local and nationwide prosperity and security.

Epilogue

A "willing suspension of disbelief," Samuel Taylor Coleridge writes, is necessary for an audience's imagination to take flight. To profit from fantastical literary concoctions, the audience must set aside standards of literal truth. Accept delusion, and the rest will follow.

In politics, suspension of disbelief paves the way to outlandish schemes, from supply-side economics to Star Wars. Professional sports is the municipal version. Overwhelming evidence shows that sports franchises and facilities do little to revive a local economy, but states and cities continue to spend hundreds of millions of dollars to get teams. Boosters promise the revival of neighborhoods, higher tax revenues, the attraction of new firms to the city, and even the amelioration of racial and ethnic strife. Ignoring the evidence, cities accept the grandiose claims. This withdrawal from reality is understandable given the intractability of urban problems. City officials face problems such as poverty, health crises ranging from AIDS to tuberculosis, violence, housing dilapidation, racial strife, crumbling infrastructures, and bad schools. Capital and middle-class flight leave them few resources. Entrenched bureaucracies and interest groups, and sensational media, feed the sense of hopelessness.

Sports offers city officials a symbolic way out. The history of American cities is the history of dramatic gestures. Bridges, highways, urban renewal, tourist malls, convention centers, and flashy subway systems are ribbon-cutting heaven. They show a city *on the move*, brazen against the odds, unwilling to settle for mediocrity. The projects might not help the city in the long run—they might even hurt it—but they do show a can-do spirit. Large-scale projects also offer booty for organized interests.

Real-estate speculators, banks, bond underwriters, builders, construction unions, and media outlets all stand to benefit from such projects.

As professional baseball celebrated its 125th anniversary in 1994, virtually every franchise was either settling into a new facility or demanding one. Stadium demands were not as pervasive in professional football, but many teams attempted to get their state and local governments to build new facilities. At the same time, dozens of cities, shut out of the exclusive club of major league sports, were petitioning for admission. The possibility of moving to a new city—both blunt and subtle threats made by league officials and team owners alike—puts host cities on the defensive. Negotiations are drawn out over years, with the costs of getting or keeping a team skyrocketing as other teams and cities establish new standards. The supply-and-demand imbalance—too many cities chasing too few teams—virtually guarantees that teams will cost too much for cities to realize any real benefits.

Yogi Berra's famous adage that "it ain't over till it's over" is ready for an update. In stadium politics, it ain't over even when it's over. Cities that thought they had commitments for new sports teams, either from the expansion of leagues or the transfer of existing teams, found themselves bitterly disappointed. St. Louis and St. Petersburg thought they had football and baseball teams for their new domed stadiums in 1993. But the NFL bypassed St. Louis in favor of Charlotte and Jacksonville in 1993, and baseball had prevented the move of the San Francisco Giants to St. Petersburg just a year earlier. Maryland Governor William Donald Schaefer spoke bitterly of the NFL's decision to bypass Baltimore in the expansion sweepstakes; he thought he had an informal commitment from the NFL to replace the dearly departed Colts.

Mother Nature is the most recent player in sports politics. After the 1994 earthquake in southern California, repair costs at the Los Angeles Memorial Coliseum and Anaheim Stadium were estimated in the tens of millions of dollars. Officials of football's Los Angeles Raiders and baseball's California Angels raised the specter of moving if state and local governments balked at paying for uninsured repairs.

Stadium-building moves in cycles. In each wave, a new model of a facility is developed to give teams a "positional" advantage over their rivals. The large stadiums from the 1950s to 1970s, for example, offered large seating capacities, highway accessibility, and better sightlines. The 1980s model appealed to the fan's nostalgia with a bandbox model brought up to date with electronic scoreboards and luxury seating. Nostalgic stadium designs might have been inspired by Philip Bess, the Chicago architect who designed an old-fashioned ballpark for the White Sox. City and club officials rejected Bess's proposal, but it received favorable notice in architecture journals and newspapers. New stadiums in Baltimore, Cleveland, and Arlington, Texas, were paeans to old stadiums like Ebbetts Field.

The latest wave begins with the premise that profit-maximization requires use of the facility beyond the ten home dates of a football team or the eighty-one dates of a baseball team. Wayne Huizinga is the leader of this new wave. In 1994 Huizinga announced plans to create an entertainment empire that extended beyond sports to movies, hotels, and theme parks. The plan would consolidate Huizinga's position in an increasingly global entertainment marketplace. Huizinga, the owner of the Blockbuster videotape rental company, got control of three major league franchises by 1994—baseball's Florida Marlins, football's Miami Dolphins, and hockey's Florida Panthers. To finance his Blockbuster Park, north of Miami, Huizinga planned an autonomous local government, complete with taxing and regulatory powers. Others also planned multipurpose complexes. The New York Mets planned to build a "permanent World's Fair" on the site of two previous fairs, with a baseball stadium, theaters, rides, and pavilions with interactive videos and other amusements. The San Francisco Giants, four times rejected for stadium projects in Bay-area referendums, planned to build an entertainment complex overlooking the city's waterfront and underneath its historic bridge.

The general public does not seem to accept the sports boosters' claims that franchises and facilities will rebuild cities. Despite the enthusiasm that surrounds the opening of a new stadium, most residents are more concerned with their everyday lives. Referendums to build new facilities often fail and always face skeptical voters. Opinion polls also show skepticism about the wisdom of sports as a public priority.

But team owners, politicians, and economic elites push the stadium projects anyway. The illusory sense of control and the very real profits and patronage are just too great to resist.

Notes

Chapter 1. Sports Politics: Teams, Local Identity, and Urban Development

1. Letter from Thomas H. Geoghegan to Timothy Wright, commissioner, Department of Economic Development, City of Chicago, May 18, 1988.

2. Thomas H. Geoghegan, interview with author, June 1992. Hereafter, unless otherwise indicated, all interviews are with the author.

3. Thomas H. Geoghegan, *Which Side Are You On?: Trying to Be for Labor When It's Flat on Its Back* (New York: Farrar, Straus and Giroux, 1991), p. 4.

4. Geohegan, interview, June 1992.

5. Robert F. Bluthardt, "The New Arenas of Debate," *Insight,* September 21, 1986. Bluthardt was chairman of the ballparks committee of Society for American Baseball Research.

6. One expert witness in the city of Oakland's eminent domain case against the Raiders franchise cited the work of Elisabeth Kubler-Ross on this subject.

7. Alan G. Ingham, Jeremy W. Howell, and Todd S. Schilperoort, "Professional Sports and Community: A Review and Exegesis," *Exercise and Sport Sciences Reviews* 15 (1987): 461.

8. See Arthur T. Johnson, *Minor League Baseball and Local Economic Development* (Champaign: University of Illinois Press, 1993); "Professional Baseball at the Minor League Level: Considerations for Cities Large and Small," *State and Local Government Review* 22 (Spring 1990), pp. 90-96; "Local Government, Minor League Baseball, and Economic Development Strategies," *Economic Development Quarterly* 5 (November 1991), pp. 313-24.

9. Matthew Goodman, "Sports Today," *Zeta,* January 1988, p. 62.

10. "Financing the Modern-Day Pyramids," *Sports inc.,* March 14, 1988.

11. Mary Norris, "Politics, Baseball, and Beer," *Wigwag,* September 1990.

12. Brooklyn has not been an independent city since the consolidation of New York's five boroughs in 1897; but, like the other boroughs of the city, it has maintained its separate identity.

13. Quoted in Richard Lipsky, *How We Play the Game: Why Sports Dominate American Life* (Boston: Beacon, 1981), p. 10.

14. Janet Lever, *Soccer Madness* (Chicago: University of Chicago Press, 1983), p. 17.

15. Alfred Schutz and Thomas Luckmann, *The Structures of the Life-World,* trans. Richard M. Zaner and H. Tristram Engelhardt, Jr. (Evanston, Ill.: Northwestern University Press, 1973), p. 63.

16. See Gerald Suttles, *The Social Construction of Communities* (Chicago: University of Chicago Press, 1972), esp. pp. 13, 149.

17. Murray Edelman, *The Symbolic Uses of Politics* (Urbana: University of Illinois Press, 1985), p. 78.

18. Mike Littwin, in his column in the *Baltimore Sun*, November 6, 1987, and January 13, 1988.

19. In his study of foreign-owned copper firms in Chile, Theodore H. Moran found that the balance of power shifted from the companies to the state as the state's bureaucratic and other elites gained more knowledge of technical processes. Greater knowledge enables the host government to make more demands on corporations already in the country and on firms seeking entry. The sports industry, by contrast, never creates the significant economic value that would attract political involvement by many groups in the city, and the franchise is highly mobile. See Moran, *Multinational Corporations and the Politics of Dependence: Copper in Chile* (Princeton: Princeton University Press, 1974).

20. Paul E. Peterson, *City Limits* (Chicago: University of Chicago Press, 1981).

21. See Charles M. Tiebout, "A Pure Theory of Local Expenditures," *Journal of Political Economy* 64 (1956), pp. 416-24; James O'Connor, *The Fiscal Crisis of the State* (New York: St. Martin's, 1973); and Jane Jacobs, *The Economy of Cities* (New York: Vintage Books, 1969); and *Cities and the Wealth of Nations: Principles of Economic Life* (New York: Vintage Books, 1984). Jacobs won fame for her attention to detail in *The Death and Life of Great American Cities* (New York: Vintage Books, 1961), but in her more recent works she has tended toward sweeping generalizations about how cities ought to pursue economic development.

22. John Mollenkopf, *The Contested City* (Princeton: Princeton University Press, 1983).

23. Outstanding examples of these studies include Clarence N. Stone and Heywood T. Sanders, eds., *The Politics of Urban Development* (Lawrence: University Press of Kansas, 1987); Mollenkopf, *Contested City*; and Chester Hartman, *The Transformation of San Francisco* (Totowa, N.J.: Rowman and Allanheld, 1984).

24. Bryan D. Jones and Lynn W. Bachelor, *The Sustaining Hand: Community Leadership and Corporate Power* (Lawrence: University Press of Kansas, 1986).

25. Douglas Yates, *The Ungovernable City: The Politics of Urban Problems and Policy Making* (Cambridge: MIT Press, 1984).

26. Matthew A. Crenson, "Urban Bureaucracy in Urban Politics: Notes toward a Developmental Theory of Urban Bureaucracy," in J. David Greenstone, ed., *Public Values and Private Power in American Politics* (Chicago: University of Chicago Press, 1982).

27. The term comes from Hugh Heclo, "Issue Networks and the Executive Establishment," in Anthony King, ed., *The New American Political System* (Washington, D.C.: American Enterprise Institute, 1978).

28. Neil J. Sullivan, *The Dodgers Move West* (New York: Oxford University Press, 1987), p. 194.

29. Ibid., p. 137.

30. See Lewis Mumford, *The Highway and the City* (New York: New American Library, 1963) for an examination of the importance of fitting different kinds of settlements with appropriate modes of transportation.

31. Sullivan, *The Dodgers Move West*, pp. 127-28.

32. Albert O. Hirschman, *Exit, Voice, and Loyalty: Responses to Decline in Firms, Organizations, and States* (Cambridge: Harvard University Press, 1970).

33. The Dodgers played at the Los Angeles Memorial Coliseum until the new stadium's construction.

Chapter 2. Sports as an Industry

1. See Table 1 in Chapter 1.

2. Quoted in "Union's Fehr Says Owners Stand Against Expansion," *Washington Post*, March 5, 1989. For a description of how political pressure forced baseball to expand, see "The Senator and the Commissioner," in David Whitford, *Playing Hardball: The High Stakes Battle for Baseball's New Franchises* (New York: Doubleday, 1993).

3. "The Business of Baseball," *Denver Post,* July 14, 1991.

4. The most succinct statement of the economics of sports and recreation is Bruce Kidd, *The Political Economy of Sport* (Vanier City, Ottawa: Canadian Association for Health, Physical Education, and Recreation, 1981). One sign of the maturity of the baseball monopoly is its control over the international labor market and its manipulation of distant markets. See also Alan M. Klein, "Baseball as Underdevelopment: The Political Economy of Sport in the Dominican Republic," *Sociology of Sport Journal* 6 (1989), pp. 95-111.

5. If all of amateur and professional sports and recreation were to be considered an industry, that industry would rank twenty-fifth in the U.S. gross national product. According to *Sports inc.*, a sports trade journal, the "gross national sports product" (G.N.S.P.) in 1987 was $47.3 billion. The sports industry is about one-tenth the size of the nation's largest industry, real estate ($483 billion). Other major industries include retail trade ($407.9 billion), health services ($198.6 billion), construction ($197 billion), and business services ($162.8 billion). Among the industries smaller than sports are social services ($40.5 billion), petroleum and coal products ($38.9 billion), and hotel and lodging ($31.9 billion). The journal estimates that the G.N.S.P. will rise to $85 billion in 1995 and $121 billion in the year 2000. See "Gross National Sports Product," *Sports inc.*, November 16, 1987, and February 2, 1989.

6. See George B. Kirsch, *The Creation of American Team Sports: Baseball and Cricket, 1838-72* (Urbana: University of Illinois Press, 1989).

7. For a good portrait of a fansumer, see "In the Stands or at Home, Many Watch Sports Events," Baltimore *Evening Sun*, April 12, 1989.

8. John A. Vernon, "Baseball, Bubble Gum, and Business," in Paul M. Sommers, ed., *Diamonds Are Forever: The Business of Baseball* (Washington, D.C.: Brookings Institution, 1992), pp. 91-106.

9. Andy Dolich, interview, February 1991.

10. See, for example, Roger Noll, "Attendance and Price Setting," in Noll, ed., *Government and the Sports Business* (Washington, D.C.: Brookings Institution, 1974), 115-57.

11. See Brent Staples, "Where Are the Black Fans?" *New York Times Sunday Magazine,* May 17, 1987, pp. 22-23. Staples argues that the baseball establishment sends clear signals about which fans it is trying to attract. Statistics indicate that blacks must perform better to remain active on major league rosters. For example, 13 percent of all black pitchers and 27 percent of all white pitchers have earned-run averages over 4.00, while 10 percent of other black players and 28 percent of other white players have lifetime batting averages of .241 or below.

12. Lawrence M. Kahn, "Discrimination in Baseball," in Sommers, *Diamonds Are Forever,* pp. 163-88.

13. "Baltimore Returns to Orioles," Baltimore *Sun,* November 22, 1991.

14. Quoted in "D.C. Isn't Without Baseball," *Washington Post,* April 1, 1988.

15. The Chicago Cubs manage to have it both ways. The Cubs' appeal stems from a tradition of day games and a beautiful old ballpark located in a tightly knit neighborhood. The image of the old-fashioned neighborhood is used to attract fans from not only the suburbs but the entire region and nation. The team's national cable broadcasting extends the "neighborhood" to the whole continent, and even to the Central American nation of Belize via satellite transmission on that nation's only television station.

16. Quoted in Howard Cosell with Peter Bonventre, *I Never Played the Game* (New York: William Morrow, 1985), p. 113.

17. The National Basketball Association, moribund in the early 1980s, has revived its fortunes by aggressive marketing based on the personalities of a few star players, like Earvin ("Magic") Johnson, Michael Jordan, and Larry Bird.

18. Ira Horowitz, "Sports Broadcasting," in Noll, *Government and the Sports Business,* pp. 310-19.

19. Dale Hofmann and Martin J. Greenberg, *Sportsbiz: Inside the Sports Business* (Champaign, Ill.: Leisure Press, 1989), p. 185.

20. David A. Klatell and Norman Marcus, *Sports For Sale: Television, Money, and the Fans* (New York: Oxford University Press, 1988), p. 68.

21. See Joan M. Chandler, "Sports as TV Product: A Case Study of 'Monday Night Football,' " in Paul D. Staudohar and James A. Mangan, eds., *The Business of Professional Sports* (Urbana: University of Illinois Press, 1991), pp. 48-60.

22. "Pay-per-View: NFL Has a Way Out, In," *Washington Post,* November 3, 1989. See also "Shifting Playoffs to Cable Discussed," *Washington Post,* December 12, 1988.

23. Quoted in "Watershed Season," *Sporting News,* January 20, 1992.

24. Football does not have a minor league system but relies on the collegiate athletic leagues to develop and supply talent. Intercollegiate sports, especially football and basketball, have become a major industry. Some universities depend on athletics to gain a high public profile and spur fund-raising campaigns. While minor league baseball foundered, college programs flourished, because of the captive audiences of students and alumni and because the shorter college playing season prevents an overload of the sport. Also, in recent years more baseball players have been developed in colleges than ever before. See James V. Koch, "The Intercollegiate Athletics Industry," in Walter Adams, ed., *The Structure of American Industry: Some Case Studies* (New York: Macmillan, 1986), pp. 325-46.

25. "Not So Minor Anymore," *Indianapolis Star,* June 30, 1991. After years of decline, the attendance at minor league games has increased robustly. In 1990, the minors drew 25,244,569 fans, breaking a record set in 1952.

26. James Quirk, "An Economic Analysis of Team Movements in Professional Sports," *Law and Contemporary Problems* 38 (Winter-Spring 1973), pp. 42-66.

27. Klein, "Baseball as Underdevelopment."

28. "For U.S. Sports, World is Rapidly Shrinking," *Washington Post*, May 17, 1989.

29. "The World Plays Catch-up," *Sports inc.*, January 2, 1989.

30. Michael K. Ozanian and Stephen Taub, "Big Leagues, Bad Business," *Financial World*, July 7, 1992, p. 38.

31. The share of skybox revenue that teams receive varies. The New York Mets split with the city the revenues from Shea Stadium's forty-six publicly financed skyboxes. The Miami Dolphins keep all of their skybox revenues but must use some of it to finance stadium bonds.

32. Hofmann and Greenberg, *Sportsbiz*, p. 172.

33. "Lean Times," *Sports inc.*, March 6, 1989.

34. These arguments are also made by Jesse W. Markham and Paul V. Teplitz, *Baseball Economics and Public Policy* (Lexington, Mass.: Lexington Books, 1981). Markham was an unofficial advisor to baseball during the commissionership of Bowie Kuhn.

35. John C. Weistart and Cym H. Lowell, *The Law of Sports* (Indianapolis: Bobbs-Merrill, 1979) remains the best overview of antitrust and other legal issues confronting leagues.

36. Raiders owner Al Davis argues that their voting rules make it difficult for the leagues to respond to the economic and legal systems. Three-quarters of the league members must agree to any substantive change. There is indeed the possibility for gridlock in the management of the league itself; redistributive issues are particularly difficult. But the great flexibility allowed the franchises makes the league responsive to its environment. Furthermore, it is important to look not only at official league policies but also at more informal league actions that benefit the franchises.

37. This was the controversial argument of Robert Bork during his 1987 hearings for confirmation for the U.S. Supreme Court. Bork argued that a department store chain's enforcement of price floors for individual franchises could be considered beneficial for the consumer. See Senate Committee on the Judiciary, *Hearings on the Nomination of Robert H. Bork to be Associate Justice of the Supreme Court of the United States,* September 17, 1987, pp. 362-69.

38. Section 1 makes illegal any contract, combination, or conspiracy that restrains trade or commerce; Section 2 imposes sanctions on every person who monopolizes, attempts to monopolize, or conspires with another to monopolize any part of trade or commerce.

39. The NFL Players Association in 1989 attempted to circumvent the antitrust privileges of football, provided by previous collective bargaining agreements, by "decertifying" itself as a union. If the union does not exist and no contract is in place, then the league does not enjoy many antitrust privileges.

40. John C. Weistart, "League Control of Market Opportunities: A Perspective on Competition and Cooperation in the Sports Industry," *Duke Law Journal*, December 1986, p. 1061.

41. Ibid., p. 1060.

42. Daniel E. Lazaroff, "The Antitrust Implications of Franchise Relocation Restrictions in Professional Sports," *Fordham Law Review*, 53 (November 1984), pp. 175-216.

43. "A Game Most Everybody Lost," *Los Angeles Times,* January 25, 1988.

44. Available from Green Bay Packers, Inc., 1265 Lombardi Avenue, Green Bay, Wisconsin 54307.

45. "Green Bay Packers Are Threatened by Football's Changing Economics," *Wall Street Journal,* December 14, 1984.

46. Packers annual report.

47. Ozanian and Taub, "Big Leagues, Bad Business," pp. 34-51.

48. The figures for baseball and football revenues and expenses come from Ozanian and Taub, "Big Leagues, Bad Business"; Andrew Zimbalist, *Baseball and Billions: A Probing Look Inside the Big Business of Our National Pastime* (New York: Basic Books, 1992), ch. 3; Gerald W. Scully, *The Business of Major League Baseball* (Chicago: University of Chicago Press, 1989), ch. 6; and confidential interviews with officials from both the league offices and the players unions of Major League Baseball and the National Football League, July 1989 and June 1992.

49. Quoted in "Baseball's Economic Future Hangs in the Balance as the National League Ponders Expansion Cities," *Sporting News,* March 25, 1991.

50. See Andrew Zimbalist, "Salaries and Performance: Beyond the Scully Model," in Sommers, ed., *Diamonds Are Forever,* pp. 109-33.

51. See "Baseball Owners Play an Expensive, Risky Game," *Los Angeles Times,* June 12, 1991.

52. "Baseball May Be About to Get Creamed," *Business Week,* December 30, 1991.

53. "NFL Strike: Socialism versus Socialism," *Village Voice,* September 28, 1982.

54. "Major League Socialism," *Forbes,* May 27, 1991.

55. The so-called superstations, like TBS (which carries Atlanta Braves games) and WGN (Chicago Cubs), are able to use national cable television stations to market their programming nationally, with some restrictions. The suggestion here is that all teams have access to all markets.

56. "Pirates De-Thrifted, Unthriving," *Washington Post,* June 28, 1989.

57. The best account of professional sports and tax privileges is Benjamin A. Okner, "Taxation and Sports Enterprises," in Noll, *Government and the Sports Business,* pp. 159-83.

58. Cited in David Harris, *The League: The Rise and Decline of the NFL,* rev. ed. (New York, Bantam Books, 1987), p. 152.

59. James F. Ambrose, "The Impact of Tax Policy on Sports," in Noll, *Government and the Sports Business,* p. 174.

60. "Yanks' Profits: Not Just Gravy," *New York Times,* July 30, 1990.

61. "The Best Team Money Can Buy," *Forbes,* May 14, 1990.

62. This illustration comes from Ambrose, "The Impact of Tax Policy," p. 173.

63. Testimony of Bowie Kuhn, House Select Committee on Professional Sports, *Inquiry into Professional Sports,* 94th Cong., 2nd sess., 1976, p. 249.

64. Scully, *The Business of Major League Baseball,* p. 132.

65. Ambrose, "The Impact of Tax Policy," p. 173.

66. "Yankees Arrange Tax Break," Albany *Times-Union,* May 30, 1991.

67. Matthew Goodman, "Sports Today," *Zeta,* January 1988, p. 63.

68. The owner of the NFL's Philadelphia Eagles, Norman Braman, paid himself a salary of $7.5 million in 1990. "Two Eagles Unperturbed by Owner's Salary," *USA Today,* July 9, 1992.

69. "Dumb Like Foxes," *Forbes,* October 24, 1988.

70. Zimbalist, *Baseball and Billions*, p. 62.

71. Ibid., p. 32. The interrelationship of franchise and outside business interests was illustrated vividly in 1984. In retaliation for the opposition of Augustus Busch to Commissioner Bowie Kuhn, Los Angeles Dodgers president Peter O'Malley revoked Budweiser's exclusive beer concession at Dodger Stadium, a privilege worth $10 million. Busch retaliated by cutting Anheuser-Busch's advertising on Dodger telecasts. See Cosell, *I Never Played the Game*, p. 294.

72. Harris, *The League*, p. 214.

73. Hofmann and Greenberg, *Sportsbiz*, p. 146.

74. Quoted in "How Are the Owners Holding Up? Just Fine, Thank You," *Sport*, June 1989; Zimbalist, *Baseball and Billions*, p. 33.

75. Janet Lever, *Soccer Madness* (Chicago: University of Chicago Press, 1983).

Chapter 3. Local Political Economy and Sports

1. Paul E. Peterson, *City Limits* (Chicago: University of Chicago Press, 1981), p. 17, 21.

2. Ibid., p. 37.

3. Ibid., p. 48.

4. Ibid., p. 147.

5. John Logan and Harvey Molotch, *Urban Fortunes: The Political Economy of Place* (Berkeley: University of California Press, 1987), pp. 70-73.

6. Bruce Kidd, "Bruce Kidd Turns Thumbs Down," *City Hall*, August 30, 1971, p. 114.

7. Clarence N. Stone and Heywood T. Sanders have called this the "politics of announcement." See their "Reexamining a Classic Case of Development Politics," in Stone and Sanders, eds., *Politics of Urban Development* (Lawrence: University Press of Kansas, 1987), pp. 178-80.

8. See Richard P. Nathan and Fred C. Dolittle et al., *Reagan and the States* (Princeton, N.J.: Princeton University Press, 1987), and George E. Peterson and Carol W. Lewis, *Reagan and the Cities* (Washington, D.C.: Urban Institute Press, 1986).

9. See Murray Edelman, *The Symbolic Uses of Politics* (Urbana: University of Illinois Press, 1985), pp. 91-92, and Paul Kantor, "The Dependent City: The Changing Political Economy of Urban Economic Development in the United States," *Urban Affairs Quarterly* 22 (June 1987), pp. 493-520.

10. Quoted in Robert A. Baade, "Is There an Economic Rationale for Subsidizing Sports Stadiums?" paper, Heartland Institute, Lake Forest, Illinois, February 1987, p. 7.

11. Quoted in "Pro Teams: A Big Value for Small Cities," *Los Angeles Times*, December 3, 1989.

12. Baade, "Is There an Economic Rationale?" p. 9.

13. See Timothy Barnekov and Daniel Rich, "Privatism and the Limits of Local Economic Development Policy," *Urban Affairs Quarterly* 25 (December 1989), pp. 212-38.

14. David Harvey, *The Limits to Capital* (Chicago: University of Chicago Press, 1982), p. 103.

15. Albert O. Hirschman, *Exit, Voice, and Loyalty: Responses to Decline in Firms, Organizations, and States* (Cambridge: Harvard University Press, 1970).

16. For good analyses, see Stephen L. Elkin, *City and Regime in the American*

Republic (Chicago: University of Chicago Press, 1987), ch. 4, and Sam Bass Warner, *The Private City: Philadelphia in Three Periods of Its Growth* (Philadelphia: University of Pennsylvania Press, 1968).

17. See Michael Lipsky, "Toward a Theory of Street-Level Bureaucracy," in Willis D. Hawley and Michael Lipsky, eds., *Theoretical Perspectives on Urban Politics* (Englewood Cliffs, N.J.: Prentice-Hall, 1974).

18. Douglas Yates, *The Ungovernable City: The Problems of Urban Politics and Policy Making* (Cambridge: MIT Press, 1984), p. 21.

19. Ibid., p. 57.

20. Matthew A. Crenson, "Urban Bureaucracy in Urban Politics: Notes toward a Developmental Theory," in J. David Greenstone, ed., *Public Values and Private Power in American Politics* (Chicago: University of Chicago Press, 1982), pp. 209-45.

21. Ibid., p. 225.

22. Ibid., p. 226.

23. Kidd, "Bruce Kidd Turns Thumbs Down," p. 114.

24. "Schaefer Pal Bids for Camden Yards Project," Baltimore *Sun,* February 22, 1988.

25. Matthew A. Crenson, "The Private Stake in Public Goods: Overcoming the Illogic of Collective Action," *Policy Sciences* 20 (1987), pp. 259-76.

26. Peterson, *City Limits,* p. 23.

27. Michael Storper and Richard Walker, *The Capitalist Imperative: Territory, Technology, and Industrial Growth* (New York: Basil Blackwell, 1989), ch. 3.

28. Ibid., pp. 80-81.

29. Ibid., p. 93.

30. See David Harvey, "The Urban Process under Capitalism: A Framework for Analysis," in *The Urbanization of Capital* (Baltimore: Johns Hopkins University Press, 1985), pp. 1-31.

31. For a provocative discussion of the perils of gigantism, see Jane Jacobs, *The Death and Life of Great American Cities* (New York: Vintage Books, 1961), ch. 15.

32. See Logan and Molotch, *Urban Fortunes,* and Floyd Hunter, *Community Power Structure: A Study of Decision Makers* (Chapel Hill: University of North Carolina Press, 1953).

33. J. Richard Aronson and Eli Schwartz, eds., *Management Policies in Local Government Finance* (Washington, D.C.: International City Management Association, 1981), pp. 305-7.

34. Logan and Molotch, *Urban Fortunes,* p. 177.

35. See my discussion of architect Philip Bess's proposals for a new stadium in Chicago in Chapter 6.

36. "Stadiums Elsewhere Don't Help Economics," *Rocky Mountain News,* June 16, 1991.

37. The stadium development plan proposed by Philip Bess in Chicago might meet this standard. See the discussion in Chapter 6.

38. A sophisticated discussion of some of these tendencies is Manuel Castells, *The Urban Question: A Marxist Approach* (Cambridge: MIT Press, 1980), ch. 9.

39. "Rx for Cities: Build a Dome," *Time,* December 27, 1987.

40. Quoted in Harry Edwards, *Sociology of Sport* (Homewood, Ill.: Dorsey Press, 1973), p. 278.

41. Robert A. Baade and Richard F. Dye, "An Analysis of the Economic Rationale for Public Subsidization of Sports Stadiums," mimeograph, July 28, 1987, p. 41.

42. "Dome Marks Its First Birthday," *St. Petersburg Times,* March 3, 1991.

43. See Deam Baim, *The Sports Stadium as a Municipal Investment* (Westport, Conn.: Greenwood, 1992). Quotations are from a conversation I had with Baim in June 1992.

44. Benjamin A. Okner, "Subsidies of Stadiums and Arenas," in Roger Noll, ed., *Government and the Sports Business* (Washington, D.C.: Brookings Institution, 1974), p. 346.

45. Robert A. Baade and Richard F. Dye, "Sports Stadiums and Area Development: A Critical Review," *Economic Development Quarterly* 1 (August 1988), p. 272.

46. *Indianapolis Star,* May 3, 1985.

47. "A Stadium Rescue: Greed, Poverty, Cost Overruns," *Chicago Tribune,* July 24, 1986.

48. Kidd, "Bruce Kidd Turns Thumbs Down," p. 114.

49. See Maureen Godsey Valente, "Local Government Capital Financing: Options and Decisions," *The Municipal Yearbook* (Washington, D.C.: International City Management Association, 1986), pp. 3-16.

50. Baade and Dye, "Analysis of Public Subsidization," p. 39.

51. Marshall Kaplan, in "Infrastructure Policy: Repetitive Studies, Uneven Responses, Next Steps," *Urban Affairs Quarterly* 25 (March 1990), pp. 371-88, concludes, after a review of the literature, that investment in infrastructure has declined in the past quarter of a century and that the gap between spending and needs is large. Michael A. Pagano, in "Fiscal Disruptions and City Responses," *Urban Affairs Quarterly* 24 (September 1988), pp. 118-37, finds that fiscal stress has caused cities to reduce direct spending on infrastructure and that this reduction has been only partially compensated with user fees. It must be kept in mind that cost overruns and ancillary costs such as land acquisition and road development increase stadium costs considerably—as much as 400 percent.

52. Mark Schneider and Fabio Fernandez, "The Emerging Suburban Service Economy," *Urban Affairs Quarterly* 24 (June 1989), pp. 537-55.

53. For an analysis of the multiplier claims for convention centers, see Farrokh Safavi, "A Cost-Benefit Model for Convention Centers," *The Annals of Regional Science* 5 (December 1971), pp. 17-37. William Grigsby, in "Some Observations on the Financial Feasibility of Philadelphia's Proposed Convention Center" (Department of City and Regional Planning, University of Pennsylvania, October 1986), argues that the convention center proposed for Philadelphia will not help the local economy because of the increases in construction costs in recent years. But plans for the center have proceeded anyway. The promotion of both stadiums and convention centers seems to follow a consistent pattern, with early promises of economic benefits and later arguments of civic image. Even though the economic argument for a Philadelphia convention center was strongly rebutted, Grigsby notes, "there is considerable momentum to proceed anyway for various reasons, including the belief that it is too late to turn back, the conviction that the city needs a world-class center to be a world-class city, and unwillingness to appear to have goofed" (personal correspondence, November 8, 1988).

54. Wilbur R. Thompson, *A Preface to Urban Economics* (Baltimore: Johns Hopkins Press, 1965), p. 206.

55. "Doomed Stadiums," *The National,* July 18, 1990.

56. Baade and Dye, "Sports Stadiums and Area Development," p. 27.

57. For example, the majority of jobs created by downtown development in Bal-

timore went to suburban commuters; the percentage of Baltimoreans working in down-town jobs in 1979 was 46.2. See Marc V. Levine, "Downtown Redevelopment as an Urban Growth Strategy: A Critical Reappraisal of the Baltimore Renaissance," *Urban Affairs Quarterly* 9 (1987), p. 113.

58. John Kasarda, "Urban Change and Minority Opportunities," in Paul E. Pe-terson, ed., *The New Urban Reality* (Washington, D.C.: Brookings Institution, 1985), pp. 33-68.

59. Mark S. Rosentraub and Samuel R. Nunn, "Suburban Investment in Profes-sional Sports," *American Behavioral Scientist* 21 (January-February 1978), pp. 393-414.

60. Ibid., pp. 412-13.

61. Baade, "Is There an Economic Rationale?" p. 15.

62. Ibid., p. 18.

63. Thompson, *Preface to Urban Economics*, p. 142.

64. See Baade, "Is There an Economic Rationale?" p. 12. One argument for con-struction of a new stadium in cities that already have a facility is that it will increase interest in the team—and hence attendance and ancillary economic activity in the city. Studies have shown, however, that factors such as the team's quality and the avail-ability of other entertainment were more important determinants in attendance. See Hal Hanson and Roger Gauthier, "Factors Affecting Attendance at Professional Sports Events," *Sociology of Sport Journal* 3 (January 1989), pp. 15-19.

65. Dale Hofmann and Martin J. Greenberg, *Sportsbiz: Inside the Sports Business* (Champaign, Ill.: Leisure Press, 1989), p. 154.

66. Baade and Dye, "Analysis of Public Subsidization," tested manufacturing ac-tivity to see if the seasonal, low-wage nature of direct stadium employment, which does little to improve the local economy, was augmented by more permanent and vigorous economic activity.

67. Baim, *The Sports Stadium as Investment*.

68. Kenneth Adams, quoted in *Los Angeles Times*, November 20, 1989.

69. Fred Hirsch, *The Social Limits to Growth* (Cambridge: Harvard University Press, 1973), p. 5.

70. Paul Kantor, with Stephen David, *The Dependent City: The Changing Political Economy of Urban America* (Glenview, Ill.: Scott, Foresman, 1988), p. 55.

71. Barry Bluestone and Bennett Harrison, *The Deindustrialization of America: Plant Closings, Community Abandonment, and the Dismantling of Basic Industry* (New York: Basic Books, 1982), pp. 8, 9.

72. Ibid., p. 92.

73. See Dennis R. Judd, *The Politics of American Cities: Private Power and Public Policy* (Glenview, Ill.: Scott, Foresman, 1988), p. 395.

74. J. Allen Whitt, "Mozart in the Metropolis: The Arts Coalition and the Urban Growth Machine," *Urban Affairs Quarterly* 23 (September 1987), pp. 15-36.

75. Irene S. Rubin and Herbert J. Rubin, "Economic Development Incentives: The Poor (Cities) Pay More," *Urban Affairs Quarterly* 23 (September 1987), pp. 37-62.

Chapter 4. Los Angeles: Raided and Raider

Epigraph: Los Angeles *Daily News* reporter Ron Rapoport was writing the song, but, he said, he got as far with it as Al Davis got with the new Raiders stadium in Irwindale. See Glenn Dickey, *Just Win, Baby: Al Davis and His Raiders* (New York: Harcourt, Brace, Jovanovich, 1991), p. 245.

1. "Davis Approves a Return to Oakland by Raiders in '92," *Los Angeles Times,* March 14, 1990.

2. Charles Lockwood and Christopher B. Leinberger, "Los Angeles Comes of Age," *Atlantic,* January 1988, p. 54.

3. Ibid., p. 32, 43.

4. Joan Didion, "Letter from Los Angeles," *The New Yorker,* April 24, 1989, p. 99.

5. Kenneth Reich, interview, August 1990.

6. See Steven A. Riess, "Power without Authority: Los Angeles' Elites and the Construction of the Coliseum," *Journal of Sport History* 8 (Spring 1981), pp. 50-63.

7. See Matthew A. Crenson, *The Un-Politics of Air Pollution: A Study of Non-Decisionmaking in the Cities* (Baltimore: Johns Hopkins Press, 1971).

8. David Harris, *The League: The Rise and Decline of the NFL,* rev. ed. (New York: Bantam Books, 1987), p. 310, 327.

9. Ibid., p. 312.

10. Ibid., p. 312-14.

11. See Amy Klobuchar, *Uncovering the Dome* (Prospect Heights, Ill.: Waveland Press, 1982) for an analysis of the Minnesota side of that story.

12. *Oakland Tribune,* June 10, 1981.

13. Dickey, *Just Win, Baby,* p. 155.

14. "Davis Reveals Offer by 49ers to Move Raiders to Seattle," *Oakland Tribune,* July 10, 1980.

15. Quoted in *Oakland Tribune,* June 14, 1980.

16. "Davis Queried on Pay-TV as Factor in Raiders Move," *Oakland Tribune,* June 18, 1981.

17. Harris, *The League,* p. 359.

18. See "Oakland Can't Afford the Raiders," *Washington Post,* April 19, 1990.

19. *Oakland Tribune,* July 10, 1980.

20. "Davis's Proposed L.A. Home Comes Under Trial Scrutiny," *Oakland Tribune* June 3, 1981.

21. "How Raiders Could Avoid Paying Back Loan," *Los Angeles Times,* July 12, 1982.

22. Interview, July 1989. Ueberroth claimed throughout negotiations for the use of sports facilities in southern California that the U.S. Olympic Committee was in financial straits. The specter of the large deficits that burdened previous Olympic Games proved to be an effective aid in bargaining. See Craig Lawson, "Intergovernmental Challenges of the 1984 Olympic Games," *Publius* 15 (Summer 1985), pp. 127-41.

23. If the LAMCC, a public body, had assumed ownership of the boxes, there have been no tax benefits.

24. Public law scholars have long argued that a political environment's complexity affects whether the parties negotiate or litigate. Contrary to those scholars' findings, however, the Raiders case went to litigation because of the environment's complexity, not its simplicity. To make the situation manageable, various parties used legalism to narrow the issues. For an overview of this literature, see Laura Nader and Henry F. Todd, Jr., "Introduction," in Nader and Todd, eds., *The Disputing Process: Law in Ten Societies* (New York: Columbia University Press, 1978), esp. pp. 12-15.

25. The effects of elevating legal issues above broader social concerns is noted by L. H. LaRue in his study of the Watergate scandal. LaRue argues that Congress's use

of the "rule of law" as a standard by which to judge President Richard Nixon narrowed the political discourse—giving the scandal an elitist slant and preventing a full discussion of the scandal's implications. The danger of legalistic definitions of issues is that "people start taking it literally, and so they become caught up in the words and lose their bearings." See LaRue, *Political Discourse* (Athens: University of Georgia Press, 1988), p. 136.

26. Lynn Mather and Barbara Yngvesson, "Language, Audience, and the Transformation of Disputes," *Law and Society Review* 15 (1980-81), p. 788.

27. "Davis to Testify on Obscure Comment about Rams' Move," *Oakland Tribune,* June 6, 1981.

28. As this essay argues below, the decision may have cut a leg off Oakland's case, too, since it eliminated consideration of the whole weblike relationship among city, league, and team.

29. "Federal Judge Cuts Raiders' Case in Half," *Oakland Tribune,* February 17, 1982.

30. A good summary of the debate over these antitrust criteria is Daniel E. Lazaroff, "The Antitrust Implications of Franchise Relocation Restrictions in Professional Sports," *Fordham Law Review* 53 (November 1984), pp. 175-93. Lazaroff holds that the per-se rule can be appropriate. An alternative view is offered by Gary R. Roberts, "The Single-Entity Status of Sports Leagues under Section 1 of the Sherman Act: An Alternative View," *Tulane Law Review* 60 (1986), pp. 562-95.

31. "News in Brief: The Southland," *Los Angeles Times,* October 2, 1981.

32. Jeremy Howell, "A Tale of Three Cities: The Relocation of Professional Football Franchises and the Dialectics of Profit and Community" (Master's thesis, University of Washington, 1984), p. 99.

33. The Fifth Amendment states that "private property [shall not] be taken for public use without just compensation." The Fourteenth Amendment states that no "State [shall] deprive any person of life, liberty, or property, without due process of law."

34. Oakland officials noted that San Diego had vaguely threatened use of eminent domain powers to prevent the transfer of their major league baseball team, the Padres, to Washington, D.C., in 1976.

35. "City's Attorney Questions Alioto," *Oakland Tribune,* June 23, 1983.

36. *City of Oakland* v. *Oakland Raiders,* California Official Reports, August 26, 1982, pp. 76, 77, 78.

37. Unlike other states, California does not specify in its constitution which uses of eminent domain are valid. This gives local communities great latitude in defining public use. Some states have defined public use as "for a general public benefit," while others make the more stringent requirement that the public directly participate in the facility or service made possible by the taking of private property.

38. The case was *Puerto Rico* v. *Eastern Sugar Associates,* First Circuit Court of the United States, 1946.

39. *Oakland Tribune,* November 20, 1981.

40. Michael Schiano, "Eminent Domain Exercised—Stare Decisis or a Warning: *City of Oakland* v. *Oakland Raiders,*" *Pace Law Review* 4 (Fall 1983), p. 192.

41. *City of Oakland* v. *Oakland Raiders,* p. 77.

42. *Los Angeles Times,* June 13, 1982.

43. David Self, interview, July 1989.

44. Melvin Durslag, interview, June 1989.

45. "Raiders Fiasco Could Pass Ball to Private Sports Management," *Los Angeles Times,* September 7, 1987.

46. Gary Miller's study of jurisdictions in the county found that while 25 of 42 cities surveyed in 1952 were heterogenous, only nine remained in this category in 1970; furthermore, only one of the thirty cities created during the intervening period was heterogenous. In short, both wealth and poverty were concentrated by incorporation. See Gary J. Miller, *Cities by Contract* (Cambridge: MIT Press, 1981), p. 133.

47. The conflict of interest questions of this private management of public development efforts was the focus of a state legislative inquiry. Hearings of the California General Assembly's Ways and Means Subcommittee on Public Employees and Bonded Indebtedness were held September 24, 1987. The hearings were called by a Los Angeles representative, Mike Roos, who opposed the Raiders' move from Los Angeles to Irwindale. Also see "The Great Raiders Scam," *LA Weekly,* September 18, 1987.

48. Miller, *Cities by Contract,* p. 56.

49. Melvin Durslag, interview, July 1989.

50. Stephen Reinhardt, interview, July 1989.

51. "Judge Scales Back Rams' Anaheim Stadium Plans," *Los Angeles Herald Examiner,* June 15, 1988.

Chapter 5. Baltimore: City of Defensive Renaissance

1. Marc V. Levine, "Downtown Redevelopment as an Urban Growth Strategy: A Critical Reappraisal of the Baltimore Renaissance," *Urban Affairs Quarterly* 9 (1987), p. 112.

2. Ibid., p. 111.

3. "The Middle Cannot Hold," *Washington Post,* May 8, 1989.

4. Paul E. Peterson, Barry G. Rabe, and Kenneth L. Wong, *When Federalism Works* (Washington, D.C.: Brookings Institution, 1986), pp. 63-68.

5. Marc V. Levine, "Economic Development in Baltimore: Some Additional Perspectives," *Urban Affairs Quarterly* 9 (1987), p. 134.

6. The Orioles are the subject of perhaps the best book about the politics and economics of professional sports, James Edward Miller, *The Baseball Business: Pursuing Pennants and Profits in Baltimore* (Chapel Hill: University of North Carolina Press, 1990). Miller shows how the operations of major league baseball, a team's management, and the players on the field affect each other. Little in the book, however, addresses the politics of stadium construction.

7. Following Charles Lindblom, *The Intelligence of Democracy: Decisionmaking through Mutual Adjustment* (New York: Free Press, 1965), incremental politics involves the careful deliberation of small events within the context of a larger political arena that sets major policy. However, sports politics takes place as a sequence of events outside the major policy deliberation arena.

8. The politics of sports in Indianapolis is described in Kimberly S. Schimmel, "Professional Sports Franchise Relocation within the Context of Urban Politics: A Case Study" (Master's thesis, Miami University, 1987).

9. Arthur T. Johnson, "Economic and Policy Implications of Hosting Sports Operations: The Case of Baltimore" (Paper delivered to North American Society for the Sociology of Sport, October 1983), p. 15.

10. Schaefer's notes and other documents relating to the Colts' move and the city's

eminent domain suit were made available to me by the corporation counsel at Baltimore's city hall. The documents will eventually be catalogued and filed in the city's archives, but they had not yet been when I examined them.

11. "Furtive Exit Was Final Colt Insult," *Baltimore Sun*, April 1, 1984.

12. "Schaefer Complains About Lack of Business and Banking Assistance in Attempt to Keep Colts," *Baltimore Sun*, March 1, 1984.

13. "Irsay Denies Plan to Shift or Sell Colts," *Baltimore Sun*, January 21, 1984.

14. Memorandum , February 29, 1984 (see note 10).

15. A term coined in 1989 by John Poindexter, a military official under President Ronald Reagan. Poindexter told congressional investigators that he had orchestrated American aid to rebels in Nicaragua without the President's explicit instructions because he knew the President wanted such involvement but was legally forbidden to order it. The President could at the same time "plausibly deny" authorizing illegal aid, while knowing that underlings like Poindexter were providing that aid.

16. See note 10.

17. See note 10.

18. After the Colts franchise of the All-America Conference then the NFL ceased operations in 1950, stockholders of the club sued. National Football League Commissioner Bart Bell promised Baltimore a new franchise if it sold 15,000 season tickets within six weeks. The franchise was awarded to a Bell protégé, Carroll Rosenbloom.

19. George W. Baker, interview, August 1989.

20. David A. Self, interview, June 1989.

21. "Irsay Ends 31-Year Marriage," *Baltimore Sun*, March 30, 1984.

22. See *Mayor and City Council of Baltimore* v. *Baltimore Football Club Inc.*, decision in U.S. District Court, December 9, 1985, p. 287.

23. "Judge Black's Ruling," *Baltimore Sun*, December 11, 1984.

24. The bylaws state that stability is a necessary precondition of the League's success. The congressional statute requires teams to stay in their host cities unless financial hardship and a lack of fan support make transfers unavoidable.

25. "Furtive Exit Final Colt Insult."

26. To say that the city paid too much attention to Irsay's personality rather than the complete array of factors leading to the Colts' departure is not to say Irsay's personality was not insulting and a proper target of enmity. Irsay did in fact lie on a regular basis and dealt shoddily with his business partners and potential business partners. See E. M. Swift, "Now You See Him, Now You Don't," *Sports Illustrated*, December 1, 1986.

27. Murray Edelman, *Constructing the Political Spectacle* (Chicago: University of Chicago Press, 1988), pp. 75-76.

28. Cited in David Harris, *The League: The Rise and Decline of the NFL*, rev. ed. (New York: Bantam Books, 1987), p. 78.

29. Edelman, *Constructing the Political Spectacle*, p. 72.

30. Letter to William Donald Schaefer, November 12, 1985 (see note 10).

31. "Colts' Future Worries Mayor," Baltimore *Evening Sun*, February 22, 1984.

32. The Maryland General Assembly had created a state sports authority in March 1986. The authority could determine the site and design for a new stadium but had to secure legislative funding and authorization to build the facility.

33. "Double-Ring Ceremony," *New York Times*, October 23, 1983.

34. Murray Edelman, *Political Language* (New York: Academic Press, 1977), p. 98.

35. See Guy Benveniste, *The Politics of Expertise* (Berkeley, Calif.: Glendissary Press, 1972).

36. Michael Peter Smith, *The City and Social Theory* (New York: St. Martin's Press, 1979), pp. 257-79.

37. *Baltimore Sun,* March 8, 1987. Also see Hal Hanson and Roger Gauthier, "Factors Affecting Attendance at Professional Sports Events," *Sociology of Sport Journal* 3 (January 1989), pp. 15-19.

38. Edelman, *Political Language,* p. 98.

39. On the neighborhood orientation of Baltimore, see Matthew A. Crenson, *Neighborhood Politics* (Cambridge: Harvard University Press, 1983), and Joseph L. Arnold, "The Neighborhood and City Hall: The Origin of Neighborhood Associations in Baltimore," *Journal of Urban History* 6 (1979).

40. Paul Kantor, "The Dependent City: The Changing Political Economy of Urban Economic Development in the United States," *Urban Affairs Quarterly* 22 (June 1987).

41. Sherry Olson, *Baltimore* (Cambridge, Mass.: Ballinger, 1976), p. 3.

42. The poll had a margin of error of plus or minus 5 percent. See "Poll on New Stadium," Baltimore *Sun,* February 17, 1987.

43. If the authority had not been created, the state's Department of State and Local Development would have overseen the project.

44. Robert A. Caro, *The Power Broker: Robert Moses and the Fall of New York* (New York: Alfred A. Knopf, 1974), p. 623.

45. Robert P. Stoker, "Baltimore: The Self-Evaluating City?" in Clarence N. Stone and Heywood T. Sanders, eds., *The Politics of Urban Development* (Lawrence: University Press of Kansas, 1987), p. 258.

46. The history of the referendum provision of Maryland's constitution does not support the argument that issues involving money should be excluded from public votes. The referendum process was instituted in 1914. The sponsor of the instituting legislation, Senator William J. Ogden of Baltimore, promoted the referendum as a means to curb corrupt and misguided fiscal practices: "Millions and millions of dollars worth of public property has been sold to these corporations by the political leaders, and the people have been bound by contracts that made them pay rates for services. . . . The legislature did it all." The support for the legislation was bipartisan; even the Republican governor of the state gushed with enthusiasm after a pro-referendum speech by the fiercely partisan William Jennings Bryan. Letter from George Callcott, professor of history, University of Maryland, Baltimore County, to William Marker, July 12, 1987.

47. Pretrial hearings, *Winfield M. Kelly Jr. and Greater Baltimore Committee Inc. v. Marylanders for Sports Sanity,* Court of Appeals of Maryland, September 1987, no. 75, appeal from the Circuit Court for Anne Arundel County, p. 25.

48. Ibid., pp. 32, 74-75.

49. Ibid., p. 78.

50. Ibid., p. 34.

51. Zan White, interview, November 1988.

52. Sen. Julian Lapides, interview, May 1989.

53. Truckson Sykes, interview, August 1990.

54. John Bowman, interview, August 1990.

55. For a good overview of this literature, see John Forester, ed., *Critical Theory and Public Life* (Cambridge: MIT Press, 1985).

56. See the discussion in Chapter 6 on the South Armour Square neighborhood's battle against a new facility for the White Sox baseball club.

57. Interview, February 1989. Interviewee requested anonymity.

58. Quoted in "The Inside Story of an Outsized Job," *Sports inc.*, October 24, 1988.

59. Dale Hofmann and Martin J. Greenberg, *Sportsbiz* (Champaign, Ill.: Leisure Press, 1989), p. 160.

60. "Phoenix Rising? Cardinals Representatives in Arizona," Baltimore *Sun,* January 7, 1988.

61. "Arizona Group Promises to Build, Lease 60 Skyboxes as Incentive to Bidwell," Baltimore *Sun,* December 16, 1987.

62. "Phoenix Rising?"

63. "Bidwell Looks Over Baltimore Site," *Washington Post,* November 12, 1987; "Arizona Officials Make 'Progress' with Cardinals," Baltimore *Evening Sun,* January 7, 1988.

64. "EBW: Maryland's First Offer to Cards Was Poorest Submitted," Baltimore *Sun,* January 12, 1988.

65. "City Sees Hopes Flickering Away," Baltimore *Sun,* January 9, 1988.

66. See John S. Nelson, "Politics as a Primarily Oral Culture" (Paper presented to the Midwest Political Science Association, April 1989).

67. "Arizona Officials Make 'Progress.' "

68. "Bidwell Holds the Cards, and He Isn't Tipping His Hand," Baltimore *Sun,* January 16, 1987.

69. "Owners Cautious, but Seem on Bidwell's Side," Baltimore *Sun,* January 16, 1988.

70. "Blast Appears Cool toward City's Lease Offer," Baltimore *Evening Sun,* January 20, 1988.

71. "Baltimore's NFL Bid Leaves D.C. Baseball Quest in Dust," *Washington Post,* December 18, 1987.

Chapter 6. Chicago: Whither the White Sox?

1. Jacqueline Grimshaw, advisor to City Hall, interview, June 1988.

2. Testimony by Jerry Reinsdorf during *Fox Television Stations* v. *Jerry Reinsdorf and Edward Einhorn and Chicago White Sox Ltd.,* Circuit Court of Cook County, complaint for declaratory judgment, September 28, 1988, p. 45.

3. Ruth Eckdish Knack, "Stadiums: The Right Game Plan?" *Planning,* September 1986, p. 6.

4. "In Play: Why Sox Future Rests with Pols," *Crain's Chicago Weekly,* July 14, 1986.

5. Roger Noll, ed., *Government and the Sports Business* (Washington: Brookings Institution, 1974).

6. Hal Hanson and Roger Gauthier, "Factors Affecting Attendance at Professional Sports Events," *Sociology of Sport Journal* 3 (January 1989), pp. 15-19. See also Philip K. Porter, "The Role of the Fan in Professional Baseball," in Paul M. Sommers, ed., *Diamonds Are Forever: The Business of Baseball* (Washington, D.C.: Brookings Institution, 1992), pp. 63-90.

7. See Chapter 2, this volume.

8. *Fox Television* v. *Jerry Reinsdorf,* p. 23.

9. Ibid., p. 51.

10. "Dome Doom for Sox," *Chicago Sun-Times*, January 13, 1985.

11. "Mayor, Suburbs Doubt Cub Move," *Chicago Sun-Times*, June 28, 1985.

12. "Dome Doom."

13. Ibid.

14. "DuPage Hunting Bulls, Bears, Too," *Chicago Sun-Times*, July 13, 1986.

15. Interview, May 1988.

16. "Feud Could Block New Sox Stadium," *Chicago Tribune*, May 14, 1987.

17. *Fox Television* v. *Jerry Reinsdorf*, p. 15.

18. Paul A. Anderson, "Decision Making by Objection and the Cuban Missile Crisis," *Administrative Science Quarterly* 28 (June 1983), pp. 201-22.

19. The plan would have required the White Sox to pay $1.5 million in annual rent and 45 percent of parking and 12 percent of concessions. Washington asked the state and Cook County to contribute funds should the construction costs exceed expectations. Washington called for the stadium area to be designated a "tax-increment" district. Under such a financing scheme, a project is financed with the taxes that are produced by the businesses that are part of the project. The proposal was based on abandoned designs of the proposed 1992 World's Fair.

20. "New Bears Stadium in South Loop?" *The New City*, February 25, 1987.

21. "Land of Opportunity," *The New City*, October 21, 1987.

22. "Mayor Receives Campaign Money from Stadium Planners," *The New City*, May 14, 1986.

23. "Alderman Roti Joins 'Anti-Stadium' Side," *The New City*, April 2, 1986.

24. "Senator Joins List of Stadium Opponents," *The New City*, March 4, 1986.

25. "McCaskey Says No to Twin Stadiums for Bears and Sox," *Chicago Sun-Times*, June 17, 1988.

26. "DuPage Hunting Bulls, Bears."

27. Jack Kneupfer, interview, June 1988.

28. "Sox Reduce Land Rush to a Crawl," *Chicago Tribune*, July 22, 1986.

29. "Stadium on the Spot," *Chicago Sun-Times*, July 14, 1986.

30. "Addison Sox Plan Ripped," *Chicago Sun-Times*, July 23, 1986.

31. "Florida Tempts Sox with TV, Radio," *Chicago Sun-Times*, May 11, 1988.

32. Letter from Robert Brown, president of the American League, to Mary O'Connell of Save Our Sox, undated.

33. "St. Pete's Passion May Prove Costly," *Tampa Tribune*, June 30, 1991.

34. "Frank Morsani Out to 'Make Things Happen,' " *St. Petersburg Times*, August 2, 1987.

35. "Study: Dome is Good Site for Baseball," *St. Petersburg Times*, December 30, 1988.

36. Editorial, *Tampa Tribune*, May 1, 1988.

37. Robert McDonald, lawyer for Tampa Bay Baseball Group, interview, August 1989.

38. The "Save Our Sox" organization, on the other hand, sent three busloads of supporters and provided them with bratwurst, sodas, and entertainment in a festive excursion like a trip to the ballpark.

39. Jacqueline Grimshaw, interview, June 1988.

40. "Dome Doom."

41. Mary Milano, interview, June 1989.

42. Curly Cohen, statement at coalition meeting, June 1988.

43. James Chapman, interview, June 1989.

44. "Comiskey Neighbors Organize for Survival," *Neighborhood Works,* November-December 1987, pp. 15, 17.

45. *Dorothy Laramore et al.* v. *Illinois Sports Facilities Authority,* United States District Court, Northern District of Illinois, Eastern Division, complaint for declaratory judgment, February 19, 1989, p. 15.

46. The author attended this meeting.

47. Mary Milano, interview, June 1989.

48. *Laramore* v. *Illinois Sports Facilities Authority,* p. 15.

49. "Residential Relocation Agreement," available from the Baker and McKenzie law firm (Chicago) and the Illinois Sports Facilities Authority. All quotations come from this report.

50. The development of the Bess proposal was underwritten by the National Endowment for the Arts, the Society for American Baseball Research (SABR), and the Graham Foundation for Advanced Studies.

51. "On Sports: One Man's Model Ballpark," *Wall Street Journal,* July 24, 1987. See also Philip H. Bess, Preface to Philip J. Lowry, *Green Cathedrals* (Manhattan, Kan.: Ag Press, 1986).

52. Philip H. Bess, interview, June 1988.

53. See Jane Jacobs, *The Death and Life of Great American Cities* (New York: Vintage Books, 1961).

54. Peter L. Berger, *To Empower People: The Role of Mediating Structures in Public Policy* (Washington, D.C.: American Enterprise Institute, 1977).

55. Philip H. Bess, interview, June 1988.

56. "Sox Park Measure Squeaks by Senate," *Chicago Sun-Times,* July 26, 1987.

57. Thomas H. Geoghegan, interview, June 1992.

58. James Chapman, interview, June 1988.

59. Sheila Radford-Hill, interview, June 1989.

Chapter 7. Sports and the Dependent City

1. "O's, Fans Share Tears, Memories," Baltimore *Sun,* October 7, 1991.

2. Harrison Donnelly, "High Stakes of Sports Economics," *Congressional Quarterly Editorial Research Reports,* April 8, 1988, p. 171

3. John Logan and Harvey Molotch, *Urban Fortunes: The Political Economy of Place* (Berkeley: University of California Press, 1987), p. 43.

4. Joe R. Feagin and Michael Peter Smith, "Cities and the New International Division of Labor: An Overview," in Feagin and Smith, *The Capitalist City* (New York: Basil Blackwell, 1987), p. 5.

5. Michael Peter Smith, *City, State, and Market* (Cambridge, Mass.: Basil Blackwell, 1988), p. 194.

6. See Michael J. Piore and Charles F. Sabel, *The Second Industrial Divide: Possibilities for Prosperity* (New York: Basic Books, 1984), pp. 40-50, 281-308.

7. Irene S. Rubin and Herbert J. Rubin, "Economic Development Incentives: The Poor (Cities) Pay More," *Urban Affairs Quarterly* 23 (September 1987), pp. 37-62.

8. Feagin and Smith, "Cities and New International Division of Labor," 21-22.

9. Ann Markusen, *Regions: The Economics and Politics of Territory* (Totowa, N.J.: Rowman and Littlefield, 1987), p. 118.

10. Paul Kantor, with Stephen David, *The Dependent City: The Changing Political Economy of Urban America* (Glenview, Ill.: Scott, Foresman, 1988), p. 168.

11. R. J. Johnston, "Regarding Urban Origins, Urbanization, and Urban Patterns," *Geography* 62 (1977).

12. David Harvey, *Consciousness and the Urban Experience* (Baltimore: Johns Hopkins University Press, 1985), p. 15.

13. Kantor, *The Dependent City,* pp. 165-66.

14. Georg Simmel, "The Metropolis and Mental Life," in Richard Sennett, ed., *Classic Essays on the Culture of Cities* (Englewood Cliffs, N.J.: Prentice-Hall, 1969), p. 53.

15. Quoted in Alan G. Ingham, Jeremy W. Howell, and Todd S. Schilperoort, "Professional Sports and Community: A Review and Exegesis," *Exercise and Sport Sciences Reviews* 15 (1987), p. 455.

16. For an evocative portrait of the hold sports can have on a community, see the description of how New Yorkers changed their daily routines to follow the progress of game six of the New York Mets–Houston Astros National League playoffs in 1986, in Roger Angell, *Season Ticket: A Baseball Companion* (Boston: Houghton Mifflin, 1988), pp. 330-33.

17. Gerald D. Suttles, *The Social Construction of Communities* (Chicago: University of Chicago Press, 1972), p. 13.

18. Janet Lever, *Soccer Madness* (Chicago: University of Chicago Press, 1983), pp. 15, 16.

19. Roger Benjamin, *The Limits of Politics: Collective Goods and Political Change in Postindustrial Societies* (Chicago: University of Chicago Press, 1980), p. 61. For the classic statement of positional goods, see Fred Hirsch, *The Social Limits to Growth* (Cambridge: Harvard University Press, 1973).

20. Michael Peter Smith, *The City and Social Theory* (New York: St. Martin's, 1979), p. 202.

21. J. Allen Whitt, "Mozart in the Metropolis: The Arts Coalition and the Urban Growth Machine," *Urban Affairs Quarterly* 23 (September 1987), p. 24.

22. Ibid.

23. See Irving Janus, *Victims of Groupthink: A Psychological Study of Foreign-Policy Decisions and Fiascoes* (Boston: Houghton Mifflin, 1972) for case studies of the way consensual orientations can affect the policy-making process.

24. Whitt, "Mozart in the Metropolis," p. 24.

25. Hugh Heclo, "Issue Networks and the Executive Establishment," in Anthony King, ed., *The New American Political System* (Washington, D.C.: American Enterprise Institute, 1978).

26. Bryan D. Jones and Lynn W. Bachelor, with Carter Wilson, *The Sustaining Hand: Community Leadership and Corporate Power* (Lawrence: University Press of Kansas, 1986), p. 73.

27. See Albert O. Hirschman, *Exit, Voice, and Loyalty: Responses to Decline in Firms, Organizations, and States* (Cambridge: Harvard University Press, 1970). For a discussion of the complexities of the voice-exit dynamic, see chapter 4.

28. John Bowman, interview, August 1990.

29. Paul Kantor, "The Dependent City: The Changing Political Economy of Urban Economic Development in the United States," *Urban Affairs Quarterly* 22 (June 1987), p. 513.

30. Paul E. Peterson, *City Limits* (Chicago: University of Chicago Press, 1981), p. 23.

31. Jones and Bachelor, *The Sustaining Hand*, p. 73.

32. Ibid., pp. 57-58.

33. Ibid., pp. 60-62.

34. Ibid., p. 81.

35. Feagin and Smith, "Cities and the New International Division of Labor," p. 17.

36. Robert F. Pecorella, "Fiscal Crises and Regime Change: A Contextual Approach," in Clarence N. Stone and Heywood T. Sanders, eds., *The Politics of Urban Development* (Lawrence: University Press of Kansas, 1987), p. 58.

37. Alexis de Tocqueville, *Democracy in America*, trans. Richard Heffner (New York: New American Library, 1956), p. 65.

38. See Bryan D. Jones, "Public Policies and Economic Growth in the American States" (Paper presented at annual meeting, American Political Science Association, September 1-3, 1988).

39. See Jane Jacobs, *Cities and the Wealth of Nations: Principles of Economic Life* (New York: Vintage Books, 1984), ch. 11, for a discussion of how monetary systems could serve as important feedback systems for local economies.

40. See Ken Auletta, *The Streets Were Paved with Gold* (New York: Random House, 1979), and Charles Morris, *The Cost of Good Intentions: New York City and the Liberal Experiment, 1960-1975* (New York: McGraw Hill, 1980). These books argue that New York City's fiscal crisis stemmed from policies that attempted to use municipal government to create and redistribute wealth.

41. Bernard H. Ross, Myron A. Levine, and Murray S. Stedman, *Urban Politics: Power in Metropolitan America* (Itasca, Ill.: F. E. Peacock, 1991), p. 390.

42. See Smith, *City, State, and Market*, p. 109.

43. Ross, Levine, and Stedman, *Urban Politics*, p. 390, 342.

44. Donald F. Kettl, *The Regulation of American Federalism* (Baltimore: Johns Hopkins University Press, 1983).

45. Ibid., p. 8.

46. Douglas Yates, *The Ungovernable City: The Politics of Urban Problems and Policy Making* (Cambridge: MIT Press, 1984), p. 34.

47. Herbert Simon, *Administrative Behavior: A Study of the Decision-Making Process in Administrative Organization* (New York: Macmillan, 1958), pp. 38-41, 80-81, 272.

48. Yates, *The Ungovernable City*, p. 141.

49. Logan and Molotch, *Urban Fortunes*, p. 209.

50. Clarence N. Stone and Heywood T. Saunders, "Reexamining a Classic Case of Development Politics: New Haven, Connecticut," in Stone and Sanders, *Politics of Urban Development*, pp. 178-79.

51. Quoted in Rubin and Rubin, "Economic Development Incentives," p. 56.

52. John Mollenkopf, *The Contested City* (Princeton: Princeton University Press, 1983), p. 9.

53. Kantor, "The Dependent City," p. 496.

54. See Barbara Ferman, *Governing the Ungovernable City: Political Skill, Leadership, and the Modern Mayor* (Philadelphia: Temple University Press, 1985).

55. Matthew A. Crenson, "Urban Bureaucracy in Urban Politics: Notes toward a Developmental Theory," in J. David Greenstone, ed., *Public Values and Private Power in American Politics* (Chicago: University of Chicago Press, 1982), p. 230.

56. Smith, *The City and Social Theory*, pp. 259-63, 275-81.

57. Pecorella, "Fiscal Crises and Regime Change," p. 64.

58. John J. Harrigan, *Political Change in the Metropolis* (Glenview, Ill.: Scott, Foresman, 1989), p. 179.

59. For a good overview of strategic planning, see Robert Mier, Kari J. Moe, and Irene Sherr, "Strategic Planning and the Pursuit of Reform, Economic Development, and Equity," *APA Journal,* Summer 1986. See also Robert Giloth, "Community Economic Development: Strategies and Practices of the 1980s," *Economic Development Quarterly* 2 (November 1988), pp. 343-50.

60. Giloth, "Community Economic Development," p. 302.

61. For an excellent discussion of the McGill Commission report and its implications, see Thomas Bender, "The End of the City?" *Democracy* 3 (1983), pp. 8-20.

Index

(*Teams without separate entries may be found under* Major League Baseball franchises *and* National Football League franchises. *Localities without separate entries may be found under* Cities and counties. *Stadiums without separate entries may be found under* Stadiums.)